S O L D

FOR SALE

OWNER WILL CARRY

123-8765

OWNER WILL CARRY are magic words that will help sell your property fast at a top price. But (FIRST) you must understand how to take back a note without being taken. This book explains how. The information in this book opens up opportunities to make money or save money for Buyers, Sellers, Real Estate Agents, Note Brokers and Investors.

3rd Edition

1st and 2nd Editions were under the title:
SELL YOUR PROPERTY FAST, How to Take Back a Mortgage Without Being Taken.

About the authors:

Bill Broadbent *(San Luis Obispo, CA)*

Bill received his BS degree from Cal Poly in 1956 and MBA from Cornell University in 1958. He has been an active real estate broker and consultant in San Luis Obispo for over 38 years. Bill is president of Arnett & Broadbent Inc., a real estate firm specializing in real estate investment brokerage and consulting. In 1976 he became a charter inductee to the Exchangor's Hall Of Fame and has won state and national recognition for his exchange transactions. Bill was the first broker in America to achieve both the prestigious SEC and CCIM designations. He has served the California Association of Realtors as local board president, state director, teacher and district representative to various committees. From 1970 to 1988 he taught an average of 4 seminars a year in a total of 18 different states.

An active broker, consultant, investor, author and educator, he is best known for his specialties of Exchanging, Consulting, and Buyer Representation, all practiced under Single Agency, a term he coined in the late 1970s.

Bill is a DOER of what he teaches. Insiders who have seen his work consider him "one of the best" when it comes to transaction structuring. He has used the techniques in this book for many years to benefit and protect his clients. In addition to his real estate investment brokerage and consulting practice, Bill has been buying trust deed and mortgage notes for his own account in over 36 states during the past 24 years. For additional background consult *http://www.arnettbroadbent.com.*

George Rosenberg *(Thousand Oaks, CA)*

A personal note to the reader: Until I retired from brokerage in 1996, I made my living as a real estate broker. I have been licensed in California since '57 and have been a broker since '69. My practice was centered around Single Agency representation and involved Exchanges, Consulting, and Home Resales.

Concerning home resales, I have tried for years to explain to agents and to consumers concepts which would either save money, make money or limit liability. My motivation to jointly author this book is that I have a vision. Someday, my vision goes, agents will act like agents; they will put their clients' interests before their own; they will learn all they can about their work; they will convey confidence so that consumers will not be afraid of an agent's always trying to sell them something.

Agents who understand the simple principles in this book will benefit their seller clients, their buyer clients, and, so, themselves. Consumers who choose to be customers (one who does not employ an agent) will begin to seek client status (one who employs an agent) when they see how a real pro works. For example, how many agents do you know who will use multiple carryback notes secured by one trust deed or mortgage when settling an estate or when parceling out equities in a divorce? Not many. But, a whole lot more will after they read this material.

My vision is about proper client representation. Creative structuring of seller carryback financing for the client's benefit is part of that representation. More, of course, is involved. But, reading this short book is a great way to begin.

COPYRIGHT

Exhibit numbers 4, 5, and 36 are reprinted by permission of the copyright owner:
Professional Publishing Corporation
880 Las Galinas Ave,
San Rafael, CA 94903-3466
www.profpub.com
Customer Service (415)472-1964   Fax (415) 472-2069

Exhibit numbers 1, 12, 23, and 32 are reprinted by permission of the copyright owner:
first tuesday
P.O. Box 20068
Riverside, CA 92516
(909) 781-7300

Exhibits 41, 43 & 44 were reprinted by permission of Wolcotts Forms, Inc.
Wolcotts forms may be purchased in most good stationery or office supply stores.

©1993 Sell Your Property Fast (1st & 2nd editions)
©1998 Owner Will Carry
This book contains all the information in the 2nd edition of *Sell Your Property Fast*. We changed the title to reach out to a broader audience. Two new chapters have been added plus other nuggets of knowledge and forms. Almost any property (real or personal) can be sold more easily for a top price when the owner will carry part of the financing.

While the major focus of the book is still real estate, the principles here apply to other assets as well. Year in and year out real estate is the best security for a note. If you are selling a non-real estate asset, it is still possible that the buyer can secure your note with real estate, providing you as a seller with a safer, more secure transaction (see Chap. 11). The more well-structured carryback paper that is generated, the more opportunities are available for everyone.

ACKNOWLEDGMENTS

The authors are grateful to the following individuals
for their influence on our careers and/or their contribution to this book.

The late Richard R. Reno, the "Grandfather of modern real estate exchanging," for his amazing doctrine that people, not property or numbers make the decision. He broadened our geographical horizons. He showed us how to help clients solve real estate problems in many different states, and instilled in us the "daring to do," which freed us from traditional thinking in real estate practice. In turn this freedom enabled us to develop and implement some of the concepts in this book.

To our good friend, the late C. Charles Chatham, for his assistance in the development of Single Agency real estate practice and the Directory, *Who's Who In Creative Real Estate*. His contribution of the art of counseling to the real estate industry helped make it possible to apply the techniques in this book. His philosophy, that "the name of the game is to benefit the client," provides a solid foundation for the professional practice of real estate.

To Ed Arnett, Bill's patient partner and good sounding board, for over three decades.

To David Bryson, CPA, for his tax guidance and review.

To Fred Crane, publisher of *first tuesday*.

To James B. McKenney, publisher of Professional Publishing Corp.

To Norman Flam, for reviewing our calculations.

To Douglas Hilton, for his excellent legal counsel, guidance and friendship for over 30 years.

To Betty Wiggin of All-American Foreclosure Service, for updating our California foreclosure procedure checklist.

To Mike Meeker, one of the best instructors in the note business, for suggesting that this book be written.

To Danny Santucci, for his tax guidance and review.

To Harry Snyder, for his editorial skills.

To Wolcott Forms, Inc., for use of their forms.

To all the real estate agents, note sellers and note brokers who offered me poorly secured and/or poorly structured paper that I (Bill Broadbent) wouldn't buy. They proved beyond a shadow of a doubt the great NEED for this book.

TABLE OF CONTENTS

CHAPTER 1:
An Important Marketing Strategy

This is NOT a California-only book! The authors only coincidentally work and sleep in sunny California. **Seller carryback financing works in EVERY state.**

We begin by defining seller carryback financing. We then discuss the terms used and explain their definitions and their functions. Some relatively new terms are introduced and explained throughout the book. Documents used are defined here and are shown throughout the book. We introduce our cast of characters and tell the part each plays. By using these characters, we hope to make our examples come alive. We focus on the advantages and disadvantages of seller carryback financing to both seller and buyer. Seller and buyer checklists for using carryback financing follow.

**References:**
- Seller carryback financing defined
- Terms used
- Documents used
- Cast of characters introduced
- Advantages to seller and to buyer of carryback financing
- Checklists for sellers and buyers for using carryback financing

CHAPTER 2:
Negotiations

"If you never remember anything else from this book, remember that all elements of a real estate transaction are **negotiable**." That quote from the chapter sets our stage. We introduce the time value of money concepts of "MORE SOONER IS BETTER" and "LESS LATER IS BETTER." Then Sam & Sally Seller meet Bob & Betty Buyer. An example of a transaction that includes a simple seller carryback negotiation and transaction follow.

**References:**
- Negotiable elements of a real estate transaction
- Time value of money concept introduced
- Example of seller carryback financing

CHAPTER 3:
Items to Consider When Drawing A Note

What items should be in a note? Better, what items must be in a note? We tell that here. Then usury (charging too much interest) and imputed interest (charging too little interest) are discussed. Late charges - when and how to use them - along with a sample late charge clause come next. Understanding the prepayment penalty and appropriate language for its use follow. Then the due-on-sale clause and a sample of same is shown. Each is related to a note and shown by example.

**References:**
- Items that need to be in a note
- Other considerations: Usury, imputed interest, late charges, prepayment penalty, due-on-sale clause

TABLE OF CONTENTS

First we had to set the table. Now comes the main course. Are two or three carryback notes better than only one? The **protective equity** concept is illustrated by example and emphasized as an important theme. This is critical information for those people who structure, buy, sell, or invest in notes. How can sellers improve their security before agreeing to carry a note? A discussion of seller carryback notes with existing assumable financing follows, first with a balloon payment, then with wraparound (all-inclusive) financing, complete with detailed examples of each. Yields to the seller are compared for each variation.

References:
* Using multiple carryback notes
* Assuming existing financing with a balloon payment
* Improving security on a note with a wraparound loan

The pros and cons of balloon payments are aired. Different methods of calculating a balloon payment are explained. We give sample wording for a balloon payment note. Not content with having floated a balloon, we now show how to defuse it, so it doesn't become a problem. Even better for both buyer and seller, we show how to avoid a balloon payment and its inherent problems.

References:
* Pros and cons of balloon payments
* Sample balloon payment wording
* How to defuse balloon payments
* How to avoid balloon payments

Now that the seller has carried back a note, we explain, then evaluate each alternative. Calculations show: How to amortize a note (several ways), how to discount a note (several ways), and how to use a financial calculator for fun and profit. Handling note collections, transfer by assignment vs. endorsement, and finding a buyer for a note are explained. Loan to value ratio ranges, discounting, and restructuring are illustrated. Examples of exchanging a note at face value are discussed. Here's another BIG bonus: New material here on the Memo of Modification. We've never seen this information anywhere else!

References:
* Alternatives: Keep, sell, exchange the note or borrow on it?
* Calculations for amortizing and discounting
* Different ways to raise cash from an existing note

TABLE OF CONTENTS

Answers some questions: Who does your real estate agent represent? How can consumers tell which agents understand how to maneuver paper? Private lenders and note investors: Who is looking out for you? Loan brokers, agents and others buying and selling notes: Do you have your agency hat on straight? And, using our Agency Disclosure Document, we show how each agent should document his or her representation in a real estate transaction.

*_References_*:
- Agency issues as applied to real estate agents, private lenders, note investors, loan brokers, note sellers, note buyers and note brokers
- Using an Agency Disclosure Document

The reader now learns what an 80-10-10 transaction is. By understanding the risks and pitfalls involved, you will learn how to turn a potential lemon into lemonade. A novice seller can lose his shirt by not knowing how to dramatically reduce the risks involved in an 80-10-10 deal. Agents learn how to protect their client and themselves. We tell you how to avoid the pitfalls. What may seem like a shaky deal can be turned into a solid transaction. Tune in here to find out how. We show you two alternative methods to dispose of a 2nd that originated in an 80-10-10 transaction. How safe is a first mortgage when the down payment is less than 10%? Let's look at a foreclosure situation, run some numbers and see!

*_References_*:
- Risks of an 80-10-10 transaction
- How to reduce most of the risk on a carryback 2nd in an 80-10-10 transaction

1. How to reduce the risk of not being paid the balloon payment.
2. How to structure a carryback note to minimize risk.
3. Using a deed of trust on another property as additional security to secure an existing T/D note.
4. How to use existing notes to give you, the seller, added protection. Here we discuss the tax consequences of assigning a secured note as collateral for another loan.
   Bet you didn't know!

When you are looking for property with seller financing, you need to know who and what to look for. You may need the help of a Buyer's agent. We tell you what to look for in property and in a Buyer's agent, to enhance your chances for a successful transaction.

*_References_*:
- How to reduce risk to the seller when s/he is asked to carry back a note:
  - When a balloon payment is involved
  - By properly structuring the note
  - By using a buyer's existing or created note

CHAPTER 10:
A "No Money Down" Transaction vs. A "Nothing Down" Deal

What's the difference? Plenty! In a "nothing down" deal the buyer has nothing to lose and the seller may lose all. In the other the seller is well-secured and the buyer has responsibility. We go into great detail with examples showing how each one works. Learn how to use the system to give you as a seller much more **protective equity!**

Agents should understand these concepts so they can benefit and protect their clients.

Properly used, these techniques mean faster sales, more transactions and commissions.

References:
• What is a "no money down" transaction?
• What is a "nothing down" transaction?
• How each one works

CHAPTER 11:
The Substitution Of Security/Collateral Alternative

Don't be frightened by the title. Or confused. Simply put, a seller may obtain better security for his carryback note than his own property! Why and how to do it? Fully discussed with supporting forms to illustrate. Many agents and consumers don't know about security substitution. Learn how safe and simple the process can be. Why and how it can be the superior alternative to subordination.

References:
• How to use something other than the property being sold to secure a carryback note

CHAPTER 12:
To Prevent Surprises, Here Is A Checklist To Use Before You Agree To Carry Back A Note Or Before You Buy an Existing Note

No, this chapter is not out of place. We needed to lay the groundwork by examples for the points discussed here. The examples shown throughout the book are used to refer to a seller's or note buyer's checklist of requirements. Here Bill Broadbent shows HIS PERSONAL LIST of 15 points to check before carrying back a note, funding a loan, or buying a note at discount! Important: This chapter provides sample forms and references to guide you.

References:
• Checklist for either carrying back a note or for buying a note
• Sample forms to use with the checklist

TABLE OF CONTENTS

EXHIBITS

INTRODUCTION

FOR SALE

OWNER WILL
CARRY

Tel. 000-000

"Owner Will Carry" or "Seller Financing" are magic words that make almost anything of significant value MORE SALABLE! As this simple diagram shows, your property will become more salable.

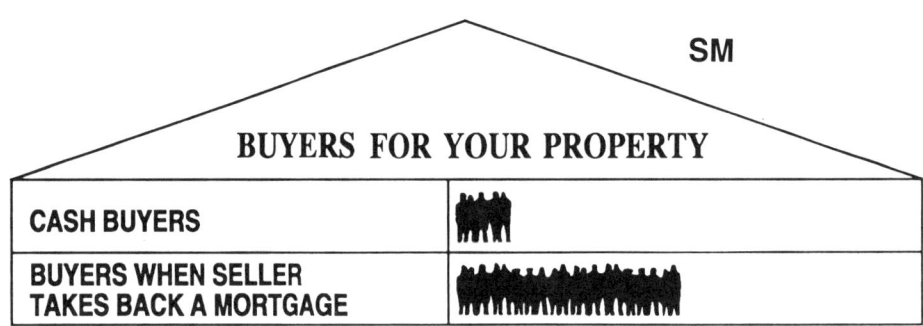

SM

BUYERS FOR YOUR PROPERTY

CASH BUYERS	
BUYERS WHEN SELLER TAKES BACK A MORTGAGE	

© 1986 Who's Who In Creative Real Estate, Inc.

There always MORE buyers with some cash for a down payment who could make monthly payments if someone would finance the balance of the purchase price. The ONLY ALTERNATIVE to either institutional financing or the rare ALL CASH BUYER is for the seller to become the lender who finances the sale.

Seller Carryback Financing Defined:
When the seller helps the buyer by acting as a lender, the seller may finance part or all of the sale. The term given to such seller financing is seller carryback financing. A seller is literally carrying back part of the financing on the property being sold.

Some advantages of seller carryback financing to the seller...
1. Getting a top price by taking terms rather than all cash.
2. Deferring taxes now on any gain by using an installment sale.
3. Receiving a higher interest rate than if you put the proceeds from a cash sale in the bank, a CD, or money market fund.
4. Monthly income secured by property you understand and whose value you know.
5. Larger number of prospective buyers and a quicker sale because you offer seller financing.

SELLER FINANCING or OWNER WILL CARRY are words you can add to your FOR SALE sign or classified advertisement. These words will attract a larger number of prospective buyers. "Owner will carry" sets your property apart from sellers who are waiting for that elusive all-cash buyer.

Seller carryback financing applies to all types of real estate:
Homes, land, mobile homes on a lot or acreage, small or large apartment buildings, condos, office buildings, farms, ranches, motels, senior care facilities, commercial, industrial, warehouse properties and special purpose properties such as theaters, hospitals and restaurants, to name just a few.

This book, *OWNER WILL CARRY, How To Take Back a Note or Mortgage Without Being Taken*, shows how to safely structure both a down payment and/or a carryback note for maximum value now. Later if the note holder needs cash for the note, it will command a top price because of its safe and secure structure.

Our major focus in this book is directed toward the sale of real estate using seller financing. The principles explained in this book would also apply to carrying a note secured by almost any asset, including but not limited to: a car, boat, airplane, mobile home (w/o land), a business (w/o real estate), stamp collection, tractor, machine, or other equipment, to name just a few examples.

A seller of one of these assets who is reluctant to accept the personal property being sold as security for the carryback note should carefully read pages 120 through 127. Some buyers may be able to secure the note with an interest in real property they own, making the security much safer than just the asset being sold. If the seller needs assistance with the process, a real estate consultant should be employed on an hourly fee basis to help structure the transaction properly and maximize the safety, security and possible future salability of the note being created.

Adding the words "Owner Will Carry" or "Seller Financing" can be the quickest way to change a "For Sale" sign to "SOLD"!

From a property seller's viewpoint:
Many sellers think they need cash. SOME MAY, OTHERS MAY NOT.
Suppose we put $100,000 cash on your coffee table, a gift for you.

Q. Would the cash still be there a year from now?
A. Probably not! You would likely spend some and invest some. To the extent you invested some, could you earn 9% or more on that money? If not, perhaps you (as a seller of property) could have carried a portion of the financing yourself. Most people think they want cash. What they really <u>need</u> is income, not a pile of cash. Ask yourself, "If you had enough income on a regular basis, would you need a pile of cash?" With enough income could you enjoy the lifestyle you desire without a lot of cash?

THINK ABOUT IT!

When a seller carries back financing to facilitate the sale of real estate, the note can provide him/her with a steady income for many years. Suppose you carry back a well secured, properly structured note and need cash at some time in the future. You can generate cash by selling all or a portion of your note at that time. Using the techniques in this book will help you get <u>MORE for your note.</u>

Many real estate agents THINK they need an all cash sale.

Agents:
Look at your marketing methods. You think a cash transaction is SIMPLE, so you don't have to be creative. True, a cash sale assures a cash commission. So can a terms sale! Even in the safely structured "No Money Down" example in Chapter 10, Sam Seller is able to pay his agent a cash commission.

A majority of listings expire, UNSOLD. Were the sellers and agents waiting for that elusive "cash to new loan" buyer?

Seller carryback financing can make the difference between a SOLD or an EXPIRED listing. Those agents who understand and utilize seller carryback financing make more sales.

Carrying back seller financing, buying and owning a note for income, or making a loan secured by real estate involves, **RISKS, REWARDS AND RESPONSIBILITIES.**

WHAT YOU BELIEVE DETERMINES YOUR SUCCESS
If you believe the information in this book will work for you, you are right. It will. If you think the information is fun to read but will not work, you are right. **95% of your success depends on what you believe. The other 5% of your success is knowing how. This book tells you how.**

ARE YOU IN ONE OR MORE OF THESE CATEGORIES?

- ❏ Accountant
- ❏ Attorney
- ❏ Business Opportunity Broker
- ❏ Commercial Property Buyer
- ❏ Commercial Property Seller
- ❏ Contractor
- ❏ Developer
- ❏ Escrow Officer
- ❏ Financial Planner
- ❏ Gift Planner
- ❏ Home Buyer
- ❏ Home Seller
- ❏ Mobile Home Dealer
- ❏ Note Investor
- ❏ Note Seller
- ❏ Note Buyer/Broker
- ❏ Private Mortgage Broker
- ❏ Real Estate Agent
- ❏ Real Estate Investor
- ❏ Rehabber (buys run down property, fixes it up & resells, for profit)

If you are in one or more of the above categories, then this book can make you money and/or save you money. By following the procedures we outline in this book, you can minimize your **risks,** understand your **responsibilities,** and increase the probability of financial **rewards.**

Steps to Finding a
Home with Seller Financing

by Robert J. Bruss

Q: Several weeks ago you explained how home buyers with bad credit can buy a house. One of the techniques was to buy a home with seller financing. I talked to my real estate agent and she says sellers in our town don't finance sales for home buyers. As I now have excellent income, but have a poor credit record due to my ex-spouse, where can I find a home I can buy with seller financing.?

A: Your agent is mistaken and apparently has a very bad attitude. Get a new agent. **There Is no town in the U.S. where home sellers will not finance sales for buyers.** Not all home sellers can finance a home sale for you, but you need just one,

The best candidates for seller financing are vacant, free and clear homes being sold by elderly people who need retirement income. I've bought many such houses and you can too.

First, find a new agent. Then ask that agent to show you only houses which are free and clear. When you find one you like, make an offer with at least a 10% cash down payment and ask the seller to carry back a 90% mortgage. In today's market a 9% interest rate is fair.

Be sure your offer specifies the exact monthly payment the seller will receive. Once the seller sees your written offer on the table, with a decent deposit check of perhaps $5,000, you can be sure the seller will think very long and hard before rejecting your offer. But if that happens, just make another offer on another free and clear house. Eventually one of your offers will be accepted. You need just one.

This is an excerpt from a <u>Los Angeles Times</u> newspaper column written by and published here with the permission of Robert J. Bruss, a San Francisco area lawyer, author and real estate broker. He may be reached at P.O. Box 280038, San Francisco, California 94128.

Think for a moment about how most agents market property. When you as a seller ask an agent how he or she will attempt to sell your house, the agent almost always responds in terms of advertising the listing, putting up signs, and holding an "open house." Indeed, if signs, advertising and open houses were the primary tools needed to effectively market property, wouldn't all properties soon be sold? Advertising, signs and open houses are part of marketing. Obviously, more is involved.

CHAPTER 1

AN IMPORTANT MARKETING STRATEGY

In a newspaper article on how to improve a home's marketability, the author suggested that sellers consider the following <u>in addition to</u> a competitive price:

- A Broker's Open House
- Bonus to Selling Agent
- Help pay Buyer's closing costs
- Subsidize extra advertising
- Improve the front entrance and aroma of the house (bake bread!)

Another article on the same subject appeared in the National Association of Realtors' magazine, *Realtor News*, which stressed "Tried and True Marketing Methods." Realtors across the nation made such suggestions as:

- Carefully check comparable properties before taking a listing
- Polish up the home and improve curb appeal
- Make needed repairs
- Reimburse buyers for a Homeowner's Warranty
- Have house available for "QUICK SHOWING"
- Impress sellers with "THE COMPETITION"

One real estate agent put out a flyer listing "52 tips to make your property more salable" without ever mentioning Seller financing, a very powerful technique to affect a sale!

While the above suggestions have varying degrees of merit, **both these articles overlooked the <u>most important</u> marketing strategy of all:**

SELLER CARRYBACK FINANCING

The availability of mortgage money varies. As we write, loans are currently inexpensive and available for owner-occupied single family homes. Some people believe that mortgage money will be less available in the future. No matter. Even though mortgage money is cheap and plentiful, **some borrowers** who would be excellent buyers still **cannot qualify** under institutional lender standards. And, there are always **some properties** that **don't meet institutional lender standards**. For that reason <u>now</u> is the time to understand seller carryback financing. This book contains principles and ideas for all seasons. Interest rates may fluctuate over the years but the principles in this book will never go out of style. These principles apply to <u>all types</u> of real property: Homes, land, mobile homes, apartments, condos, office buildings, farms, commercial and industrial property. Many of these principles can be applied to notes secured by personal property, such as the assets of a business that is being sold. <u>THESE PRINCIPLES APPLY AND WILL WORK IN ANY STATE!</u> **Be sure to conform the paperwork and forms to the laws of your state and get professional legal and tax advice to accomplish your objective.**

Seller Carryback Financing Defined:

When a seller assists the buyer by acting as the lender, the seller may finance part or all of the sale. The term given to such seller financing is carryback financing. A seller instead of a financial institution, is literally carrying back part or all of the financing on the property.

Seller carryback financing is vital to a successful sales program. It is so important that if more sellers and agents understood the principles of seller carryback financing, more real estate sales activity would be generated across the country than with any other marketing tool!

The primary reason we wrote this book is to show you how to properly structure and use seller carryback financing. Many listing (seller's) agents are not aware that seller carryback financing can make their listings more salable. Seller carryback paper (any note secured by real property or personal property) can provide a seller with an interest return (yield) on their note that exceeds savings accounts, certificates of deposit (CDs) and money market funds. Following the suggestions in this book will make seller carryback notes safer for sellers who want to keep their notes. These same suggestions will also make carryback notes <u>more salable for sellers who may later need to sell all or part of their note to raise cash</u>. Many sellers are not aware that owner financing, if properly structured, can be converted to cash. Several possibilities are outlined later in this book.

Holding a note secured by real property involves three R's: RISK, RESPONSIBILITY and REWARD:

RISK <u>can best be minimized</u> by proper structuring of the transaction in which the note is created.

RESPONSIBILITY means YOUR responsibility to understand the rules that relate to trust deed and mortgage notes. REWARDS are available to those who understand the rules. Those who don't know the rules should employ someone who does to represent them. Understanding each of the three R's will benefit property sellers, property buyers, real estate and business opportunity agents, note holders, note sellers, note brokers, and individuals who invest in notes for income.

When a seller agrees to carry back a note to finance the sale of his property, there is some RISK involved. This book shows how to <u>reduce the RISK</u> if the seller follows certain guidelines. This book shows you ***How To Take Back A Note or Mortgage Without Being Taken!***

Terms used in the book:

We use the terms deed of trust or trust deed interchangeably throughout the book to identify the security for a seller carryback note. Both mean the same. If you are from a state that uses mortgages instead of trust deeds, think and use the term mortgage. In states where Land Contracts or Contracts For Deed are routinely used, then think Land Contract or Contract For Deed. All of these instruments are sometimes referred to by real estate agents and investors as "paper."

Introducing the cast of characters in this book:

Our cast of characters is fictional. Any similarity to persons living or dead is purely coincidental.

Arthur Agent (represents either the buyer or seller of real estate)
Sam and Sally Seller
Bob and Betty Buyer
Corporate America (a term used to reference large institutional note buyers)
Dan Deadbeat (a high risk buyer, who seldom pays his bills)
Evelyn Exchangor (builds her estate using notes and property equities)
Insecurity Bank (the Friendly Lender with picky policies)
IRS (the Infernal Revenue Service)
Irving Investor (buys and holds real estate as an investment)
Mobile Melvin (an agent who specializes in the sale of pre-owned mobile homes)
Ned Notebroker (Agent for Sellers or Buyers of privately held notes)
Nancy Notebuyer (buys and sells notes as a business)
Norman Noteholder (buys and holds notes for income)
Steve Speculator (buys and sells real estate using notes in exchange for equities)

The formula for our examples: The **KISSS** formula (**K**eep **I**t **S**imple, **S**ensible and **S**afe!)

To keep our examples simple, let's use a $100,000 house.

If you are from a lower-priced area of the country, then divide by two.

If you are from a high-priced area on the East Coast or California, multiply by three or four.

If you're from Texas where everything is supposed to be bigger, then add three or four zeros.

Monthly payments shown in many examples have been rounded to the nearest dollar.

How does a seller benefit by carrying back financing?

Sam Seller wants to sell his property. Suppose when he sells he could get a:

1. Larger number of prospective buyers because he offers "seller financing."
2. Fast sale at a top price by taking terms rather than all cash.
3. Way to defer paying taxes now on the gain. Tax bracket changes in the 1997 Tax

Law applicable to capital gains will make installment sales more attractive for some property sellers.

4. Higher interest rate than if he put the cash from his sale into a bank, savings account, CD or money market fund.
5. Monthly income secured by a property he understands and whose value he knows.
6. Cash payment for all or a portion of the note he carries.
7. In many states seller carryback notes are exempt from usury limits.

There are more buyers today for well structured, privately held real estate notes than at any other time in our history. Also a growing market of buyers for other types of cash flows has evolved during the last decade. A recent report indicates there are 58 different types of cash flows available.

Sam Seller's motivation would be strong. Why would he not help a buyer finance part of the sale? There is some risk, and Sam still needs to do some checking on a specific buyer by following our checklist in Chapter 12. Seller carryback financing helps most properties sell faster!

Just as the benefits listed above work for Sam Seller, the flip side of each benefits Bob Buyer.

How does a buyer benefit when a seller carries the financing?

1. **In some areas of the country less than half of potential home buyers can meet institutional lender qualifications.**
2. Though Bob Buyer may pay a top price, he may get more favorable terms.
3. As Sam Seller is permitted by tax law to defer his taxes with an installment sale, Bob Buyer is dealing with a motivated seller. Sam is usually not required to pay taxes on his deferred gain until he receives some payments on principal (an installment sale, Internal Revenue Code Section 453). An exception to this rule is covered in Chapter 5.
4. Although Bob Buyer may be paying Sam Seller a higher interest rate than Sam would earn by depositing money in a bank savings account, Bob's interest rate may be less than he would pay for a loan from Insecurity Bank.
5. Lower closing costs. Even if the interest rate were the same, Sam Seller has not charged Bob a loan origination fee of between 1% and 2% of the loan. Insecurity Bank would do that. Nor has Sam Seller charged Bob an appraisal fee or a variety of additional costs and fees normally charged by Insecurity Bank. In some cash to new loan transactions a Buyer's charges can run as high as 6 to 8% of the price of the home.
6. Seller carryback notes secured by the property sold (in California & some other states) carry no personal liability. The property is the sole security for the debt.
7. **For some buyers seller financing can make the difference between owning and NOT owning a home.**

Lenders have tightened their credit requirements. They are being picky. And, in some cases, rightly so.

*"O.K., folks, let's move along. I'm sure you've all
seen someone qualify for a loan before."*

© 1992, New Yorker Magazine. Reprinted with permission.

"WE CAN'T MAKE YOU A LOAN...."

Institutional lenders may not be willing to make a loan based on policies which
relate <u>either to the people concerned and/or the property involved</u>. Examples would
include but are not limited to:

PEOPLE PROBLEMS
Lenders tend to categorize people. People who fall into the categories listed below
are frequently avoided by some lenders. Do any of these categories apply to you?

- ❑ Are you self employed?
- ❑ Do you have multiple real estate loans?
- ❑ Are you an active real estate investor whose income is primarily from rentals?
- ❑ Do you spend more than about a third of your monthly income for housing?
- ❑ Are your credit card plus car payments more than about a third of your income?
- ❑ Are you a nonresident alien?
- ❑ Have you had any credit problems?

And that's only a partial list of reasons why institutions may say, "We can't make
you a loan...."

PROPERTY PROBLEMS that institutional lenders can get picky about include but
are not limited to the following:

- Almost any type property other than residential (1 to 4) units
- Land/Improvement ratio heavily weighted toward land, e.g., house on 40 acres
- Zoning, e.g., a single family home on a lot zoned commercial or other non-conforming zoning
- Old house that doesn't have a concrete foundation
- Easements or access problems
- Co-op apartments, small 1 bedroom houses, vacation cabins, etc.
- Condominiums where less than a majority of the project/units are owner occupied.
- Special purpose buildings, e.g., church, restaurant, car wash, chicken ranch, bowling alley, service station, theater, etc.

> **Seller carryback financing can overcome all of the above obstacles (both people and property). Sellers can provide the financing where institutions can't or won't.**

DOCUMENTS USED:
What documents are used in a sale involving seller carryback financing?

1. Offer To Purchase

The document may be called an Agreement to Purchase, Purchase Contract, Deposit Receipt, or a Real Estate Purchase Contract and Receipt for Deposit. This document contains the offer and shows details of the sales or purchase price, down payment, institutional loan, if any, and/or the seller's carryback loan. It also contains other terms and conditions of purchase.

2. Mortgage or trust deed to secure the promissory note

In states where mortgages are used:
The note may be built into the mortgage document or it may be a separate document. A note is a promise to pay a certain amount of money during a certain time period. A mortgage encumbers (places a lien) on the owner's interest in the real property as security for the note.
There are two parties to a mortgage.

    a. The mortgagor is the buyer/payor.
    b. The mortgagee is the seller/lender on carryback notes; otherwise, only the lender.

In trust deed states:
The note is a separate document. It also shows who owes what, to whom and when it is payable. The note or promise to pay money is a negotiable instrument (can be assigned to others). A trust deed provides security for the note by encumbering (using) the property as security.
There are three parties to a trust deed:

a. The **Trustor** is the person (buyer/payor) who conveys the real property to the trustee as security. Terminology differs in some states. For example, in Oregon the buyer/payor is called a Grantor in the deed of trust.
b. The **Beneficiary** is the payee of the note (seller/lender on carry-back notes; otherwise, only the lender).
c. The **Trustee** holds title for the protection of the seller/beneficiary until the note is paid off.

The trustee also releases (reconveys) the trust deed as security when the beneficiary advises the trustee that the note has been paid in full.

In the event the trustor/payor defaults, the beneficiary may notify the Trustee of the default and ask the trustee to begin a <u>nonjudicial</u> foreclosure on the trust deed by filing a NOTICE OF DEFAULT. <u>Nonjudicial</u> means you do not go to court to foreclose. The beneficiary also has the option of going to court to obtain a judicial foreclosure.

The trustor/payor will either bring the note current or pay it off within the statutory time limit or the property will be sold at a trustee's sale (a privately held public sale/auction) to the highest bidder. Frequently the <u>only</u> bidder is the note's beneficiary.

PROPERTY DISCLOSURES

Seller Checklists

1. Preliminary Title Report or Commitment To Insure
When you offer your property for sale, with or without an agent, purchase a Preliminary Title Report or Commitment To Insure issued by a licensed title insurance company. The title company will normally credit you the cost of this report when they issue a title insurance policy at the closing of your sale. Having this report in advance will eliminate the buyer's usual "subject to approval of seller's title" contingency which appears in most offers. Much better to know about any bugs in the woodwork before serious negotiations begin.

2. Termite Inspection Report
Speaking of bugs, unless you own vacant land, order a Termite Inspection Report prior to starting your marketing. You will eliminate the buyer's contingency to review the Termite Report by knowing about any damage and the cost necessary to correct it.

3. Real Estate Transfer Disclosure Statement
In California, when selling a property containing 1 to 4 residential units, a seller must provide a buyer with a Real Estate Transfer Disclosure Statement (CA Civil Code 1102, et seq.). While not a warranty, this disclosure gives a buyer notice of any facts that may materially affect the value of the property. Such notice reduces the probability of litigation. Following California's lead, several other states have now adopted similar legislation to require property condition disclosures. With the support of the National Association of Realtors (NAR), this idea is spreading to other states. Such disclosures benefit all parties: Buyers, sellers, and agents.

© 1992, Washington Post Writer's Group. Reprinted with permission.

Even if your state laws may not require you (a seller) to prepare a Real Estate Transfer Disclosure Statement showing Condition of the Property (**EX#1, pgs 24-25), prepare one for the buyer!** You do not need a form for this if your state does not have one. A simple letter telling the buyer what you would want to know about the property's defects if you were buying will do the job. We have included a two page form, which may be used in any state, on pages 24 and 25. The more you can tell a buyer up front, the fewer contingencies the buyer will have. If you own an older property, providing an inspection by a qualified professional inspection service may reassure the buyer that the property is in good condition.

4. Other Ideas
For vacant land not connected to city services, percolation tests for future septic systems are useful. Drilling a test hole to prove water is available also enhances value and marketability. Installing a well and pump will add the most value.

Buyer Checklists:

1. Abstract of title
A condensed summary showing the history or recorded documents relating to a property's title. It should include all liens and encumbrances affecting the property. An abstract is no more than a historical record. Without a policy of title insurance, an abstract is only as good as the attorney who prepares it. The national trend seems to be moving away from abstracts and toward title insurance policies. A title insurance policy protects buyers and/or land contract purchasers. A mortgagee's policy protects lenders, and holders of notes secured by Deeds of Trust or Mortgages. Prior to writing a Title Insurance Policy a title company will issue either a Commitment to Insure or a Preliminary Title Report showing the condition of title that they are willing to insure.

2. Preliminary Title Report or Commitment To Insure

Review the Preliminary Title Report or Commitment To Insure for loans or judgments that have been paid off but still show on the Report. Even though a note has been paid, the recorded security instrument remains as a lien on title until the trustee/mortgagee releases the security. In states where mortgages are used, a mortgage release is called a Satisfaction of Mortgage **(EX #2, pg 26)**. In states where trust deeds are used, a trust deed release is called a Full Reconveyance **(EX #3, pg 27)**. Look for unpaid property taxes and other unpaid liens which show up on the title report. If you find such liens, contact the title insurance company and ask a title officer how to remove the liens. Ask the title officer to get you copies of other recorded documents that are referenced on the title report. These items can affect your ownership and/or your use of the property.

3. Environmental concerns:

Particularly important these days, beware of potential hazardous waste situations:

Asbestos, radon, toxic chemicals, lead paint etc. Contamination on adjacent or nearby properties could impact your property. Inspectors who can determine the presence or history of such materials on the property are available. A qualified inspector can conduct tests which tell you what materials are there and who to contact in the event removal is necessary. Be sure to check the credentials and references of any inspection firm or consultant you hire. The report you get is only as good as the person who prepares it.

Don't ignore this issue. If you do, the liability may stay with you even though you later sell the property. A Hazardous Materials Addendum could be an appropriate addition to a Sales Contract or Deposit Receipt **(EX #4, pg 29)**.

In California a new law requires disclosure if the property is within one or more Natural Hazard zones. The hazard zones are:

> **Special Flood Hazard Area**
> **Area of Potential Flooding**
> **Very High Fire Hazard Severity Zone**
> **Wildland Area That May Contain Substantial Forest Fire Risks & Hazards**
> **Earthquake Fault Zone**
> **Seismic Hazard Zone**

These are in addition to disclosures such as Agency, Lead Paint, Seller Financing Disclosure and the Transfer Disclosure Statement (TDS).

CONDITION OF PROPERTY

(Seller's Representations)

This disclosure statement is prepared for the following:

☐ Seller's listing agreement

☐ Purchase agreement

☐ Exchange agreement

☐ Counteroffer

☐ _____

Dated _____ , 19_____

at _____ , California

Entered into by_____

_____

Regarding property referred to as:_____

_____

REAL ESTATE TRANSFER DISCLOSURE STATEMENT

THIS DISCLOSURE STATEMENT CONCERNS THE REAL PROPERTY SITUATED IN THE CITY OF _____, COUNTY OF _____, STATE OF CALIFORNIA, DESCRIBED AS _____. THIS STATEMENT IS A DISCLOSURE OF THE CONDITION OF THE ABOVE DESCRIBED PROPERTY IN COMPLIANCE WITH SECTION 1102 OF THE CIVIL CODE AS OF _____, 19____. IT IS NOT A WARRANTY OF ANY KIND BY THE SELLER(S) OR ANY AGENT(S) REPRESENTING ANY PRINCIPAL(S) IN THIS TRANSACTION, AND IS NOT A SUBSTITUTE FOR ANY INSPECTIONS OR WARRANTIES THE PRINCIPAL(S) MAY WISH TO OBTAIN.

COORDINATION WITH OTHER DISCLOSURE FORMS

This Real Estate Transfer Disclosure Statement is made pursuant to Section 1102 of the Civil Code. Other statutes require disclosures, depending upon the details of the particular real estate transaction (for example: special study zone and purchase-money liens on residential property).

Substituted Disclosures: The following disclosures have or will be made in connection with this real estate transfer and are intended to satisfy the disclosure obligations on this form, where the subject matter is the same:

☐ Inspection reports completed pursuant to the contract of sale or receipt for deposit.

☐ Additional inspection reports or disclosures: _____

SELLER'S INFORMATION: The Seller discloses the following information with the knowledge that even though this is not a warranty, prospective Buyers may rely on this information in deciding whether and on what terms to purchase the subject property. Seller hereby authorizes any agent(s) representing any principal(s) in this transaction to provide a copy of this statement to any person or entity in connection with any actual or anticipated sale of the property.

> THE FOLLOWING ARE REPRESENTATIONS MADE BY THE SELLER(S) AND ARE NOT THE REPRESENTATIONS OF THE AGENT(S), IF ANY. THIS INFORMATION IS A DISCLOSURE ONLY AND IS NOT INTENDED TO BE A PART OF ANY CONTRACT BETWEEN THE BUYER AND SELLER.

Seller ☐ is, ☐ is not, occupying the property.

A. The subject property has the items checked below **(read across)**:

☐ Range	☐ Oven	☐ Microwave
☐ Dishwasher	☐ Trash Compactor	☐ Garbage Disposal
☐ Washer/Dryer Hookups	☐	☐ Rain Gutters
☐ Burglar Alarms	☐ Smoke Detector(s)	☐ Fire Alarm
☐ T.V. Antenna	☐ Satellite Dish	☐ Intercom
☐ Central Heating	☐ Central Air Conditioning	☐ Evaporator Cooler(s)
☐ Wall/Window Air Conditioning	☐ Sprinklers	☐ Public Sewer System
☐ Septic Tank	☐ Sump Pump	☐ Water Softener
☐ Patio/Decking	☐ Built-in Barbecue	☐ Gazebo
☐ Sauna	☐ Pool ☐ Child Resistant Barrier*	☐ Spa ☐ Hot Tub ☐ Locking Safety Cover*
☐ Security Gate(s)		
☐ Window Screens	☐ Window Security Bars	☐ Quick Release Mechanism on Bedroom Windows*

☐ Automatic Garage Door Opener(s)*, Number Remote Controls:_____

Garage: ☐ Attached, ☐ Not Attached, ☐ Carport

Pool/Spa Heater: ☐ Gas, ☐ Solar

Water Heater: ☐ Gas, ☐ Electric ☐ Anchored, Braced, or Strapped*

Water Supply: ☐ City, ☐ Well ☐ Private Utility or Other _____

Gas Supply: ☐ Utility, ☐ Bottled

Exhaust Fan(s) in _____ 220 Volt Wiring in _____

Fireplace(s) in _____ ☐ Gas Starter _____

☐ Roof(s): Type_____ Age: _____ (approx.)

☐ Other: _____

Are there, to the best of your (Seller's) knowledge, any of the above that are not in operating condition? ☐ Yes ☐ No

If yes, then describe: _____

_____ ☐ See additional description in attached addendum.

B. Are you (Seller) aware of any significant defects/malfunctions in any of the following? ☐ Yes ☐ No

If yes, check appropriate boxes below.

☐ Interior Walls ☐ Ceilings ☐ Floor ☐ Exterior Walls ☐ Insulation ☐ Roof(s) ☐ Windows ☐ Doors
☐ Foundation ☐ Slab(s) ☐ Driveways ☐ Sidewalks ☐ Walls/Fences ☐ Electrical Systems ☐ Plumbing/Sewers/Septics
☐ Other Structural Components (describe): _____

If any of the above is checked, explain: _____

_____ ☐ See additional explanation in attached addendum.

* This garage door opener or child resistant pool barrier may not be in compliance with the safety standards relating to automatic reversing devices as set forth in Chapter 12.5 (commencing with Section 19890) of Part 3 of Division 13 of, or with the pool safety standards of Article 2.5 (commencing with Section 115920) of Chapter 5 of Part 10 of Division 104 of, the Health and Safety Code. The water heater may not be anchored, braced or strapped in accordance with Section 19211 of the Health and Safety Code. Window security bars may not be quick-release mechanisms in compliance with the 1995 Edition of the California Building Standards Code.

‑‑‑‑‑‑‑‑‑‑‑‑‑‑‑‑‑‑‑‑‑‑‑‑‑‑ *PAGE ONE OF TWO-PAGE DISCLOSURE* ‑‑‑‑‑‑‑‑‑‑‑‑‑‑‑‑‑‑‑‑‑‑‑‑‑‑

C. Are you (Seller) aware of any of the following:

1. Substances, materials, or products which may be an environmental hazard such as, but not limited to, asbestos, formaldehyde, radon gas, lead-based paint, fuel or chemical storage tanks, and contaminated soil or water on the subject property . . . . ☐ Yes ☐ No
2. Features of the property shared in common with adjoining landowners, such as walls, fences, and driveways, whose use or responsibility for maintenance may have an effect on the subject property . . . ☐ Yes ☐ No
3. Any encroachments, easements or similar matters that may affect your interest in the subject property . . . . ☐ Yes ☐ No
4. Room additions, structural modifications, or other alterations or repairs made without necessary permits . ☐ Yes ☐ No
5. Room additions, structural modifications, or other alterations or repairs not in compliance with building codes . . . . ☐ Yes ☐ No
6. Landfill (compacted or otherwise) on the property or any portion thereof . . . . ☐ Yes ☐ No
7. Any settling, from any cause, or slippage, sliding, or other soil problems . . . . ☐ Yes ☐ No
8. Flooding, drainage, or grading problems . . . . ☐ Yes ☐ No
9. Major damage to the property or any of the structures from fire, earthquake, floods, or landslides . . . . ☐ Yes ☐ No
10. Any zoning violations, nonconforming uses, violations of "setback" requirements . . . . ☐ Yes ☐ No
11. Neighborhood noise problems or other nuisances . . . . ☐ Yes ☐ No
12. CC&Rs or other deed restrictions or obligations . . . . ☐ Yes ☐ No
13. Homeowners' Association which has any authority over the subject property . . . . ☐ Yes ☐ No
14. Any "common area" (facilities such as pools, tennis courts, walkways, or other areas co-owned in undivided interest with others) . . . . ☐ Yes ☐ No
15. Any notices of abatement or citations against the property . . . . ☐ Yes ☐ No
16. Any lawsuits by or against the seller threatening to or affecting this real property including any lawsuits alleging a defect or deficiency in this real property or "common areas" (facilities such as pools, tennis courts, walkways, or other areas co-owned in undivided interest with others) . . . . ☐ Yes ☐ No

If the answer to any of these is yes, explain:_____

_____

_____ ☐ See additional explanation in attached addendum.

Seller certifies that the information herein is true and correct to the best of the Seller's knowledge as of the date signed by the Seller.

Seller: _____ Date: _____, 19 _____
Seller: _____ Date: _____, 19 _____

SELLER'S AGENT'S INSPECTION DISCLOSURE (To be completed only if the Seller is represented by an agent in this transaction): THE UNDERSIGNED, BASED ON THE ABOVE INQUIRY OF THE SELLER(S) AS TO THE CONDITION OF THE PROPERTY AND BASED ON A REASONABLY COMPETENT AND DILIGENT VISUAL INSPECTION OF THE ACCESSIBLE AREAS OF THE PROPERTY IN CONJUNCTION WITH THAT INQUIRY, STATES THE FOLLOWING:

☐ Agent notes no items for disclosure.
☐ Agent notes the following items:

_____

_____

Agent: _____ By: _____ Date: _____, 19 _____
(Broker representing Seller — Please print)   (Associate Licensee or Broker — Signature)

BUYER'S AGENT'S INSPECTION DISCLOSURE (To be completed only if the agent who has obtained the offer is other than the agent above): THE UNDERSIGNED, BASED ON A REASONABLY COMPETENT AND DILIGENT VISUAL INSPECTION OF THE ACCESSIBLE AREAS OF THE PROPERTY, STATES THE FOLLOWING:

☐ Agent notes no items for disclosure.
☐ Agent notes the following items:

_____

_____

Agent: _____ By: _____ Date: _____, 19 _____
(Broker obtaining the Offer — Please print)   (Associate Licensee or Broker — Signature)

BUYER(S) AND SELLER(S) MAY WISH TO OBTAIN PROFESSIONAL ADVICE AND/OR INSPECTIONS OF THE PROPERTY AND TO PROVIDE FOR APPROPRIATE PROVISIONS IN A CONTRACT BETWEEN BUYER(S) AND SELLER(S) WITH RESPECT TO ANY ADVICE/INSPECTIONS/DEFECTS.
A REAL ESTATE BROKER IS QUALIFIED TO ADVISE ON REAL ESTATE. IF YOU DESIRE LEGAL ADVICE CONSULT YOUR ATTORNEY.

Buyer's Broker:	**Seller's Broker:**
Agent (Broker obtaining the Offer): _____	Agent (Broker representing Seller): _____
Date: _____, 19 ___	Date: _____, 19 ___
By:_____	By:_____
(Associate Licensee or Broker — Signature)	(Associate Licensee or Broker — Signature)
I have read and received a copy of this statement.	**I have read and received a copy of this statement.**
Date: _____, 19 ___	Date: _____, 19 ___
Buyer: _____	Seller: _____
Buyer: _____	Seller: _____
Broker's Approval: _____ ___/___/___	Broker's Approval: _____ ___/___/___

SECTION 1102.3 OF THE CIVIL CODE PROVIDES A BUYER WITH THE RIGHT TO RESCIND A PURCHASE CONTRACT FOR AT LEAST THREE DAYS AFTER THE DELIVERY OF THIS DISCLOSURE IF DELIVERY OCCURS AFTER THE SIGNING OF AN OFFER TO PURCHASE. IF YOU WISH TO RESCIND THE CONTRACT, YOU MUST ACT WITHIN THE PRESCRIBED PERIOD.

FORM 304   01-97   ©1997 first tuesday, P.O. BOX 20069, RIVERSIDE, CA 92516 (909) 781-7300

Owner Will Carry © 1998 by Bill Broadbent, SEC, CCIM, & George Rosenberg

EXHIBIT 2
SATISFACTION OF MORTGAGE

Recording Requested By:

When Recorded Return To:

Property Parcel No.

Satisfaction of Mortgage

I (we) is (are) the owner (s)   and   holder(s) of a certain mortgage deed executed by

to

dated   19   , recorded in Official Records Book
                ,Page   , in the office of the Clerk of the Circuit Court of   County,

State of   , securing   certain note   in the principal sum of

Dollars, and certain promises and obligations set forth in said mortgage deed, upon the property situate
in said State and County described as follows;

- LEGAL DESCRIPTION -

> **PLEASE CHECK WITH YOUR TITLE INSURANCE COMPANY OR ATTORNEY FOR THE APPROPRIATE FORM TO USE IN YOUR STATE** if you need to release or satisfy a mortgage.

hereby acknowledge   full payment and satisfaction of said note   and mortgage deed, and surrender
the same as cancelled, and hereby direct   the Clerk of said Circuit Court to cancel the same of record.

Witness   hand   and seal   , this   day of   , 19
Signed, sealed and delivered in the presence of:

_____   _____
Witness Signature   Grantor Signature

_____   _____
Print name   Print name

_____   _____
Witness Signature   Address

_____
Printed name

_____   _____
Witness Signature   Co-Grantor Signature

_____   _____
Print name   Print name

_____   _____
Witness Signature   Address

_____
Printed name

STATE OF_____)   I hereby Certify that on this day, before me, an
                                       officer duly authorized to administer oaths and
COUNTY OF_____)   take acknowledgements, personally appeared

_____   _____

Notary Seal et al

EXHIBIT 3

Order No.
Escrow No.
Loan No.

FULL RECONVEYANCE (For Deed of Trust)

WHEN RECORDED MAIL TO:

Mr. and Mrs. Bob Buyer
77 Park Avenue
Anytown, USA

SPACE ABOVE THIS LINE FOR RECORDER'S USE

FULL RECONVEYANCE

FIRST AMERICAN TITLE INSURANCE COMPANY, a Corporation, Trustee under the Deed of Trust executed by _____ Bob Buyer and Betty Buyer, husband and wife _____

Trustor, and recorded _October 10, 1992_ as Document No. _98765_ in Book_____,
page_____, of Official Records in the Office of the County Recorder of ____SLO_____
County, California, having been requested in writing by the holder of the obligation secured by said Deed of Trust, to reconvey the estate granted to Trustee under said Deed of Trust, does hereby reconvey to the person or persons legally entitled thereto, without warranty, all the estate, title and interest acquired by Trustee under said Deed of Trust.

DESCRIPTION   Lot 3 of Tract No. 890, Whispering Pines Subdivision in the County of SLO, State of California as per map recorded in Book 12, Pages 4 and 5 of Maps, in the office of the County Recorder of said County.

IN WITNESS WHEREOF, said FIRST AMERICAN TITLE INSURANCE COMPANY, Trustee, has caused its corporate name and seal to be hereto affixed by its Assistant Secretary, thereunto duly authorized.

Dated:

FIRST AMERICAN TITLE INSURANCE COMPANY

After note is paid off and
returned to Trustee with
reconveyance fee.

By

Assistant Secretary

STATE OF CALIFORNIA   }
COUNTY OF _____ }ss.
                                                }
On _____ before me,

_____,

personally appeared_____

_____,

personally known to me (or proved to me on the basis of satisfactory

evidence) to be the person(s) whose name(s) is/are subscribed to the

within instrument and acknowledged to me that he/she/they executed

the same in his/her/their authorized capacity(ies), and that by

his/her/their signature(s) on the instrument the person(s) or the entity

upon behalf of which the person(s) acted, executed the instrument.

WITNESS my hand and official seal.

Signature_____

(This area for official notarial seal)

EXHIBIT 4

HAZARDOUS MATERIALS DISCLOSURE

This is in reference to the Agreement dated _____ between _____
and _____, concerning the property located at _____
_____.

Various materials utilized in the construction of improvements to property may contain materials that have been or may in the future be determined to be toxic, hazardous, or undesirable. These materials may need to be specially handled or removed from the property. For example, some electrical transformers and other electrical components can contain PCBs. Asbestos has been used in a wide variety of building components such as fire-proofing, air duct insulation, acoustical tiles, spray-on acoustical materials, linoleum, floor tiles, and plaster. Due to current or prior uses, the property or improvements may contain materials such as metals, minerals, chemicals, hydrocarbons, biological or radioactive materials, and other substances which are considered, or in the future may be determined to be, toxic wastes, hazardous materials, or undesirable substances. Such substances may be in above-ground and below-ground containers on the property or may be present on or in soils, water, building components, or other portions of the property in areas that may not be accessible or noticeable.

Current and future federal, state, and local laws and regulations may require the clean-up of such toxic, hazardous, or undesirable materials at the expense of those persons who in the past, present, or future have had any interest in property including, but not limited to, current, past and future owners and users of the property. The parties are advised to consult with independent legal counsel of their choice to determine the potential liability with respect to toxic, hazardous, or undesirable materials. The parties should also consult with such legal counsel to determine what provisions regarding toxic, hazardous, or undesirable materials they may wish to include in purchase and sale agreements, leases, options, and other legal documentation related to transactions they contemplate entering into with respect to the property.

The real estate salespersons and brokers in this transaction have no expertise with respect to toxic wastes, hazardous materials, or undesirable substances. Proper inspections of the property by qualified experts are an absolute necessity to determine whether or not there are any current or potential toxic wastes, hazardous materials, or undesirable substances in or on the property. The real estate salespersons and brokers in this transaction have not made, nor will make, any representations, either expressed or implied, regarding the existence or nonexistence of toxic wastes, hazardous materials, or undesirable substances in or on the property. Problems involving toxic wastes, hazardous materials, or undesirable substances can be extremely costly to correct. It is the responsibility of the parties to retain qualified experts to deal with the detection and correction of such matters.

The parties are directed to seek further information concerning any and all future correctional measures, if any, from appropriate governmental agencies.

The undersigned acknowledge that they have read and understand this disclosure and have received a copy.

_____   Date _____

_____   Date _____

_____   Date _____

_____   Date _____

  **PROFESSIONAL PUBLISHING**

Owner Will Carry © 1998 by Bill Broadbent, SEC, CCIM, & George Rosenberg

NCR (No Carbon Required)

DISCLOSURE OF INFORMATION ON LEAD-BASED PAINT AND LEAD-BASED PAINT HAZARDS
(Required by Law for Sales of Property Built Prior to 1978)

This disclosure statement concerns the real property situated in the City of _____,
County of _____, State of _____, described as _____

LEAD WARNING STATEMENT

Every purchaser of an interest in residential real property on which a residential dwelling was built prior to 1978 is notified that such property may present exposure to lead from lead-based paint that may place young children at risk of developing lead poisoning. Lead poisoning in young children may produce permanent neurological damage, including learning disabilities, reduced intelligence quotient, behavioral problems, and impaired memory. Lead poisoning also poses a particular risk to pregnant women. The seller of any interest in residential real property is required to provide the buyer with any information on lead-based paint hazards from risk assessments or inspections in the seller's possession and notify the buyer of any known lead-based paint hazards. A risk assessment or inspection for possible lead-based paint hazards is recommended prior to purchase.

SELLER'S DISCLOSURE (initial [a] and [b])

[____] [____] (a) Presence of lead-based paint and/or lead-based paint hazards (check one below):

Check one
☐ Known lead-based paint and/or lead-based paint hazards are present in the housing (explain).
_____
☐ Seller has no knowledge of lead-based paint and/or lead-based paint hazards in the housing.

[____] [____] (b) Records and reports available to the seller (check one below):

Check one
☐ Seller has provided the purchaser with all available records and reports pertaining to lead-based paint and/or lead-based paint hazards in the housing (list documents below).
_____
☐ Seller has no reports or records pertaining to lead-based paint and/or lead-based paint hazards in the housing.

BUYER'S ACKNOWLEDGMENT (initial [c], [d], and [e])

[____] [____] (c) Buyer has received copies of all information listed above.

[____] [____] (d) Buyer has received the pamphlet *Protect Your Family from Lead in Your Home,* or other approved pamphlet.

[____] [____] (e) Buyer has (check one below):

Check one
☐ Received a 10-day opportunity (or mutually agreed upon period) to conduct a risk assessment or inspection for the presence of lead-based paint and/or lead-based paint hazards; or
☐ Waived the opportunity to conduct a risk assessment or inspection for the presence of lead-based paint and/or lead-based paint hazards.

LISTING AGENT'S ACKNOWLEDGMENT (initial)

[____] (f) Agent representing the seller has informed the seller of the seller's obligations under 42 U.S.C. 4852d and is aware of his or her responsibility to ensure compliance.

CERTIFICATION OF ACCURACY

The following parties have reviewed the information above and certify, to the best of their knowledge, that the information provided by the signatory is true and accurate.

Seller _____ Date _____   Buyer _____ Date _____

Seller _____ Date _____   Buyer _____ Date _____

Listing Broker _____ Date _____   Selling Broker _____ Date _____

By (Agent) _____   By (Agent) _____

Rev. by _____
Date _____

42 United States Code § 4852d

§ 4852d. Disclosure of information concerning lead upon transfer of residential property
(a) Lead disclosure in purchase and sale or lease of target housing

(1) Lead-based paint hazards

Not later than 2 years after October 28, 1992, the Secretary [of HUD] and the Administrator of the Environmental Protection Agency shall promulgate regulations under this section for the disclosure of lead-based paint hazards in target housing which is offered for sale or lease. The regulations shall require that, before the purchaser or lessee is obligated under any contract to purchase or lease the housing, the seller or lessor shall:

(A) provide the purchaser or lessee with a lead hazard information pamphlet, as prescribed by the Administrator of the Environmental Protection Agency under section 406 of the Toxic Substances Control Act [15 U.S.C.A. § 2686];

(B) disclose to the purchaser or lessee the presence of any known lead-based paint, or any known lead-based paint hazards, in such housing and provide to the purchaser or lessee any lead hazard evaluation report available to the seller or lessor; and

(C) permit the purchaser a 10-day period (unless the parties mutually agree upon a different period of time) to conduct a risk assessment or inspection for the presence of lead-based paint hazards.

(2) Contract for purchase and sale

Regulations promulgated under this section shall provide that every contract for the purchase and sale of any interest in target housing shall contain a Lead Warning Statement and a statement signed by the purchaser that the purchaser has:

(A) read the Lead Warning Statement and understands its contents;

(B) received a lead hazard information pamphlet; and

(C) had a 10-day opportunity (unless the parties mutually agreed upon a different period of time) before becoming obligated under the contract to purchase the housing to conduct a risk assessment or inspection for the presence of lead-based paint hazards.

(3) Contents of Lead Warning Statement

The Lead Warning Statement shall contain the following text printed in large type on a separate sheet of paper attached to the contract:

"Every purchaser of any interest in residential real property on which a residential dwelling was built prior to 1978 is notified that such property may present exposure to lead from lead-based paint that may place young children at risk of developing lead poisoning. Lead poisoning in young children may produce permanent neurological damage, including learning disabilities, reduced intelligence quotient, behavioral problems, and impaired memory. Lead poisoning also poses a particular risk to pregnant women. The seller of any interest in residential real property is required to provide the buyer with any information on lead-based paint hazards from risk assessments or inspections in the seller's possession and notify the buyer of any known lead-based paint hazards. A risk assessment or inspection for possible lead-based paint hazards is recommended prior to purchase."

(4) Compliance assurance

Whenever a seller or lessor has entered into a contract with an agent for the purpose of selling or leasing a unit of target housing, the regulations promulgated under this section shall require the agent, on behalf of the seller or lessor, to ensure compliance with the requirements of this section.

(5) Promulgation

A suit may be brought against the Secretary of Housing and Urban Development and the Administrator of the Environmental Protection Agency under section 20 of the Toxic Substances Control Act [15 U.S.C.A. § 2619] to compel promulgation of the regulations required under this section and the Federal district court shall have jurisdiction to order such promulgation.

(b) Penalties for violations

(1) Monetary penalty

Any person who knowingly violates any provision of this section shall be subject to civil money penalties in accordance with the provisions of section 3545 of this title.

(2) Action by Secretary

The Secretary is authorized to take such lawful action as may be necessary to enjoin any violation of this section.

(3) Civil liability

Any person who knowingly violates the provisions of this section shall be jointly and severally liable to the purchaser or lessee in an amount equal to 3 times the amount of damages incurred by such individual.

(4) Costs

In any civil action brought for damages pursuant to paragraph (3), the appropriate court may award court costs to the party commencing such action, together with reasonable attorney fees and any expert witness fees, if that party prevails.

(5) Prohibited act

It shall be a prohibited act under section 409 of the Toxic Substances Control Act [15 U.S.C.A. § 2689] for any person to fail or refuse to comply with a provision of this section or with any rule or order issued under this section. For purposes of enforcing this section under the Toxic Substances Control Act [15 U.S.C.A. § 2601 et seq.], the penalty for each violation applicable under section 16 of that Act [15 U.S.C.A. § 2615] shall not be more than $10,000.

(c) Validity of contracts and liens

Nothing in this section shall affect the validity or enforceability of any sale or contract for the purchase and sale or lease of any interest in residential real property or any loan, loan agreement, mortgage, or lien made or arising in connection with a mortgage loan, nor shall anything in this section create a defect in title.

(d) Effective date

The regulations under this section shall take effect 3 years after October 28, 1992.

(Pub.L. 102-550, Title X, § 1018, Oct. 28, 1992, 106 Stat. 3910.)

FORM 110.74 (6-97)

Now that you know some basic concepts of seller carryback financing, let's discuss the negotiations involved. Begin by looking at:

CHAPTER 2

NEGOTIATIONS

THE ELEMENTS OF A REAL ESTATE TRANSACTION

PRICE

TERMS

INTEREST RATES

CASH PAYMENTS

CLOSING COSTS (who pays)

IMPOUND ACCOUNTS

TITLE COMPANY TO USE

ESCROW COMPANY OR CLOSING ATTORNEY TO USE

RELEASE OF LOAN LIABILITY FOR SELLER

PERSONAL PROPERTY INCLUDED OR NOT

TIME OF POSSESSION

REPAIRS OR DEFERRED MAINTENANCE

APPRAISAL

SELLER CARRYBACK FINANCING

Q. WHAT DO ALL OF THE ABOVE ELEMENTS HAVE IN COMMON?

A. They are all νεγοτιαβλε !

Does that word look like Greek to you? Those are Greek letters. The word is **NEGOTIABLE.** Some people act as if they don't understand its meaning. Few transactions have as many negotiable elements as a real estate transaction. You will have far more difficulty negotiating loan terms and conditions with Insecurity Bank than with a Seller who is carrying back a trust deed note or mortgage to facilitate the sale of his/her property.

If you remember nothing else from this book, remember that <u>all elements</u> of a real estate transaction **are negotiable.** It is sometimes difficult to be objective about your own situation. If you are not good at negotiating, employ a knowledgeable agent to represent and negotiate for you!

NEGOTIATING TERMS ON A SELLER CARRYBACK NOTE

Although all note amounts and terms are negotiable, the first items most commonly negotiated between buyer and seller on a note are:
- Amount of the note (how much of the purchase price the seller will carry back)
- Interest rate
- Monthly payment
- Due date (or balloon payment, if any)

When structuring a carryback note, to minimize a discount, the due date is normally more important than the interest rate or the monthly payment.

The last three elements above, not the amount of the note, influence the time value of money, our next topic.

AN IMPORTANT FINANCIAL PERSPECTIVE
UNDERSTANDING THE TIME VALUE OF MONEY.

Time affects the value of money. When you receive money, either now or later, makes that money either more valuable (now) or less valuable (later). **A dollar to be received in the future is worth less than a dollar received today.** To understand this concept, think of the flow of dollars as follows:

#1. "MORE SOONER IS BETTER" APPLIES WHEN YOU ARE RECEIVING MONEY.

If you carry back a note for 10 years at 10% interest, each payment you will receive is worth a different amount, depending on when (the time) you receive it. Suppose you can invest that money at more than 10% as it comes in. The faster the money comes in, the faster you can reinvest that money to earn more money. So, when you are on the receiving end of money, assuming you can invest that money at a higher rate of interest (or return) than you are receiving, "MORE SOONER IS BETTER". If you can't earn more than 10%, you may be better off holding the carryback note for income.

What do sellers want, or should sellers want when negotiating the terms of a note?

From Sam Seller's perspective as a seller carrying back financing, he will be on the receiving end of money. "MORE SOONER IS BETTER." The faster Sam can get his money back, the better for him. The sooner the note pays off, the more the note is worth today.

#2. "LESS LATER IS BETTER" APPLIES WHEN YOU ARE PAYING MONEY.

If you are now paying on that 10 year note at 10% interest, and, if you know how to earn more than 10% interest on another investment, you may want to borrow money for as long as possible. Your payments will be lower and the excess cash can then be invested to earn you more than 10%. When you are paying money, "LESS LATER IS BETTER". However, if you can't earn more than 10%, you may be better off paying your note as quickly as possible, and saving a large amount of interest.

What do buyers want, or should buyers want when negotiating terms of a note?

From Bob Buyer's perspective as the purchaser, he is on the paying end of money. "LESS LATER IS BETTER." The less money Bob Buyer pays out and the longer he can take to repay at an interest rate less than he can earn on another investment, the more he benefits. This can best be illustrated in the following example.

Suppose Bob is planning to buy an investment property he believes will appreciate in value in years to come. He plans to use leverage (borrowed money) to finance this property purchase. Bob will be making loan payments. The lower his interest rate, the longer the loan term, the lower his payments will be. This allows him to handle a larger loan, control more property and, if appreciation occurs, he will increase his profit margin over time. Using debt to acquire assets that produce income and/or grow in value, like buying a business or income producing real estate, can be a productive use of debt. This is different from using debt to live beyond one's means (buying expensive toys or unnecessary consumer goods), which is an unproductive use of debt.

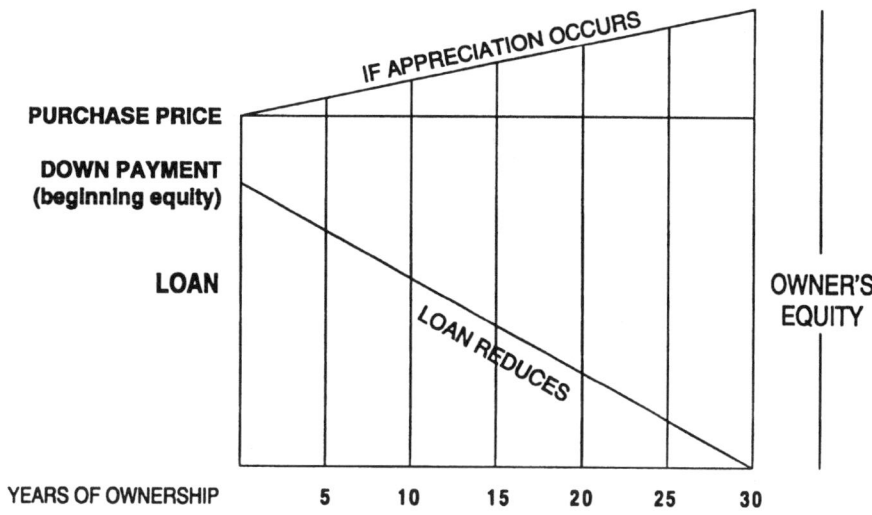

The concepts of "MORE SOONER IS BETTER" and "LESS LATER IS BETTER" apply when you can earn a higher interest rate than you are receiving OR when you can earn a higher interest rate than you are paying. "MORE SOONER IS BETTER" and "LESS LATER IS BETTER" may not be great grammar, but each concept can be good business. The authors of this book would like to thank Peter Fortunato for sharing this concept and the quoted words over a decade ago.

THE WONDER OF COMPOUNDING:
WHENEVER POSSIBLE HAVE YOUR MONEY EARN INTEREST ON INTEREST, WHICH IN TURN EARNS MORE INTEREST ON INTEREST, ETC. THIS IDEA OF MONEY GROWING BY ITSELF IS CALLED THE COMPOUNDING EFFECT. Some of the world's greatest financial geniuses have called compounding "the eighth wonder of the world." Compounding is a two edged sword that works for you when you are receiving money and reinvesting it on a regular basis. If you are in debt and either not paying the interest or are continuing to borrow to pay the interest (as we do with our national debt), the amount owed compounds, then the compounding effect works against you.

Here is our favorite example of how the compounding effect of money works in a positive way: Ben, age 22, invests $1,000 per year compounded annually at 10% for eight (8) years, until he is 30 years old. For the next 35 years, until he is 65, Ben invests not one penny more, while his savings compound.

Arthur, age 30, invests $1,000 per year for thirty five (35) years, until he is 65 years old. His investment also earns 10% compound interest per year. At age 65, will Arthur or Ben have the most money? Guess before looking at the end.

YEAR	BEN	AT YR END	ARTHUR	AT YR END
1	1,000	1,100	0	0
2	1,000	2,310	0	0
3	1,000	3,641	0	0
4	1,000	5,105	0	0
5	1,000	6,716	0	0
6	1,000	8,487	0	0
7	1,000	10,436	0	0
8	1,000	12,579	0	0
9	0	13,837	1,000	1,100
10	0	15,221	1,000	2,310
11	0	16,743	1,000	3,641
12	0	18,418	1,000	5,105
13	0	20,259	1,000	6,716
14	0	22,285	1,000	8,487
15	0	24,514	1,000	10,436
16	0	26,965	1,000	12,579
17	0	29,662	1,000	14,937
18	0	32,628	1,000	17,531
19	0	35,891	1,000	20,384
20	0	39,480	1,000	23,523
21	0	43,428	1,000	26,975
22	0	47,771	1,000	30,772
23	0	52,548	1,000	34,950
24	0	57,802	1,000	39,545
25	0	63,583	1,000	44,599
26	0	69,941	1,000	50,159
27	0	76,935	1,000	56,275
28	0	84,628	1,000	63,002
29	0	93,091	1,000	70,403
30	0	102,400	1,000	78,543
31	0	112,640	1,000	87,497
32	0	123,904	1,000	97,347
33	0	136,295	1,000	108,182
34	0	149,924	1,000	120,100
35	0	164,917	1,000	133,210
36	0	181,409	1,000	147,631
37	0	199,549	1,000	163,494
38	0	219,504	1,000	180,943

Did you guess who would come out ahead? If you really understand how compounding works, you will understand that **the value of money is directly related to the time when it is received.** If the compounding effect takes place in a tax sheltered environment, such as an IRA account, Keogh or Self-Directed Pension or Profit Sharing Plan, the results are even more dramatic. Learn how to make the compounding effect work for you.

THE ADVANTAGE OF TAX DEFERRED COMPOUNDING
(Tax Free using a Roth IRA)

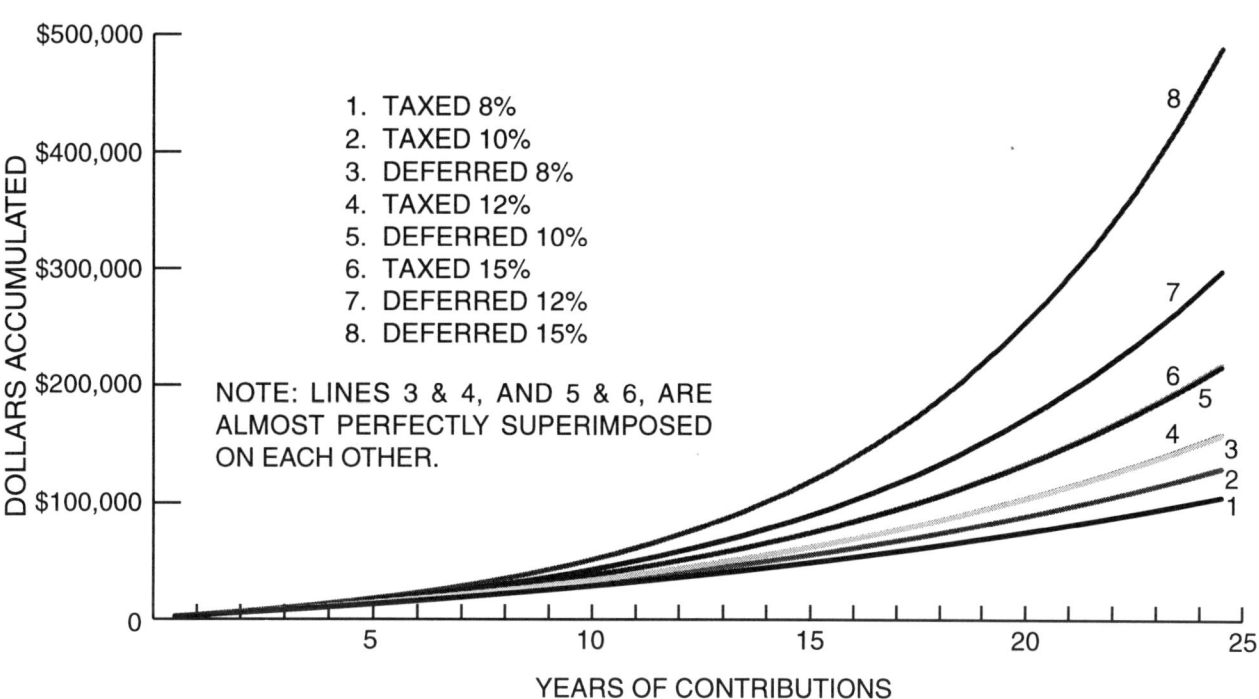

1. TAXED 8%
2. TAXED 10%
3. DEFERRED 8%
4. TAXED 12%
5. DEFERRED 10%
6. TAXED 15%
7. DEFERRED 12%
8. DEFERRED 15%

NOTE: LINES 3 & 4, AND 5 & 6, ARE ALMOST PERFECTLY SUPERIMPOSED ON EACH OTHER.

This chart assumes a $2,000 annual contribution at the beginning of each year, with the earnings taxed annually at 33%. It shows after-tax and deferred-tax earnings accumulated at fixed rates of return at 8%, 10%, 12% & 15%.

SELLER CARRYBACK FINANCING EXAMPLE

The more equity a seller has in his property, the easier it is for the seller to structure carryback financing. Statistics differ on the subject, but some experts estimate that up to half the homes in America have no existing debt. Suppose Sam and Sally Seller own their home on Park Ave. <u>free and clear of debt</u>. A realistic, written appraisal by a licensed, professional fee appraiser, one not in the real estate marketing business, indicates a value of $100,000. Sam and Sally Seller own a motor home and want to spend their retirement years traveling.

Bob and Betty Buyer are a young couple in their mid-twenties who want to buy a home. They have saved $18,000 cash toward a down payment. They want to buy Sam Seller's house and make the following offer to purchase:

Price of Seller's home on Park Ave.	$100,000
Cash down payment by Buyers	$ 18,000
Seller to carry back a note secured by a first trust deed on their property for	$ 82,000

The Seller's note will earn interest at 9% per year. The note will be amortized over 30 years.

Amortization refers to a series of periodic payments of principal and interest which pay off a loan over a set period of time. The word "amortize" is derived from the French "amortir," which means to kill. A loan is literally killed when it is paid off. In this example, amortizing an $82,000, 30 year loan at 9% interest will require a monthly payment of $660 principal and interest (rounded).

Let's look at the items to be negotiated on the note in this sale:

Sellers want:
1. A due-on-sale provision. If Bob and Betty Buyer sell in the future, the Sellers may want the loan paid off, or, at least want the opportunity to determine the credit and financial strength of the new buyer/borrower. It also gives them an opportunity to adjust to current interest rates.
2. A balloon payment due on the note five years from closing. The entire unpaid balance will be due and payable five years from closing.
3. A late charge of 6 percent of the payment if it is not made within 10 days of its due date.
4. Buyer to pay all closing costs.

Buyers want:
1. No due-on-sale provision. If they sell, their note would be assumable.
2. No balloon payment. Where will they get the money to pay in five years?
3. No late charge. Buyers try to pay on time but accidents happen.
4. Sellers to pay all closing costs.

A negotiated compromise
Seldom in the real world do we get everything EXACTLY the way we want. Each party may begin by asking for their dream. A seller should not ignore a low first offer. He/she should always make a counter offer. Some buyers need the satisfaction of having tried to get a "great buy." Expect some give and take on each side through negotiation and compromise. Here is a likely compromise:

1. A due-on-sale provision will give Sellers some control in the event Buyers sell. Sellers still have the option of approving a new buyer.
2. A balloon payment in 10 years, not five. The loan balance will be lower and buyers should be able to refinance.
3. A late charge of 6 percent of the payment if not paid within 15 days.
   This allows buyers a reasonable time to pay without penalty.
4. Buyer and Seller agree to share closing costs equally.

See **EX#6** on the following pages for an example of a Residential Purchase Agreement.

NCR (No Carbon Required) **STANDARD RESIDENTIAL PURCHASE AGREEMENT**

DEFINITIONS

BROKER includes cooperating brokers and all sales persons. *DAYS* means calendar days unless otherwise specified. *DATE OF ACCEPTANCE* means the date Seller accepts the offer or the Buyer accepts the counter offer. *DELIVERED* means personally delivered, transmitted by facsimile machine, by a nationally recognized overnight courier, or by deposit in the U.S. Mail, postage prepaid. In the event of mailing, the document will be deemed delivered three (3) business days after deposit; in the event of overnight courier, one (1) business day after deposit; and if by facsimile, at time of transmission provided that a transmission report is generated and retained by the sender reflecting the accurate transmission of the document. *DATE OF CLOSING* means the date title is transferred. *TERMINATING THE AGREEMENT* means that both parties are relieved of their obligations and all deposits will be returned to Buyer less expenses incurred by or on account of Buyer to date of termination. *PROPERTY* means the real property and any personal property included in the sale.

AGENCY RELATIONSHIP CONFIRMATION. The following agency relationship is hereby confirmed for this transaction and supersedes any prior agency election:

LISTING AGENT: _____ is the agent of (check one):
(Print Firm Name)

☐ the Seller exclusively; or ☐ both the Buyer and the Seller.

SELLING AGENT: _____ (if not the same as the Listing Agent) is the agent of (check one):
(Print Firm Name)

☐ the Buyer exclusively; or ☐ the Seller exclusively; or ☐ both the Buyer and the Seller.

Note: This confirmation DOES NOT take the place of the AGENCY DISCLOSURE form (P.P. Form 110.42 CAL) required by law.

_____ hereinafter designated as BUYER, offers to purchase the real property situated in _____, County of _____, California, described as _____,
FOR THE PURCHASE PRICE OF $_____ (_____
_____ dollars) on the following terms and conditions:

☐ Buyer does ☐ Buyer does not intend to occupy the property as his or her residence.

1. **FINANCING TERMS AND LOAN PROVISIONS.**
   A. $_____ **DEPOSIT** evidenced by ☐ check, or ☐ other: _____,
   held uncashed until acceptance and not later than three (3) business days thereafter deposited with: _____
   B. $_____ **ADDITIONAL CASH DEPOSIT** to be placed in escrow ☐ within _____ days after acceptance, ☐ upon receipt of Loan Commitment per Item 2. ☐ Other: _____
   C. $_____ **BALANCE OF CASH PAYMENT** needed to close, not including closing costs.
   D. $_____ **NEW FIRST LOAN:** ☐ CONVENTIONAL, ☐ FHA, ☐ VA, ☐ Other financing acceptable to Buyer:
   ☐ FIXED RATE: For ____ years, interest not to exceed _____%, payable at approximately $_____ per month (principal and interest only), with the balance due in not less than _____ years.
   ☐ ARM: For ____ years, initial interest rate not to exceed _____%, with initial monthly payments of $_____ and maximum lifetime rate not to exceed _____%.
   ☐ Buyer will pay loan fee or points not to exceed _____.
   ☐ Lender to appraise property at no less than purchase price.
   ☐ If FHA or VA, Seller will pay _____% discount points, and other fees and costs not to exceed $_____.
   ☐ OTHER TERMS: _____.
   E. $_____ **EXISTING FINANCING:** ☐ FIRST LOAN, ☐ SECOND LOAN:
   ☐ ASSUMPTION OF, ☐ SUBJECT TO existing loan of record described as follows: _____
   F. $_____ **SELLER FINANCING:** ☐ FIRST LOAN, ☐ SECOND LOAN, ☐ THIRD LOAN, secured by the property.
   ☐ Seller Financing Addendum, P.P. Form 131.1-3 CAL, is attached and made a part of this Agreement.
   G. $_____ **OTHER FINANCING:** _____
   H. $_____ **TOTAL PURCHASE PRICE (not including closing costs).**

2. **LOAN APPROVAL.** Conditioned upon Buyer's ability to obtain a commitment for new financing, as set forth above, from a lender or mortgage broker of Buyer's choice, and/or consent to assumption of existing financing provided for in this Agreement, **within _____ days after acceptance.** Buyer will in good faith use his or her best efforts to qualify for and obtain the financing and will complete and submit a loan application **within five (5) days after acceptance.** Buyer ☐ will, ☐ will not provide a pre-qualification letter from lender or mortgage broker based on Buyer's application and credit report **within _____ days after acceptance.** In the event a loan commitment or consent is obtained but not timely honored without fault of Buyer, Buyer may terminate this Agreement.

Buyer [_____] [_____] and Seller [_____] [_____] have read this page.

CAUTION: The copyright laws of the United States forbid the unauthorized reproduction of this form by any means including scanning or computerized formats.

PROFESSIONAL PUBLISHING

Owner Will Carry © 1998 by Bill Broadbent, SEC, CCIM, & George Rosenberg

Property Address _____

3. **BONDS AND ASSESSMENTS.** In the event there is a bond or assessment which has an outstanding principal balance and is a lien upon the property, the current installment will be prorated between Buyer and Seller as of the date of closing. Payments not yet due will be assumed by Buyer WITHOUT CREDIT toward the purchase price, EXCEPT AS FOLLOWS: _____

    This Agreement is conditioned upon both parties verifying and approving in writing the amount of any bond or assessment to be assumed or paid **within ten (10) days after receipt** of the preliminary title report. In the event of disapproval, the disapproving party may terminate this Agreement.

4. **PROPERTY TAX. Within five (5) days after acceptance,** Seller will deliver to Buyer for his or her approval a copy of the latest property tax bill. Buyer is advised that: (a) the property will be reassessed upon change of ownership which may result in a tax increase; and (b) the tax bill may not include certain exempt items such as school taxes on property owned by seniors. Buyer should make further inquiry at the assessor's office. **Within ten (10) days after receipt** of the tax bill, Buyer will in writing approve or disapprove the tax bill. In the event of disapproval, Buyer may terminate this Agreement.

5. **EXISTING LOANS.** Seller will, **within three (3) days after acceptance,** provide Buyer with copies of all notes and deeds of trust to be assumed or taken subject to. **Within five (5) days after receipt** Buyer will notify Seller in writing of his or her approval or disapproval of the terms of the documents. Approval will not be unreasonably withheld. **Within three (3) days after acceptance,** Seller will submit a written request for a current Statement of Condition on the above loan(s). Seller warrants that all loans will be current at close of escrow. Seller will pay any prepayment charge imposed on any existing loan paid off at close of escrow. Buyer will pay the prepayment charge on any loan which is to remain a lien upon the property after close of escrow. The parties are encouraged to consult his or her lender regarding prepayment provisions and any due on sale clauses.

6. **DESTRUCTION OF IMPROVEMENTS.** If the improvements of the property are destroyed, materially damaged, or found to be materially defective as a result of such damage prior to close of escrow, Buyer may terminate this Agreement by written notice delivered to Seller or his or her Broker, and all unused deposits will be returned. In the event Buyer does not elect to terminate this Agreement, Buyer will be entitled to receive, in addition to the property, any insurance proceeds payable on account of the damage or destruction.

7. **EXAMINATION OF TITLE.** In addition to any encumbrances assumed or taken "subject to," Seller will convey title to the property subject only to: [1] real estate taxes not yet due; and [2] covenants, conditions, restrictions, rights of way and easements of record, if any, which do not materially affect the value or intended use of the property.

    Within three (3) days after acceptance, Buyer will order a Preliminary Title Report and copies of CC&Rs and other documents of record if applicable. **Within ten (10) days after receipt,** Buyer will report to Seller in writing any valid objections to title contained in such report (other than monetary liens to be paid upon close of escrow). If Buyer objects to any exceptions to the title, Seller will use due diligence to remove such exceptions at his or her own expense **before close of escrow.** If such exceptions cannot be removed before close of escrow, this Agreement will terminate, unless Buyer elects to purchase the property subject to such exceptions. If Seller concludes he or she is in good faith unable to remove such objections, Seller will so notify Buyer **within ten (10) days after receipt** of said objections. In that event Buyer may terminate this Agreement.

8. **EVIDENCE OF TITLE** will be in the form of a CLTA or ALTA owner's policy of title insurance, issued by _____, paid by ☐ Buyer, ☐ Seller, ☐ Other _____. **NOTE:** In addition to coverage under a CLTA policy, the ALTA policy may offer additional coverage for a number of unrecorded matters. Buyer should discuss the choice of a CLTA or ALTA policy with the title company of their choice at the time escrow is opened. In the event a lender requires an ALTA lender's policy of title insurance, ☐ Buyer, ☐ Seller will pay the premium.

9. **PRORATIONS.** Rents, real estate taxes, interest, payments on bonds and assessments assumed by Buyer, and homeowners association fees will be prorated as of the date of recordation of the deed. Security deposits, advance rentals, or considerations involving future lease credits will be credited to Buyer.

10. **CLOSING.** Full purchase price to be paid and deed to be recorded ☐ on or before _____, OR ☐ within _____ **days after acceptance.** Both parties will deposit with an authorized escrow holder, to be selected by Buyer, all funds and instruments necessary to complete the sale in accordance with the terms of this Agreement. ☐ Where customary, signed escrow instructions will be delivered to escrow holder **within _____ days after acceptance.** Escrow fee to be paid by _____. County/City transfer tax(es), if any, to be paid by _____. Homeowner association transfer fee to be paid by _____.
    THIS PURCHASE AGREEMENT TOGETHER WITH ANY ADDENDA WILL CONSTITUTE JOINT ESCROW INSTRUCTIONS TO THE ESCROW HOLDER.

11. **PHYSICAL POSSESSION.** Physical possession of the property, with keys to all property locks, alarms, and garage door openers, will be delivered to Buyer (*check one*):
    ☐ On the date of recordation of the deed, not later than _____ ☐ a.m., ☐ p.m.;
    ☐ On the _____ day after recordation, not later than _____ ☐ a.m., ☐ p.m.
    In the event possession is to be delivered **before or after recordation,** such possession is conditioned upon the execution by both parties of a written occupancy agreement.

12. **FIXTURES.** All items permanently attached to the property, including light fixtures and bulbs, attached floor coverings, all attached window coverings, including window hardware, window and door screens, storm sash, combination doors, awnings, TV antennas, burglar, fire, smoke and security alarms (unless leased), pool and spa equipment, solar systems, attached fireplace screens, electric garage door openers with controls, outdoor plants and trees (other than in movable containers), are included in the purchase price free of liens, EXCLUDING: _____

Buyer [_____] [_____] and Seller [_____] [_____] have read this page.

FORM 101-R.2 CAL (6-97)   COPYRIGHT © 1994–97 BY PROFESSIONAL PUBLISHING, 880 LAS GALLINAS AVE., SAN RAFAEL, CA 94903   (415) 472-1964 FAX (415) 472-2069

PROFESSIONAL PUBLISHING

Owner Will Carry © 1998 by Bill Broadbent, SEC, CCIM, & George Rosenberg

Property Address _____

13. CONDITION OF PROPERTY. Regardless of any disclosures made or conditions discovered by the parties or their agents, Seller agrees that upon delivery of possession to the Buyer: (a) all built-in appliances included in the sale, and the electrical, plumbing, heating and cooling systems will be in working order and free of leaks; (b) the roof will be free of leaks; (c) all broken or cracked glass, including mirrors and shower/tub enclosures and broken seals between double-pane windows, will be replaced; (d) and existing window and door screens that are damaged will be repaired. The following items are specifically excluded from the above: _____
_____

Seller's obligations under this provision are not intended to create a duty to repair an item that may fail after possession is delivered. **Buyer and Seller acknowledge that Broker is not responsible for any alleged breach of these covenants.**

14. MAINTENANCE. Until possession is delivered, Seller will maintain all structures, landscaping, grounds, and pool in the same general condition as of the date of acceptance or physical inspection, whichever is later. Seller agrees to deliver the property in a neat and clean condition with all debris and personal belongings removed.

15. PERSONAL PROPERTY. The following personal property, on the premises when inspected by Buyer, is included in the purchase price and will be transferred to Buyer free of liens and properly identified by a Bill of Sale **at close of escrow.** No warranty is made as to the condition of the property: _____.

16. TRANSFER DISCLOSURE STATEMENT (TDS). Seller will comply with Civil Code §1102 by providing Buyer with a completed Real Estate Transfer Disclosure Statement (P.P. Form 110.21-23 CAL). The completed statement will consist of disclosure by Seller, Listing Agent, and Selling Agent.

☐ Buyer has received and read the completed TDS.
☐ Seller will provide to Buyer the completed TDS **within _____ days after acceptance.**

Buyer and Seller agree that any new reports or other documents received by Buyer after receipt of the TDS are automatically deemed an amendment to the TDS. If any disclosure or a material amendment of any disclosure is delivered after the execution of an offer to purchase, Buyer will have **three (3) days** after delivery in person **or five (5) days** after deposit in the mail to terminate his or her offer by delivery of a written notice of termination to Seller or Seller's Agent.

Seller agrees to hold all Brokers in the transaction harmless and to defend and indemnify them from any claim, demand, action or proceedings resulting from any omission or alleged omission by Seller in his or her Real Estate Transfer Disclosure Statement or supplement.

17. SUPPLEMENT TO STATUTORY DISCLOSURE STATEMENT. Within _____ days after acceptance, Seller will provide the following or comparable disclosure supplement(s) to Buyer:
☐ P.P. FORM 110.31-33 CAL, SUPPLEMENT TO TDS, ☐ P.P. FORM 110.35-36 CAL, CONDOMINIUM DISCLOSURE SUPPLEMENT,
☐ P.P. FORM 110.72, NOTICE RE: SEPTIC SYSTEMS, ☐ Other _____
☐ P.P. FORM 110.90-92 CAL, STANDARD DISCLOSURES AND DISCLAIMERS, ☐ P.P. FORM 110.74 LEAD-BASED PAINT DISCLOSURE.

18. SAFETY BOOKLETS. By initialing below, Buyer acknowledges receipt of the following booklets:
[_____] [_____] Homeowner's Guide to Earthquake Safety and Environmental Hazards or Commercial Guide to Earthquake Safety
[_____] [_____] Approved Lead-Based Paint Pamphlet

19. ACCESS TO PROPERTY. Seller agrees to provide reasonable access to the property to Buyer and inspectors, appraisers, and all other professionals representing Buyer.

20. WALK-THROUGH INSPECTION. Buyer will have the right to conduct a walk-through inspection of the property **within _____ days prior to close of escrow,** to verify Seller's compliance with the provisions under Item 12, FIXTURES, Item 13, CONDITION OF PROPERTY, Item 14, MAINTENANCE, and Item 15, PERSONAL PROPERTY. This right is not a condition of this Agreement, and Buyer's sole remedy for an alleged breach of these items is a claim for damages. Utilities are to remain turned on until the close of escrow.

21. COMPLIANCE WITH LOCAL LAWS. Seller will comply with any local laws applicable to the sale or transfer of the property, including but not limited to: Providing inspections and/or reports for compliance with local building and permit regulations, including septic system inspection reports; compliance with minimum energy conservation standards; and compliance with water conservation measures. All required inspections and reports will be ordered **within three (3) days after acceptance** and will be paid by ☐ Seller, ☐ Buyer. If Seller does not agree **within _____ days after receipt** of a report to pay the cost of any repair or improvement required to comply with such laws, Buyer may terminate this Agreement. It is understood that if Seller has given notice that necessary permits or final approvals were not obtained for some improvements, Seller will not be responsible for bringing the improvements into compliance unless otherwise agreed.

22. OPTIONAL PROVISIONS. The provisions in this Item 22, **if initialed by Buyer are included in this Agreement.**

22-A. [_____] [_____] **PEST CONTROL INSPECTION.** Within _____ days after acceptance, ☐ Buyer, ☐ Seller, will obtain at his or her expense a current written report of an inspection by a licensed structural pest control operator of the main building (excluding the roof covering), and all attached structures plus the following: _____

The inspector will be requested to provide a separate report for: **"Section 1"**—Any portion of the structure(s) where infestation or infection is evident, and **"Section 2"**—Where conditions are present which are deemed likely to lead to infestation or infection, but where no infestation or infection exists at this time. **Within three (3) days** after receipt of the report, Seller may: (a) elect to pay the entire cost of work recommended in said report (including work recommended in both Section 1 and Section 2); or (b) elect to pay none or only a portion of the cost of such work. Written notice of such election will be delivered to Buyer or his or her Broker, together with the report.

In the event Seller does not agree to pay for all the recommended work (including work recommended in both Section 1 and Section 2), Buyer may: (a) elect to pay the balance of the cost of any Section 1 work not paid for by Seller; (b) elect to have any remaining Section 2 work done at Buyer's expense; OR (c) terminate this Agreement. Written notice of Buyer's elections will be delivered to Seller or his or her Broker **within seven (7) days after receipt of Seller's notice.**

Work to be performed at Seller's expense may be performed in whole or in part by the Seller; provided that, upon completion of

Buyer [_____] [_____] and Seller [_____] [_____] have read this page.

Page 3 of 7
FORM 101-R.3 CAL (6-97)*   COPYRIGHT © 1994–97 BY PROFESSIONAL PUBLISHING, 880 LAS GALLINAS AVE., SAN RAFAEL, CA 94903   (415) 472-1964   FAX (415) 472-2069

PROFESSIONAL PUBLISHING

Property Address _____

Seller's work but before the area has been closed up, the property is reinspected by a licensed structural pest control operator at Seller's expense who certifies that the inspected property is free of evidence of active infestation or infection. As soon as they are available, copies of inspection reports, certifications, or other proof of completion of the work will be delivered to Brokers of Buyer and Seller, who are authorized to receive the documents on behalf of their principals.

Funds for work to be done at Seller's expense after close of escrow will be held in escrow and disbursed by the escrow holder upon receipt of a certification by a licensed structural pest control operator that the property is free of evidence of active infestation or infection.

22-B. [____] [____] **SELLER TO PAY FOR WORK SHOWN IN EXISTING PEST CONTROL REPORT. Within 24 hours after acceptance,** Seller will furnish Buyer a copy of the existing pest control report dated _____ by _____. Seller agrees to pay for both Section 1 and Section 2 work, if any, recommended in said report, or perform the work himself or herself as stated in Item 22-A. **Within fifteen (15) days after acceptance,** Buyer will notify Seller in writing of approval or disapproval of the report. In case of disapproval, Buyer may terminate this Agreement.

22-C. [____] [____] **WAIVER OF PEST CONTROL INSPECTION.** Buyer has satisfied himself or herself about the condition of the property and agrees to purchase the property without the benefit of a structural pest control inspection. Buyer acknowledges that he or she has not relied upon any representations by either the Broker or the Seller with respect to matters that would normally be covered in a pest control inspection.

22-D. [____] [____] **INSPECTIONS OF PHYSICAL CONDITION OF PROPERTY.** Buyer will have the right to retain, at his or her expense, licensed experts including but not limited to engineers, geologists, architects , contractors, surveyors, and structural pest control operators to inspect the property for any structural and nonstructural conditions, including matters concerning roofing, electrical, plumbing, heating, cooling, appliances, well, septic system, pool, boundaries, geological and environmental hazards, toxic substances including asbestos, formaldehyde, radon gas, and lead-based paint. Buyer, if requested by Seller in writing, will promptly furnish, at no cost to Seller, copies of all written inspection reports obtained. Buyer will approve or disapprove in writing all inspection reports obtained **within _____ days after acceptance.** In the event of Buyer's disapproval, Buyer may elect to terminate this Agreement.

22-E. [____] [____] **MAINTENANCE RESERVE.** Seller agrees to leave in escrow a maintenance reserve in the amount of $ _____. If, in the reasonable opinion of a qualified technician, any of the equipment listed under Item 13, CONDITION OF PROPERTY, is not in working order, Buyer will furnish Seller a copy of the technician's inspection report and/or submit written notice to Seller of non-compliance of any of the terms under Item 13, CONDITION OF PROPERTY, **within seven (7) days after occupancy is delivered.**

In the event Seller fails to make the repairs and/or corrections **within five (5) days after receipt of said report or notice,** Seller authorizes the escrow holder to disburse to Buyer against bills for such repairs or corrections the sum of such bills, not to exceed the amount reserved. Said reserve will be disbursed to Buyer or returned to Seller **not later than fifteen (15) days after date occupancy is delivered.**

22-F. [____] [____] **HOME PROTECTION CONTRACT** paid for by ☐ Buyer, ☐ Seller, will become effective **upon close of escrow** for not less than one year at a cost not to exceed $ _____. The Brokers have informed both parties that such protection programs are available, but do not approve or endorse any particular program. Unless this provision is initialed, Buyer understands that such a protection plan is waived.

22-G. [____] [____] **COMMON INTEREST DEVELOPMENT DISCLOSURE. Within fifteen (15) days after acceptance,** Seller, at his or her expense, agrees to provide to Buyer the management documents and other information required by California Civil Code §1368. **Within five (5) days after receipt,** Buyer will notify Seller in writing of approval or disapproval of the documents and information. In case of disapproval, Buyer may terminate this Agreement.

Any delinquent assessments including penalties, attorney's fees, and other charges that are or could become a lien on the property will be credited to Buyer at close of escrow.

22-H. [____] [____] **FLOOD HAZARD ZONE.** Buyer has been advised that the property is located in a special flood hazard area designated by the Federal Emergency Management Agency (FEMA). It will be necessary to purchase flood insurance in order to obtain any loan secured by the property from any federally regulated financial institution or a loan insured or guaranteed by an agency of the U.S. Government. The purpose of the program is to provide flood insurance at reasonable cost. For further information consult your lender or insurance carrier.

22-I. [____] [____] **EARTHQUAKE FAULT OR SEISMIC HAZARD ZONE DISCLOSURES.** The property is situated in a Earthquake Fault Zone or Seismic Hazard Zone as designated under §§2621–2625 and §§2690–2699.6 of the California Public Resources Code. Construction or development of any structure for human occupancy may be restricted. No representations on the subject are made by Seller or Broker. Buyer may make further independent inquiries at appropriate governmental agencies concerning the use of the property under the terms of the above statutes. **Within seven (7) days after acceptance,** Buyer will notify Seller in writing of satisfaction or dissatisfaction of said inquiries. In case of dissatisfaction Buyer may terminate this Agreement.

22-J. [____] [____] **PROBATE/CONSERVATORSHIP SALE.** Pursuant to the California Probate Code, this sale is subject to court approval at which time the court may allow open competitive bidding. An "AS IS" Addendum (P.P. Form 101-AI) ☐ is, ☐ is not attached and made a part of this Agreement.

22-K. [____] [____] **RENTAL PROPERTY.** Buyer to take property subject to rights of parties in possession on leases or month-to-month tenancies. **Within seven (7) days after acceptance,** Seller will deliver to Buyer for his or her approval copies of the following documents: (a) existing leases and rental agreements with tenants estoppel certificates; (b) any outstanding notices sent to tenants; (c) a written statement of all oral agreements with tenants; (d) existing defaults by Seller or tenants; (e) claims made by or to tenants; (f) a statement of all tenants deposits held by Seller; (g) a complete statement of rental income and expenses; (h) and any service and equipment rental contracts with respect to the property which run beyond close of escrow. Seller warrants all of this documentation to be true and complete.

Buyer [_____] [_____] and Seller [_____] [_____] have read this page.

CAUTION: The copyright laws of the United States forbid the unauthorized reproduction of this form by any means including scanning or computerized formats.

FORM 101-R.4 CAL (6-97)   COPYRIGHT © 1994–97 BY PROFESSIONAL PUBLISHING, 880 LAS GALLINAS AVE., SAN RAFAEL, CA 94903   (415) 472-1964   FAX (415) 472-2069

PROFESSIONAL PUBLISHING

Owner Will Carry © 1998 by Bill Broadbent, SEC, CCIM, & George Rosenberg

Property Address _____

Within seven (7) days after receipt of documents, Buyer will notify Seller in writing of approval or disapproval of the documents. In case of disapproval, Buyer may terminate this Agreement. During the escrow period of this transaction Seller agrees that no changes in the existing leases or rental agreements will be made, nor new leases or rental agreements longer than month to month entered into, nor will any substantial alterations or repairs be made or undertaken without the written consent of the Buyer. Security deposits, advance rentals, or considerations involving future lease credits will be credited to Buyer in escrow.

22-L. [____] [____] **RENT CONTROL ORDINANCE.** Buyer is aware that a local ordinance is in effect which regulates the rights and obligations of property owners. It may also affect the manner in which future rents can be adjusted.

22-M. [____] [____] **TAX DEFERRED EXCHANGE (INVESTMENT PROPERTY).** In the event that Seller wishes to enter into a tax deferred exchange for the property, or Buyer wishes to enter into a tax deferred exchange with respect to property owned by him or her in connection with this transaction, each of the parties agrees to cooperate with the other party in connection with such exchange, including the execution of such documents as may be reasonably necessary to complete the exchange; provided that: (a) the other party will not be obligated to delay the closing; (b) all additional costs in connection with the exchange will be borne by the party requesting the exchange; (c) the other party will not be obligated to execute any note, contract, deed or other document providing for any personal liability which would survive the exchange; and (d) the other party will not take title to any property other than the property described in this Agreement. It is understood that a party's rights and obligations under this Agreement may be assigned to a third party intermediary to facilitate the exchange. The other party will be indemnified and held harmless against any liability which arises or is claimed to have arisen on account of the exchange.

23. **CONTINGENT ON SALE.** (Please check one of the following):
   A. [____] **CONTRACT IS NOT CONTINGENT** upon the sale or close of any property owned by Buyer.
   B. [____] **CONTRACT IS CONTINGENT** on Buyer's Property at _____,
   which is in escrow and concerning which all contingencies [____] have, [____] have not been satisfied, closing on or before _____. If Buyer's escrow is terminated, abandoned, or does not close on time, this Agreement will terminate without further notice unless the parties agree otherwise in writing.
   C. [____] **CONTRACT IS CONTINGENT** on Buyer accepting an offer for his or her property at _____ **within ____ days after acceptance** of this Agreement, and that sale closing on or before _____. Seller will have the right to continue to offer the property for sale. When Buyer has accepted an offer on the sale of his or her property, Buyer will promptly provide a written notice of the sale to Seller. If Buyer's purchase agreement is subject to the sale of another property, it does not qualify without the written consent of Seller. Upon providing notice of the qualified sale, this Agreement will still be contingent on Buyer's property closing as specified in this Item 23-C. If Seller accepts a bonafide written offer from a third party prior to Buyer accepting an offer on the sale of his or her property, Seller may give Buyer written notice of that fact. **Within 72 hours of receipt of the notice,** Buyer will waive the contingency on the sale and close of his or her property, or this Agreement will terminate without further notice. Upon waiver of the contingency, Buyer will provide evidence that funds needed to close escrow will be available and Buyer's ability to obtain financing is not contingent upon the sale and/or close of any property.

24. **LIQUIDATED DAMAGES.** By initialing in the spaces below,
   [_____] [_____] **Buyer agrees**   [_____] [_____] **Buyer does not agree**
   [_____] [_____] **Seller agrees**   [_____] [_____] **Seller does not agree**
   that in the event Buyer defaults in the performance of this Agreement, Seller will retain as liquidated damages the deposit set forth in Items 1-A and 1-B, and that said liquidated damages are reasonable in view of all the circumstances existing on the date of this Agreement. If the property is a dwelling with no more than four (4) units, one of which Buyer intends to occupy as his or her residence, the liquidated damages will not exceed three percent (3%) of the purchase price and any deposit in excess of that amount will be refunded to Buyer. In the event that Buyer defaults and has not made the deposit required under Item 1-B, or refuses to execute liquidated damage provision with respect to additional deposits, then Seller will have the option of retaining the initial deposit(s) that have been made, or terminating the obligations of the parties under this Item 24 and recovering such damages from Buyer as may be allowed by law. The parties understand that in case of dispute mutual cancellation instructions are necessary to release funds from escrow or trust accounts.

25. **DEFAULT.** In the event Buyer defaults in the performance of this Agreement (unless Buyer and Seller have agreed to liquidated damages), Seller may, subject to any rights of Broker, retain Buyer's deposit to the extent of damages sustained and may take such actions as he or she deems appropriate to collect such additional damages as may have been actually sustained. Buyer will have the right to take such action as he or she deems appropriate to recover such portion of the deposit as may be allowed by law. **In the event that Buyer defaults, or unless Buyer and Seller have agreed to liquidated damages, Buyer agrees to pay the Broker(s) any commission that would be payable by Seller in the absence of such default.**

26. **MEDIATION OF DISPUTES.** If a dispute arises out of or relates to this Agreement or its breach, by initialing in the "agree" spaces below the parties agree to first try in good faith to settle the dispute by voluntary non-binding mediation before resorting to court action or arbitration, unless the dispute is a matter excluded under Item 27—ARBITRATION.
   [_____] [_____] **Buyer agrees**   [_____] [_____] **Buyer does not agree**
   [_____] [_____] **Seller agrees**   [_____] [_____] **Seller does not agree**

Buyer [_____] [_____] and Seller [_____] [_____] have read this page.

FORM 101-R.5 CAL (6-97)   COPYRIGHT © 1994-97 BY PROFESSIONAL PUBLISHING, 880 LAS GALLINAS AVE., SAN RAFAEL, CA 94903   (415) 472-1964 FAX (415) 472-2069

PROFESSIONAL PUBLISHING

Owner Will Carry   © 1998 by Bill Broadbent, SEC, CCIM, & George Rosenberg

41

Property Address _____

27. ARBITRATION OF DISPUTES. Any dispute or claim in law or equity arising out of this Agreement will be decided by neutral binding arbitration in accordance with the California Arbitration Act (C.C.P. §1280 et seq.), and not by court action except as provided by California law for judicial review of arbitration proceedings. Judgment upon the award rendered by the arbitrator may be entered in any court having jurisdiction. The parties will have the right to discovery in accordance with Code of Civil Procedure §1283.05.

The parties agree that the following procedure will govern the making of the award by the arbitrator: (a) a Tentative Award will be made by the arbitrator within 30 days following submission of the matter to the arbitrator; (b) the Tentative Award will explain the factual and legal basis for the arbitrator's decision as to each of the principal controverted issues; (c) the Tentative Award will be in writing unless the parties agree otherwise; provided, however, that if the hearing is concluded within one (1) day, the Tentative Award may be made orally at the hearing in the presence of the parties. Within 15 days after the Tentative Award has been served or announced, any party may serve objections to the Tentative Award. Upon objections being timely served, the arbitrator may call for additional evidence, oral or written argument, or both. If no objections are filed, the Tentative Award will become final without further action by the parties or arbitrator. Within thirty (30) days after the filing of objections, the arbitrator will either make the Tentative Award final or modify or correct the Tentative Award, which will then become final as modified or corrected.

The following matters are excluded from arbitration: (a) a judicial or non-judicial foreclosure or other action or proceeding to enforce a deed of trust, mortgage, or real property sales contract as defined in Civil Code §2985; (b) an unlawful detainer action; (c) the filing or enforcement of a mechanic's lien; (d) any matter which is within the jurisdiction of a probate court, or small claims court; or (e) an action for bodily injury or wrongful death, or for latent or patent defects to which Code of Civil Procedure §337.1 or §337.15 applies. The filing of a judicial action to enable the recording of a notice of pending action, for order of attachment, receivership, injunction, or other provisional remedies, will not constitute a waiver of the right to arbitrate under this provision.

NOTICE: By initialing in the ["agree"] space below you are agreeing to have any dispute arising out of the matters included in the "Arbitration of Disputes" provision decided by neutral arbitration as provided by California law and you are giving up any rights you might possess to have the dispute litigated in a court or jury trial. By initialing in the ["agree"] space below you are giving up your judicial rights to discovery and appeal, unless those rights are specifically included in the "Arbitration of Disputes" provision. If you refuse to submit to arbitration after agreeing to this provision, you may be compelled to arbitrate under the authority of the California Code of Civil Procedure. Your agreement to this arbitration provision is voluntary.

We have read and understand the foregoing and agree to submit disputes arising out of the matters included in the "Arbitration of Disputes" provision to neutral arbitration.

[_____] [_____] **Buyer agrees**   [_____] [_____] **Buyer does not agree**
[_____] [_____] **Seller agrees**   [_____] [_____] **Seller does not agree**

28. ATTORNEY FEES. In any action or proceeding involving a dispute between Buyer and Seller arising out of the execution of this Agreement or the sale, whether for tort or for breach of contract, and whether or not brought to trial or final judgment, the prevailing party will be entitled to receive from the other party a reasonable attorney fee to be determined by the court or arbitrator(s).

29. EXPIRATION OF OFFER. This Offer will expire unless acceptance is delivered to Buyer or to _____ (Buyer's Broker) on or before _____ ☐ a.m. ☐ p.m., _____, 19___.

30. COUNTERPARTS. This Agreement may be executed in one or more counterparts, each of which is deemed to be an original.

31. CONDITIONS SATISFIED/WAIVED IN WRITING. Each condition or contingency, covenant, approval or disapproval will be satisfied according to its terms or waived by written notice delivered to the other party or his or her Broker.

32. TIME. Time is of the essence of this Agreement; provided, however, that if either party fails to comply with any contingency in this Agreement within the time limit specified, this Agreement will not terminate until the other party delivers written notice to the defaulting party requiring compliance **within 24 hours after receipt** of notice. If the party receiving the notice fails to comply **within the 24 hours,** the non-defaulting party may terminate this Agreement without further notice.

33. SURVIVAL. The omission from escrow instructions of any provision in this Agreement will not waive the right of any party. All representations or warranties will survive the close of escrow.

34. ENTIRE AGREEMENT. This document contains the entire agreement of the parties and supersedes all prior agreements or representations with respect to the property which are not expressly set forth. This Agreement may be modified only in writing signed and dated by both parties. **Both parties acknowledge that they have not relied on any statements of the real estate Agent or Broker which are not expressed in this Agreement.**

35. ADDENDA. The following addenda are attached and made a part of this Agreement:
☐ Addendum No. 1 _____
☐ Addendum No. 2 _____

36. ADDITIONAL TERMS AND CONDITIONS.
_____
_____
_____
_____

Buyer [_____] [_____] and Seller [_____] [_____] have read this page.

CAUTION: The copyright laws of the United States forbid the unauthorized reproduction of this form by any means including scanning or computerized formats.

FORM 101-R.6 CAL (6-97)   COPYRIGHT © 1994–97 BY PROFESSIONAL PUBLISHING, 880 LAS GALLINAS AVE., SAN RAFAEL, CA 94903   (415) 472-1964 FAX (415) 472-2069   **PROFESSIONAL PUBLISHING**

Owner Will Carry   © 1998 by Bill Broadbent, SEC, CCIM, & George Rosenberg

Property Address _____

LIMITATION OF AGENCY: A real estate broker or agent is qualified to advise on real estate. If you have any questions concerning the legal sufficiency, legal effect, insurance, or tax consequences of this document or the related transactions, consult with your attorney, accountant or insurance advisor.

The undersigned Buyer acknowledges that he or she has thoroughly read and approved each of the provisions of this offer and agrees to purchase the property for the price and on the terms and conditions specified. Buyer acknowledges receipt of a copy of this offer.

Buyer _____ Date _____ Time _____

Buyer _____ Date _____ Time _____

ACCEPTANCE

Seller accepts the foregoing Offer and agrees to sell the property for the price and on the terms and conditions specified.

NOTICE: The amount or rate of real estate commissions is not fixed by law. They are set by each Broker individually and may be negotiable between the Seller and Broker.

37. **COMMISSION.** Seller agrees to pay in cash the following real estate commission for services rendered, which commission Seller hereby irrevocably assigns to Broker(s) from escrow:

    _____% of the accepted price, or $_____, to the listing Broker: _____, and

    _____% of the accepted price, or $_____, to the selling Broker: _____

    without regard to the agency relationship. Escrow instructions with respect to commissions may not be amended or revoked without the written consent of the Broker(s).

    If Seller receives liquidated or other damages upon default by Buyer, Seller agrees to pay Broker(s) the lesser of the amount provided for above or one half of the damages after deducting any costs of collection, including reasonable attorney fees.

    Commission will also be payable upon any default by Seller, or the mutual rescission by Buyer and Seller without the written consent of the Broker(s), which prevents completion of the purchase. This Agreement will not limit the rights of Broker and Seller provided for in any existing listing agreement.

    In any action for commission the prevailing party will be entitled to reasonable attorney fees whether or not the action is brought to trial or final judgment.

38. **PROVISIONS TO BE INITIALED.** The following items must be "agreed to" by both parties to be binding on either party. In the event of disagreement, Seller should make a counter offer.

    Item 24. LIQUIDATED DAMAGES   **Item 26.** MEDIATION OF DISPUTES   **Item 27.** ARBITRATION OF DISPUTES

Seller acknowledges receipt of a copy of this Agreement. Authorization is given to the Broker(s) in this transaction to deliver a signed copy to Buyer and to disclose the terms of purchase to members of a Multiple Listing Service, Board or Association of REALTORS® at close of escrow.

39. **SUBJECT TO:** _____

Seller _____ Date _____ Time _____

Seller _____ Date _____ Time _____

Receipt of Seller's acceptance acknowledged by Buyer or authorized agent [_____] [_____] on (date) _____

Rev. by _____
Date _____

FORM 101-R.7 CAL (6-97)   COPYRIGHT © 1994–97 BY PROFESSIONAL PUBLISHING, 880 LAS GALLINAS AVE., SAN RAFAEL, CA 94903   (415) 472-1964   FAX (415) 472-2069

PROFESSIONAL PUBLISHING

Owner Will Carry © 1998 by Bill Broadbent, SEC, CCIM, & George Rosenberg

Here is a small, but important chapter of nitty gritty, in the "You'd better think of that" part of a note. How you negotiate these elements can save you money and may MAKE you money.

CHAPTER 3

ITEMS TO CONSIDER WHEN DRAWING A NOTE

What items need to be in a note?

See **EX #7** on the following page. Each item is numbered to correspond to its description below.

A note needs several dates.

(1)   Origination date
      The date the note was drawn. It is a reference date and should conform to the same reference date on the security (deed of trust, mortgage, or Security Agreement). The security instrument references a "note or notes of even date."

(2)   Date interest begins (most often it is different from the origination date)
      When a note calls for interest payments, interest usually begins from the closing date of the sale.

(3)   Date of the first payment
      The day of the month (or period) when each payment is due. The payor must pay on or before this date. It is also the reference point (beginning of the grace period) to determine when late charges apply. Payments may be monthly, quarterly, semi-annual, annual or whatever specific dates the parties agree on.

(4)   Date the balloon payment, if any, is due
      This usually is the date that the final payment of principal and interest is due and payable. See Chapter 5 for a complete discussion of balloon payments.

(5)   Principal amount of the note
      Sometimes referred to as the face amount, principal or original amount of the note. It is the amount owed and the amount to be paid by the payor.

(6)   Name of the payor(s) (who pays)
      The borrower. (Bob Buyer & Betty Buyer on the seller carryback note in this book)

(7)   Name of the payee(s) (who receives the payment)
      In this book the property seller on a carryback note. (Sam Seller and Sally Seller)

(8)   Location where payments are to be sent
      The payor must know where to make his regular payment. If the payee moves, he should notify the payor where to send the payment.

(9)   Interest rate (typically written as an annual rate even though the payment is paid monthly)
      A vital element in the note. What the seller receives as a rate of return must be clearly spelled out.

(10) Amount of the payment to be made in each period
      This figure should be specific to avoid misunderstanding.

EXHIBIT 7

DO NOT DESTROY THIS NOTE: When paid, this note and the Deed of Trust must be surrendered to the First American Title Insurance Company with request for reconveyance.

INSTALLMENT NOTE

(INTEREST INCLUDED)

(This note contains an acceleration clause)

$ (5) 82,000.00 _____ _____ Anytown _____ , California, (1) October 1, 1992 _____

In installments and at the times hereinafter stated, for value received (6) Bob Buyer and Betty Buyer _____

promise___ to pay to

(7)   Sam Seller and Sally Seller

(8)
or order, at 123 Elm Street, Anytown, CA _____
the principal sum of (5)   Eighty Two Thousand and no/100------------------------------------ Dollars,
with interest from (2)   October 1, 1992 _____ on the amounts of principal remaining from time to time
unpaid, until said principal sum is paid, at the rate of (9)   Nine _____ per cent, per annum. Principal and interest due
in monthly installments of (10)   Six Hundred Sixty and no/100------------------------------ Dollars,
($ 660.00 _____), or more on the (3) 1st day of each and every month, beginning on the (3) 1st day
of November _____ 19 92   and continuing until (4)   October 1, 2002   , at which
time the entire remaining balance of principal and interest shall be due and payable.

In the event any payment is not paid within 15 days of the due date, Trustor shall pay to Beneficiary a late charge of 6% of the payment due.

and continuing until said principal sum and the interest thereon has been fully paid. AT ANY TIME, THE PRIVILEGE IS RESERVED TO PAY MORE THAN THE SUM DUE. Each payment shall be credited first, on the interest then due; and the remainder on the principal sum; and interest shall thereupon cease upon the amount so credited on the said principal sum. Should default be made in the payment of any of said installments when due, then the whole sum of principal and interest shall become immediately due and payable at the option of the holder of this note.

If the trustor shall sell, convey or alienate said property, or any part thereof, or any interest therein, or shall be divested of his title or any interest therein in any manner or way, whether voluntarily or involuntarily, without the written consent of the beneficiary being first had and obtained, beneficiary shall have the right, at its option, except as prohibited by law, to declare any indebtedness or obligations secured hereby, irrespective of the maturity date specified in any note evidencing the same, immediately due and payable.

Should suit be commenced to collect this note or any portion thereof, such sum as the Court may deem reasonable shall be added hereto as attorney's fees. Principal and interest payable in lawful money of the United States of America. This note is secured by a (11) certain DEED OF TRUST to the FIRST AMERICAN TITLE INSURANCE COMPANY, a California corporation, as TRUSTEE.

_____
Bob Buyer

_____
Betty Buyer

_____

_____

39

(11) Attorney's fee clause

A buyer/payor might like to avoid this, but it is a necessity for the seller/payee. If a payor doesn't pay or a misunderstanding arises and ruins everyone's day, it is best NOT to be on the paying end of attorney's fees. Their hourly rates continue to rise with inflation and can mount up quickly.

EX #8: Deed of Trust securing the note in EX #7

Knowing which items should be in a note is important, but only a beginning. Whoever draws the note must be aware of other issues. These are some issues you must consider:

Usury

Usury means charging a rate of interest on a loan that exceeds the interest rate limit allowed by state law. The usury limit may be different within the same state, depending on the purpose for which the loan is made (business or personal). In California loans which are arranged by a licensed California real estate broker, unlike other loans, secured by real estate, may be exempt from usury limits. A different usury ceiling may apply to unsecured loans.

In California seller carryback Trust Deed notes are not subject to the usury limit.

Other loans may be subject to usury limits. See **EX #9, pgs 183-184** in the back of the book which covers California. Article 15 of the California Constitution, which covers state usury rules, is repeated. Read it. The language is understandable and its provisions, the ones naming those who are exempt from the rules, are worth knowing. Each state has its own rules regarding usury. **CHECK YOUR STATE'S LAWS. Penalties on usury violations can be substantial!** A licensed mortgage loan broker, real estate agent, or attorney who specializes in real estate loans should be helpful.

If you lend money secured by real estate, consider the use of a SAVINGS CLAUSE in the note. This clause is used in a note as a safety valve in the event that the note's interest rate inadvertently exceeds the maximum legal rate. It states that the amount of interest paid above the legal maximum permitted is deemed a principal payment on the note.

How could this happen? In a California Federal District Court case, *in re Dominguez 995 Fed. 2d 883*, The court remarked that, as California's legal maximum interest rate constantly changes according to a formula, it is difficult for lay persons to always know the rate. A SAVINGS CLAUSE **may be** a valid way to prevent a lender from forfeiting all interest received. Check with your attorney.

Imputed Interest

The opposite of usury (charging too much interest) is charging too little interest. **From a legal standpoint it is OK not to charge any interest!** But, from an **income tax** standpoint, if a certain minimum interest rate is not charged, the IRS will IMPUTE (put in place) a certain rate of interest. Imputed interest rate rules fall under Internal

EXHIBIT 8

Inst.No. **98765**
OFFICIAL RECORDS
SAN LUIS OBISPO CO. CA

OCT 10 1992

JAMES TRUSTWORTHY
County Clerk-Recorder
TIME **8:00 AM**

SPACE ABOVE THIS LINE FOR RECORDER'S USE

DEED OF TRUST WITH ASSIGNMENT OF RENTS
(This Deed of Trust contains an acceleration clause)

This DEED OF TRUST, made   October 1, 1992   , between

Bob Buyer and Betty Buyer, husband and wife   herein called TRUSTOR,

whose address is   999 Main Street   Anytown   CA
(Number and Street)   (City)   (State)

FIRST AMERICAN TITLE INSURANCE COMPANY, a California corporation, herein called TRUSTEE, and

Sam Seller and Sally Seller, husband and wife as joint tenants

, herein called BENEFICIARY,

WITNESSETH: That Trustor grants to Trustee in Trust, with Power of Sale, that property in the city of
Anytown,   County of   SLO   , State of California, described as:

Lot 3 of Tract No. 890, Whispering Pines Subdivision in the
County of SLO, State of California as per map recorded in Book
12, Pages 4 and 5 of Maps, in the office of the County Recorder
of said County.

If the trustor shall sell, convey or alienate said property, or any part thereof, or any interest therein, or shall be divested of his title or any interest therein in any manner or way, whether voluntarily or involuntarily, without the written consent of the beneficiary being first had and obtained, beneficiary shall have the right, at its option, except as prohibited by law, to declare any indebtedness or obligations secured hereby, irrespective of the maturity date specified in any note evidencing the same, immediately due and payable.

Together with the rents, issues and profits thereof, subject, however, to the right, power and authority hereinafter given to and conferred upon Beneficiary to collect and apply such rents, issues and profits.

For the Purpose of Securing (1) payment of the sum of $ 82,000.00   with interest thereon according to the terms of a promissory note or notes of even date herewith made by Trustor, payable to order of Beneficiary, and extensions or renewals thereof, and (2) the performance of each agreement of Trustor incorporated by reference or contained herein (3) Payment of additional sums and interest thereon which may hereafter be loaned to Trustor, or his successors or assigns, when evidenced by a promissory note or notes reciting that they are secured by this Deed of Trust.

To protect the security of this Deed of Trust, and with respect to the property above described, Trustor expressly makes each and all of the agreements, and adopts and agrees to perform and be bound by each and all of the terms and provisions set forth in subdivision A, and it is mutually agreed that each and all of the terms and provisions set forth in subdivision B of the fictitious deed of trust recorded in Orange County August 17, 1964, and in all other counties August 18, 1964, in the book and at the page of Official Records in the office of the county recorder of the county where said property is located, noted below opposite the name of such county, namely:

COUNTY	BOOK	PAGE	COUNTY	BOOK	PAGE	COUNTY	BOOK	PAGE	COUNTY	BOOK	PAGE
Alameda	1288	556	Kings	858	713	Placer	1028	379	Sierra	38	187
Alpine	3	130-31	Lake	437	110	Plumas	166	1307	Siskiyou	506	762
Amador	133	438	Lassen	192	367	Riverside	3778	347	Solano	1287	621
Butte	1330	513	Los Angeles	T-3878	874	Sacramento	5039	124	Sonoma	2067	427
Calaveras	185	338	Madera	911	136	San Benito	300	405	Stanislaus	1970	56
Colusa	323	391	Marin	1849	122	San Bernardino	6213	768	Sutter	655	585
Contra Costa	4684	1	Mariposa	90	453	San Francisco	A-804	596	Tehama	457	183
Del Norte	101	549	Mendocino	667	99	San Joaquin	2855	283	Trinity	108	595
El Dorado	704	635	Merced	1660	753	San Luis Obispo	1311	137	Tulare	2530	108
Fresno	5052	623	Modoc	191	93	San Mateo	4778	175	Tuolumne	177	160
Glenn	469	76	Mono	69	302	Santa Barbara	2065	881	Ventura	2607	237
Humboldt	801	83	Monterey	357	239	Santa Clara	6626	664	Yolo	769	16
Imperial	1189	701	Napa	704	742	Santa Cruz	1638	607	Yuba	398	693
Inyo	165	672	Nevada	363	94	Shasta	800	633			
Kern	3756	690	Orange	7182	18	San Diego	SERIES 5	Book 1964, Page 149774			

shall inure to and bind the parties hereto, with respect to the property above described. Said agreements, terms and provisions contained in said subdivisions A and B, (identical in all counties, and printed on the reverse side hereof) are by the within reference incorporated herein and made a part of this Deed of Trust for all purposes as fully as if set forth at length herein, and Beneficiary may charge for a statement regarding the obligation secured hereby, provided the charge therefor does not exceed the maximum allowed by law.

The undersigned Trustor, requests that a copy of any notice of default and any notice of sale hereunder be mailed to him at his address hereinbefore set forth.

Signature of Trustor

STATE OF CALIFORNIA   }
COUNTY OF _____   }ss.
                              }

On _____ before me,   Bob Buyer

_____ ,   Betty Buyer

personally appeared_____

_____ ,

personally known to me (or proved to me on the basis of satisfactory
evidence) to be the person(s) whose name(s) is/are subscribed to the within
instrument and acknowledged to me that he/she/they executed the same in
his/her/their authorized capacity(ies), and that by his/her/their signature(s) on
the instrument the person(s) or the entity upon behalf of which the person(s)
acted, executed the instrument.

WITNESS my hand and official seal.

Signature_____

Revenue Code Section 483 and §1271 through §1274A. The Internal Revenue Service has a formula to determine what that rate will be at any time. If you plan to carry a note at less than 9% interest, see your accountant or attorney for the current imputed interest rate formula.

(Read the next paragraph only if you are technically curious. Otherwise, skip it. Imputed interest rate calculations present a classic example of bureaucracy.)

If seller financing is $2.8 million **or less** the interest rate on that financing must be at least 9% **or** *the relevant Applicable Federal Rate **(AFR),** whichever is lower.* The relevant Applicable Federal Rate as of this 1998 publishing date is below 9% but it fluctuates. The relevant Applicable Federal Rate is the lower of: 1) those rates in effect in the month the sales contract is *written* (not closed) or, 2) the rates in effect in the prior two months. Each month IRS issues a set of Applicable Federal Interest Rates. The IRS bases the rates on yields of treasury securities with roughly comparable terms to maturity. The short-term Applicable Rate is for seller financing that lasts up to 3 years. The median Applicable Rate is based on the yields for Treasury securities with terms of more than three years, up to and including 9 years. The long-term Applicable Rate is for financing maturities of 10 years or more. Within those classifications are four others, based on how often the payments of principal and interest are to be made on the note: monthly, quarterly, semi-annually, or annually. These rates also set a floor for the amount of interest the seller may charge a buyer of real estate without the IRS *imputing* a higher rate of interest. As we said, a study in bureaucracy!

See your accountant for the present imputed interest formula. When buying or selling property, always have competent counsel review the tax consequences PRIOR TO ACCEPTING AN OFFER TO PURCHASE. The same recommendation applies when buying or selling a note.

CAUTION: Re: VARIABLE OR ADJUSTABLE INTEREST RATES ON CARRYBACK NOTES:

Some sellers would like to copy lending institutions by carrying a secured note that has a variable rate of interest (one that is adjusted periodically). **BE CAREFUL.** In California such loans are regulated under Civil Code §1916.5 et seq. The law limits the amount of change in interest rate and the frequency of change. Federal regulations also have an impact. In some states usury may be an issue. DO NOT attempt to set up an adjustable rate carryback note without help from a VERY GOOD REAL ESTATE ATTORNEY.

Late charges
Example of a late charge clause in a note:
IN THE EVENT ANY PAYMENT IS NOT PAID WITHIN 10 DAYS OF THE DUE DATE, TRUSTOR SHALL PAY TO BENEFICIARY A LATE CHARGE OF SIX PER CENT (6%) OF THE PAYMENT DUE.
A late charge provision is a penalty clause inserted in a note to discourage the payor from being late. Most institutional and private investors who hold notes secured by real estate allow a grace period (usually 10 to 15 days) before the late charge is

applied. In California a 10 day grace period (no penalty) is required by Civil Code §2954.4 for single family, owner-occupied dwellings. States may have late charge limitations in either the amount or percentage imposed by law at the state level. California does! Check your state.

Consider adding this provision:
If the payee waives its right to impose a late payment charge for one or more installments, it shall not act as a waiver of this provision, nor limit payee's right to collect late payment charges for subsequent defaults in timely payment.

Prepayment Penalty

If a seller does not want his loan paid in full before the due date, the seller may put wording in the note that the buyer must pay several months of interest in addition to the principal due in order to pay off the note. Such wording is called a prepayment penalty.

For the seller a prepayment penalty is an exception to the "MORE SOONER IS BETTER" rule. The reason: Suppose a property seller is in a low tax bracket. He structures the note payments so that the gain on the sale is spread over a period of years where much or all of the gain is taxed in a lower tax bracket. An early payoff could accelerate the remaining gain and push the seller into a higher tax bracket. If that were to happen, then the "MORE SOONER IS BETTER" rule may not be good for that seller. In Chapter 11 we will discuss the use of a Substitution Of Security Agreement. That alternative could avoid the prepayment penalty problem and be beneficial to both parties.

A prepayment penalty may be good for a lender but is not good for a borrower. A note does not permit prepayment when the words **"or more"** are omitted from the note in describing the periodic payment amount. For example: Payable $100 per month until paid. Without the words "**or more**" prepayment of the note may not be permitted. Smart buyers will negotiate **"or more"** wording which permits them to prepay all or a portion of their note without penalty. A note which permits prepayment may impose a prepayment penalty. California places some limits on prepayment penalties on loans involving owner-occupied single family dwellings,and permits prepayment in certain circumstances regardless of the provisions in the note. See California Civil Code § 2954.9.

CHECK YOUR STATE! What may not be legal in some states is wording which prohibits a buyer from paying off a loan before the due date. Such language is called a "lockout." Check your state law for this one too.

Due-on-sale

This clause gives the beneficiary/mortgagee the right but not the obligation to accelerate the note's due date when a buyer sells his property. Most notes use an "alienation clause" as the due-on-sale clause. When the borrower alienates title (transfers title to another), an alienation clause gives the beneficiary/mortgagee the right to accelerate the note balance, which is then immediately payable. The note holder need not accelerate but may negotiate some new terms on the note. A "due-on-sale" clause is the common reference for this. Here is some sample wording. In

California this clause must appear in both the note and the trust deed for 1 to 4 unit residential dwellings only (CC § 2924.5).

If the trustor shall sell, convey or alienate said property, or any part thereof, or any interest therein, or shall be divested of his title in any manner or way, whether voluntarily or involuntarily, without the written consent of the beneficiary being first had and obtained, beneficiary shall have the right, at its option, to declare any indebtedness or obligations secured hereby, irrespective of the maturity date specified in any note evidencing the same, immediately due and payable.

In states using mortgages, substitute mortgagor for trustor and mortgagee for beneficiary.

IMPORTANT
INTEREST RATE, SIZE AND FREQUENCY OF PAYMENTS, LATE CHARGES, PREPAYMENT PENALTIES, DUE-ON-SALE CLAUSES

ALL ARE NEGOTIABLE BETWEEN A WILLING BUYER AND A WILLING SELLER, within statutory limits imposed by the state. Consult a mortgage loan broker who specializes in private lender financing or a real estate-oriented attorney for details on any limits in your state.

When creating a seller carryback note, be aware of the three most important variables:
1. Term (how long until payoff)
2. Payment amount.
3. Interest rate

Term is the most important variable. The shorter the term, the higher the value. MORE SOONER IS BETTER to maximize the value of a note.

New Federal regulations: Section 32 loans
In October 1995 "High Cost Mortgage" legislation (frequently referred to as Section 32 loans) became effective. This federal law is consumer focused and apparently does not include business loans or purchase money (seller carryback) mortgages. It does affect loans originated on owner occupied homes.

Why do we mention it in a book on seller financing?

It is not clear in all states whether a "substantial" modification and/or extension** of the terms of a seller carryback note make it a loan transaction. If the carryback note changes are substantial, then Section 32 rules may apply. Section 32 loans require disclosure periods before closing the loan, APR calculations, no balloon payments in less than five years, some limits on the fees charged, and other requirements.

**See the St.Claire Corp. Tax Memo 1997-171 on page 94.

Those people who originate loans on owner occupied single family homes or investors who fund or buy them as investments from brokers want to be sure the Section 32 requirements have been complied with. Otherwise the penalites are substantial.

Sam and Sally Seller's transaction with Bob and Betty Buyer

Selling price on Park Ave.	$100,000
Cash down payment by Buyer	18,000
Seller carryback financing	$ 82,000

A 30 year note all due in 10 years. The monthly payment is $660 (rounded) including 9% interest.

CHAPTER 4

Now, let's look at four (4)
ALTERNATIVE FINANCING STRUCTURES

Sam and Sally Seller could carry the entire note and secure it by a first trust deed as discussed earlier. However, this limits their flexibility in the future if they need some cash. People's circumstances change. Suppose three years from now the Sellers need a small amount of cash. They could borrow it, using the note as collateral but may have to tie up an $82,000 asset to secure the cash. They could sell their note at a discount, but larger notes are sometimes more difficult to sell and may be discounted more than smaller notes when the primary buyers are private investors.

IDEA #1

To provide for future flexibility, Sam and Sally Seller could take back two smaller notes instead of one. Their security is NO DIFFERENT than if they carried back only ONE large note. *Splitting a carryback into two separate notes is a good strategy for future flexibility as it helps avoid some of the adverse tax consequences of disposition or hypothecation. These tax issues are covered in Chapter 6, page 101. When a note holder doesn't need a lot of cash s/he can sell or borrow against the smaller note and keep the larger one.*

Note secured by a 1st trust deed for	$60,000 @ $483/mo.
Note secured by a 2nd trust deed for	$22,000 @ $177/mo.
Total notes carried by Seller	$82,000 @ $660/mo.

Should Sam Seller need $15,000 cash, he could either borrow against or sell the $22,000 second and not disturb the income stream from the first note. Although the first trust deed note would be easier to sell, because it is more secure, a private lender or note buyer like Norman Noteholder, who buys and holds small notes, may still feel secure with the 2nd. It has an 18% **protective equity** ($18,000 down payment) behind the last dollar of the second loan. But, if Norman buys the note for $15,000, he has more protection. He has Bob's $18,000 equity in the house plus the $7,000 discount (the difference between $22,000, the note balance, and $15,000, his purchase price of the note).

Suppose Norman does not buy the note but instead lends $15,000. He has the same protection. If Norman Noteholder (who keeps notes) loaned Sam Seller $15,000 and secured it with Sam's $22,000 second trust deed note from Bob Buyer as collateral, Norman would feel secure. When he either makes the loan or buys Sam's 2nd, Norman has $25,000 worth of **protective equity** behind his $15,000 investment even though Bob Buyer has only $18,000 equity in the property.

	Norman's position	Bob Buyer's Actual debt structure
Current value of Park Ave.	$ 100,000	$ 100,000
First loan	$ 60,000	$ 60,000
Norman's loan	$ 15,000	secured by a $ 22,000 2nd
Subtract Total loans	$ 75,000	$ 82,000
Protective Equity	**$ 25,000**	**$ 18,000**
	(Norman)	**(Bob's Equity)**

Protective equity is normally the current market value of the property less the total debt. In the above example, as Norman lends Sam Seller only $15,000 in this example, Norman's **protective equity** is $25,000. **Comparing the amount of cash invested plus any senior debt to the property's value is frequently referred to as the "Investment To Value" (ITV) ratio**. The $60,000 first loan plus $15,000 invested by Norman = $75,000. The $75,000 total loans ÷ $100,000 value = 75% Investment To Value.

IMPORTANT: Like the stock market, real estate prices fluctuate over time. Even though the overall long term (20 years +) trend in real estate prices may be up, a weak national, regional, or local economy may cause a decline in property values. Just ask someone who lived in Texas in the early 1980s when real estate values declined 30% to 70%. Remember Arizona and New England in the late '80s and early '90s? Property values fell drastically. Even California, the Golden State, for decades nationally envied for its above average appreciation in real estate, experienced a peaking of property values in the late '80s only to be followed by a decline that lasted about seven years. **Protective equity** is the lender's cushion against possible loss. The larger the **protective equity,** the more protection for the lender. As the concept of **protective equity** is so important, we are emphasizing it in **bold type** throughout the book. The same concept applies for note buyers. Some uninformed note sellers, novice note buyers, and real estate agents seem oblivious to its importance.

Having substantial protective equity is the best way to take back a mortgage without being taken.

IDEA #2

Instead of one larger note in first position and a smaller note in 2nd position, you could have the smaller note ($22,000) in first position and the larger note ($60,000) in 2nd position. The smaller note in first position, being extremely well-secured, could be sold for cash at a smaller discount than the same note on the same terms in 2nd position behind a $60,000 first loan.

–OR–

For even greater flexibility Sam Seller could carry back three notes:

First loan	$ 50,000	@	$403/mo.
Second loan	$ 20,000	@	$158/mo.
Third loan	$ 12,000	@	$ 99/mo.
Total loans	$ 82,000		$660/mo.

As long as Sam owns ALL THE NOTES his security position is the same.

NOTE:

Many institutional investors (corporate America) are not interested in buying 2nd mortgages that are less than half the size of the first mortgage.

IDEA #3

Suppose Sam Seller's property is NOT free and clear of debt:

Selling Price	$100,000
Existing 1st loan @ 8% interest, is assumable or not callable	$ 50,000
Seller's Equity	$ 50,000

Bob and Betty Buyer are able to make a cash down payment of $20,000 and assume the 8% first loan. The Buyers ask the Sellers to carry back a note secured by a 2nd trust deed on the seller's property for $30,000. The carryback note will be payable <u>interest only monthly</u> at 11% per annum ($30,000 x 11%= $3,300 divided by 12 = $275/mo. payment) and will be all due and payable four years from closing.

Let's say Bob is in business for himself. Though he has good credit, he does not qualify for an 80% of value real estate loan with a 10% interest rate at Insecurity Bank. Many agents miss an opportunity in such circumstances when they don't understand seller carryback financing. Using seller carryback financing can be a win-win transaction for both buyer and seller. Sam doesn't know where he can earn 11% on his money and, even though Bob pays 11% interest on the 2nd, Bob's overall cost of money in this transaction is less than if he took out a new loan with Insecurity Bank at 10% interest.

Let's analyze Bob's cost of money:

There is $80,000 in total financing	=	100.0%
Made up of a $50,000 1st loan	=	62.5%
and a $30,000 2nd loan	=	37.5%
Bob is paying 8% interest on 62.5% of his debt (8% x 62.5%)	=	5.00%
Bob is paying 11% interest on 37.5% of his debt (11% x 37.5%)	=	4.13%
Bob's average interest cost in this case is		**9.13%**

Owner Will Carry © 1998 by Bill Broadbent, SEC, CCIM, & George Rosenberg

The Seller's $50,000 equity would be purchased as follows:
Cash down payment $20,000
Seller's carryback second $30,000

EX #10, pg 56 IS A COPY OF THAT PROPOSED CARRYBACK NOTE. IT IS CALLED A STRAIGHT NOTE AS IT IS PAYABLE INTEREST ONLY "OR MORE" AND THE BALANCE IS ALL DUE AND PAYABLE AT A FUTURE DATE.

Here is how the Buyers plan to pay their balloon (due in 4 years):

Bob's business will have an established track record by then. Betty Buyer plans to return to work in 2 years when their youngest child starts school. After Betty's year or more on the job, their combined income will be sufficient for them to qualify for a new loan to pay off both the 1st and 2nd loans on their home.

When a seller's property has no debt or has an assumable first loan at an attractive interest rate, the opportunity for seller carryback financing should be actively pursued. This is first accomplished by an agent <u>employed in writing</u> by the buyer who represents the buyer. See Bob Bruss' column on page 14. The above example illustrates a situation where cash to a new loan, even if the buyer could qualify, is not the best move for Bob Buyer. A new loan would cost Bob more. Selling for all cash might not be best for the Sellers if they don't <u>need</u> cash and can't earn a return of 11% or more on that money. This is an example where selling for all cash is not the best alternative for either the Buyer or Seller.

The same circumstances present a different opportunity for a seller's agent. Can some type of wraparound financing be structured? Let's discuss that thought next.

IDEA #4

The All-Inclusive Trust Deed note (AITD) or All-Inclusive Mortgage (AIM)
An All-Inclusive note is sometimes referred to as a "wrap" or wraparound loan. The new note wraps around the old note. **CAVEAT**: THE UNDERLYING OR WRAPPED LOAN MUST BE ASSUMABLE TO AVOID POSSIBLE ACCELERATION (due-on-sale) BY THE LENDER.

Selling Price	$100,000
Cash down payment	<u>$20,000</u>

The note structure looks like this:
All-Inclusive note secured by a deed of trust (10% interest)	$80,000
Less: Assumable 1st loan (8%, 25 years remaining) included in the All-Inclusive note:	<u>$50,000</u>
Seller's equity in the All-Inclusive note (effectively in 2nd position)	$30,000

Instead of financing a $30,000 2nd trust deed note, the Sellers carry back an All-Inclusive Trust Deed note in the amount of $80,000 at an interest rate of 10%. This note is amortized over 30 years ($702/mo.) but is all due and payable four years

EXHIBIT 10

STRAIGHT NOTE

DO NOT DESTROY THIS NOTE: When paid, this note and the Deed of Trust must be surrendered to the First American Title Insurance Company with request for reconveyance.

STRAIGHT NOTE

$ __30,000.00__ _____Anytown_____, California,_____May 1, 1991_____

_____On or before June 1, 1995_____after date,

for value received,____Bob Buyer and Betty Buyer_____promise__ to pay

to_____Sam Seller and Sally Seller_____

_____

_____, or order,

at____123 Elm Street, Anytown, CA_____

the sum of____Thirty Thousand and no/100--Dollars,

with interest from_____May 1, 1991_____until paid, at the rate of_____-11-_____

per cent, per annum, payable____$275.00 per month, interest only or more, with the____

first payment due June 1, 1991 and continuing until June 1, 1995 when all unpaid interest and principal shall be due and payable.

Should interest not be so paid, it shall thereafter bear like interest as the principal, but such unpaid interest so compounded shall not exceed an amount equal to simple interest on the unpaid principal at the maximum rate permitted by law. Should default be made in the payment of any installment of interest when due, then the whole sum of principal and interest shall become immediately due and payable at the option of the holder of this note. Should suit be commenced to collect this note or any portion thereof, such sum as the Court may deem reasonable shall be added hereto as attorney's fees. Principal and interest payable in lawful money of the United States of America. This note is secured by a certain DEED OF TRUST to the FIRST AMERICAN TITLE INSURANCE COMPANY, a California corporation, as TRUSTEE.

_____   _____
Bob Buyer   Betty Buyer

_____   _____

from closing. The Buyers, as discussed above, have thought through a plan to handle the balloon payment when it comes due.

Buyers make their monthly payment on AITD to Sellers of	$702
Sellers continue to make payments on the old loan of	$386
The monthly cash flow that Sellers keep is	$316

The cash flow to the Sellers is greater here than if they carried back a 2nd trust deed note at 11% as in the previous example, Idea #3. The cash flow or interest only payment on that note was $275/mo. Also, Sellers are making a better return on their $30,000 equity in the AITD.

Here is the Seller's return on their equity in the $80,000 AITD note: ($702/mo. incl. 10% interest, 30 year amortization)

Annual interest income (A) on AITD note:

MO/YEAR	PAYMENT	INTEREST	PRINCIPAL	BALANCE
Wraparound note				$80,000.00
1993 TOTALS	8424.00	7980.02	443.98	79,556.02
1994 TOTALS	8424.00	7933.52	490.48	79,065.54
1995 TOTALS	8424.00	7882.17	541.83	78,523.71
1996 TOTALS	8424.00	7825.43	598.57	77,925.14
TOTALS	$33,696.00	$31,621.14 **(A)**	$2,074.86	

Less: Annual interest expense (B): (on the $50,000 first loan, $386/mo. incl. 8% interest, 25-year remaining amortization)

MO/YEAR	PAYMENT	INTEREST	PRINCIPAL	BALANCE
Underlying loan (assumable)				$50,000.00
1993 TOTALS	4632.00	3976.29	655.71	49,344.29
1994 TOTALS	4632.00	3921.89	710.11	48,634.18
1995 TOTALS	4632.00	3862.94	769.06	47,865.12
1996 TOTALS	4631.99	3799.11	832.88	47,032.24
TOTALS	$18,528.00	$15,560.23 **(B)**	$2,967.76	

4 YEAR TOTAL INTEREST INCOME ON WRAP: $31,621.14 **(A)**

4 YEAR TOTAL INTEREST EXPENSE ON WRAP $15,560.23 **(B)**

TOTAL PROFIT ON 4 YEAR WRAP LOAN (**A - B**) $16,060.91

AVERAGE ANNUAL PROFIT ON WRAP LOAN $ 4,015.23

$4,015.23 AVERAGE ANNUAL PROFIT ÷ $30,000 EQUITY = 13.4% RETURN

There is some principal reduction on both the AITD and the first loan:

The balance due on the $80,000 AITD after 48 months will be $77,925

The balance due on the underlying first loan after 48 months will be $47,032

Payoff due Sellers at the end of 48 months $30,893

IDEA #4 works better for Sam Seller than IDEA #3.

In IDEA #3 Sam Seller carried back a second loan of $30,000 payable interest only monthly @ 11%. The cash flow to the Sellers on this loan was $275 per month.

In IDEA #4 Sam Seller also earns the benefit of the principal reduction, $893, on the first loan, thus receiving $893 more at the end of 48 months than if he had carried back a $30,000 2nd as in idea #3.

When the additional $223.25 (1/4 of $893) is added to their $4,015 net interest income, the Seller's yield or return on their $30,000 equity in the AITD increases to over 14% per annum. Their cash flow was $316 per month. The Seller's cash flow is 13% more using the AITD than a simple 2nd TD note in Idea #3. **This illustrates that unless Sam Seller has the ability to earn more than 13% or has a real need for cash, then a cash to new loan transaction may not be as good for him.**

When carrying back an AITD rather than a 2nd trust deed note, the seller need not worry about the buyer making payments on the first loan. The buyer makes only one payment on the AITD to the Seller and the Seller continues to make the payment on the first loan. A safer strategy for the buyer might be to find a neutral collection agency where the buyer can send his payment and the collection agent will disburse two checks. One covers the payment on the first loan and the other pays the seller. Otherwise, if the seller took the buyer's payment and did not pay the underlying loan, the buyer would be at risk of losing his property.

EX #11, pg 59 AN ALL-INCLUSIVE TRUST DEED AND NOTE: Notice that both the note and trust deed language allow the borrower to step into the seller's/lender's shoes if the seller/lender fails to pay the underlying loan.

What about wraparound seller carryback financing when legal title does not transfer?

Such seller carryback instruments are called: Contract For Sale, Sales Contract, Contract For Deed, Land Contract. All mean about the same. When a property is sold on some type of sales contract, the underlying note structure and the All-Inclusive or Wraparound structure is similar to an All-Inclusive trust deed note or All-Inclusive mortgage except legal title does not transfer.

When using the above instruments that do not transfer legal title, the seller retains "bare legal title" and the buyer has "equitable title" (the right to obtain absolute ownership to the property). The situation is similar to car financing. The lender has "bare legal title" evidenced by the legal owner's slip. The buyer has "equitable title" evidenced by the registered owner's slip. The buyer has the right to gain full title when the note is paid off. In real estate when either a specific amount is paid toward principal on the contract or when the contract is paid in full, the seller will deed

EXHIBIT 11

DO NOT DESTROY THIS NOTE: When paid, this note and the Deed of Trust securing same,
must be surrendered to the First American Title Insurance Company with request for reconveyance.

ALL INCLUSIVE PROMISSORY NOTE SECURED BY LONG FORM
ALL-INCLUSIVE DEED OF TRUST
(Installment Note, Interest Included)

$ __80,000.00__ _____ Anytown _____, California, _____ October 1 __, 19 92

In installments as herein stated, for value received, I/we promise to pay to __Sam Seller and Sally Seller,__
__husband and wife as joint tenants__

or order, at __123 Elm Street, Anytown, CA__

the sum of __Eighty Thousand and no/100------------------------------------__ Dollars,

with interest from __October 1, 1992__ on unpaid principal at the rate of __Ten__ percent per

annum; principal and interest payable in installments of __Seven Hundred Two and no/100 ($702.00)__

__----------------__ Dollars or more on the___1st___ day of each __and every__

month, beginning on the _____1st___ day of __November___19 92 , and continuing until ☒☒☒☒☒☒

☒☒☒☒☒☒☒☒☒☒☒☒☒☒☒☒☒☒☒ October 1, 1996 at which time all unpaid interest
and principal shall be due and payable.

Each payment shall be credited first on interest then due and the remainder on principal; and interest shall cease upon the principal so credited.

The total principal amount of this Note also includes the unpaid principal balance of the promissory note(s) ("Senior Note(s)") secured by Senior Deed(s) of Trust more particularly described as follows:

1. A promissory note which had an original amount of $ __52,600.00__ dated __October 1, 1987__
    _____ in favor of __Insecurity Bank__
    _____ wherein __Sam Seller and Sally Seller, husband and__
    __wife as joint tenants__ is Payor.

2. (If applicable:) A promissory note which had an original amount $ _____ dated _____
    _____ in favor of_____
    _____ wherein _____
    _____ is Payor.

At all times the equity of the Payee of this Note shall be the difference between the unpaid balance of this Note and the total unpaid balance of the Senior Note(s) secured by the Senior Deed(s) of Trust now of record.

When the total of the unpaid balance of this Note, accrued interest thereon, and all other sums due pursuant to the terms of the All-Inclusive Deed of Trust securing this Note, at any time, is equal to or less than the unpaid balance of principal and interest then due under the terms of the Senior Note(s), Payee, at his option, shall cancel this Note and deliver same to Maker and execute a request for full reconveyance of the Deed of Trust securing this Note.

By Payee's acceptance of this Note, Payee agrees that, provided Maker is not in default under the terms of this Note, Payee shall pay all installments of principal and interest which become due under the terms of the Senior Note(s). In the event Maker shall be in default on this Note, Payee's obligation to make such payments is deferred until the default is cured. Should Payee default in any of the installments as to the payment of the Senior Note(s) secured by the Senior Deed(s) of Trust, the Maker may make said payments directly to the holder of such Senior Note(s); any and all payments so made shall be credited to this Note. Notwithstanding any covenants contained in the Senior Note(s), if any, or Deed(s) of Trust securing same, Payee shall have no further duty under this Note when: (i) the lien of the All-Inclusive Deed of Trust has been extinguished by foreclosure sale, or (ii) the All-Inclusive Deed of Trust has been duly reconveyed after payment in full of the Secured Note and subsequent to the payment by Payee herein of Maker's portion of the Senior Note(s) which Payee herein is required to pay to the holder of said Senior Note(s).

Should Maker be in default under the terms of this Note, and Payee consequently incurs any penalties, charges or other expenses on account of the Senior Note(s) during the period of such default, the amount of such penalties, charges and expenses shall be added to the principal amount of this Note and shall be immediately payable by Maker to Payee.

Notwithstanding anything to the contrary herein contained, the right of Maker to prepay all or any portion of the principal of this Note is limited to the same extent as the right to prepay the principal of the Senior Note(s). If any prepayments of principal of this Note shall, by reason of the application of any portion thereof by Payee to the prepayment of the Senior Note(s), constitute such prepayment for which the holders of the Senior Note(s) are entitled to receive a prepayment penalty or consideration, the amount of such prepayment penalty or consideration shall be paid by Maker to Payee upon demand, and any such amount shall not reduce the unpaid principal of principal or interest hereunder.

Should default be made in payment of any installment when due, Payee may declare all sums hereunder due at the option of the holder of this Note. Principal, interest and all other sums due hereunder shall be payable in lawful money of the United States. If action be instituted on this Note, I/we promise to pay such sums as the Court may fix as attorneys' fees. This Note is secured by a **LONG FORM ALL-INCLUSIVE DEED OF TRUST to FIRST AMERICAN TITLE INSURANCE COMPANY,** a California corporation, as Trustee.

_____ **(Maker)**   _____ **(Maker)**
Bob Buyer   Betty Buyer

The undersigned hereby accept(s) the foregoing All-Inclusive Promissory Note and agree(s) to perform each and all of the terms thereof on the part of Payee to be performed.

Executed as of the date and place first above written.

_____ **(Payee)**   _____ **(Payee)**
Sam Seller   Sally Seller

(IT IS RECOMMENDED THAT, PRIOR TO THE EXECUTION OF THIS NOTE, THE PARTIES CONSULT WITH THEIR ATTORNEYS WITH RESPECT THERETO.)

EXHIBIT 12

NOTE INFORMATION STATEMENT
for All Inclusive Deeds of Trust, Wraparound Mortgages, or (Wrap) Contracts of Sale

HISTORY OF TRANSACTION

How was this note acquired? Purchased_____   Created_____   Carryback_____

If carryback:Selling Price/property $_____   Down Payment $_____

SECURITY

Type of Real Estate_____

Address_____

Legal Description_____

Market Value $_____   Appraisal?_____   Date_____   Copy included?_____

SENIOR LIENS (IN ORDER OF PRIORITY)

1st: Payable to_____   Account #_____

Date_____   Original Amount $_____   Payment $_____   Interest_____ %

Estimated Current Balance_____   Form of Security_____   Impounds T&I___Y___No

Balloon Payment Due Date_____   Est Amt $_____

2nd: Payable to_____   Account #_____

Date_____   Original Amount $_____   Payment $_____   Interest_____ %

Estimated Current Balance_____   Form of Security_____   Impounds T&I___Y___No

Balloon Payment Due Date_____   Est Amt $_____

3rd: Payable to_____   Account #_____

Date_____   Original Amount$_____   Payment $_____   Interest_____ %

Estimated Current Balance_____   Form of Security_____   Impounds T&I___Y___No

Balloon Payment Due Date_____   Est Amt $_____

DESCRIPTION OF NOTE AITD or WRAP

( ) Deed of Trust ( ) Mortgage ( ) Other_____   ( ) 1st ( ) 2nd ( ) 3rd

Date of Note_____   Original Balance $_____

Current Balance $_____   Interest Rate_____ % Payment $_____

Payable ( )Monthly ( )Annually ( )Other_____   Payment Due Date_____

Due and Payable_____, 19____   Balloon Payment $_____

Are Payments Current?_____   Is record of previous payments included?_____

Impounds for Taxes & Ins._____

SPECIAL CLAUSES

List special clauses in any of the notes.

_____

_____

When complete return to;

"bare legal title" to the buyer.

> **CAUTION: Sales contracts for real estate are treated somewhat differently by the courts in each state. Seek legal counsel before using one, particularly in California. Do not use a fixed-rate AITD note to wrap around a large adjustable rate loan. An increase in interest and payment on the senior loan could eliminate the cash flow between the payment on the senior loan and the AITD note.**

WHEN SELLING AN AITD NOTE, WRAPAROUND MORTGAGE OR CONTRACT FOR DEED WITH UNDERLYING MORTGAGE(S) A BUYER WILL WANT TO KNOW THE INFORMATION IN **EX #12**. THIS FORM IS ON PAGE 60.

DEFINING "EXCESS MORTGAGE OVER BASIS"

Suppose Sam Seller bought an investment or trade or business property in 1974 for $60,000. In 1988 it appraised for $115,000. Sam refinanced the property with an assumable loan for $80,000, paid off his $50,000 loan and generated $30,000 cash from which refinancing costs must be paid. With a cost basis of $60,000 (1974) and a new loan of $80,000 (1988) Sam now has a loan that is $20,000 higher than his $60,000 cost basis in the property. While this creates an "excess mortgage over basis" situation, no problem yet!

Problem:

It's 1992 and Sam wants to sell his property. He and his wife plan to travel the country in their motor home. Prices have dropped since 1988 and Sam's property is now worth $95,000 to $100,000. Sales activity is slow. Suppose Sam sells his property for $100,000 with $10,000 cash down and carries back a trust deed note for $10,000. The buyer assumes Sam's $80,000 loan. From an income tax standpoint Sam has received $30,000 ($10,000 cash from Bob Buyer plus $20,000, the amount by which his loan is higher than his adjusted cost basis). That $30,000 is considered cash received in the year of the sale even though Sam receives only $10,000 actual cash. Sam has a $40,000 gain ($100,000 sale price less his $60,000 cost basis). $30,000 ($10,000 down payment + $20,000 loan over basis) of this gain will be taxed in the year of the sale and the additional $10,000 gain will be recognized when the note is paid off. Sam could owe the government more in taxes than the $10,000 cash he receives from the sale.

Solution:

Sam could take $10,000 down and carry back a wraparound loan, either an AITD or Contract of Sale for the $90,000 balance. He would remain responsible for the $80,000 loan. As the AITD or Contract of Sale is an installment sale, Sam spreads the tax on his $40,000 gain over a period of years (the term of the note).

The "Upside Down" problem.

Suppose Sam's adjusted cost basis (ACB: what he paid for his house plus any improvement costs added) was $60,000 and he later refinanced with an $80,000 loan. Due to a real estate recession, property values declined to where Sam's house is only worth $75,000. Sam is "Upside Down" in his property. His loan balance exceeds the value of his home. If he stops paying on his mortgage the lender will foreclose. He might try to arrange a "Short Sale" where Insecurity Bank writes off a portion of their loan and allows Bob Buyer to pay off the existing loan (at a discount) with a loan from another lender. Sam receives nothing and has a $20,000 gain due to his excess mortgage over basis ($80,000 Mtg less $60,000 ACB = $20,000). Prior to the Taxpayer Relief Act of 1997 this $20,000 gain would have been taxed as income received because the debt was forgiven by the lender. Except for Sam's principal residence the same rule would still apply. The Taxpayer Relief Act of 1997 offers a capital gain exemption on the sale of a principal residence of $250,000 for a single person and $500,000 for a married couple. To qualify, the taxpayer must have owned and occupied the home for two of the last five years. This exclusion could be used again after two years on another home that qualifies. This exclusion replaces the old " once in a lifetime" exclusion and the reinvestment provisions.

IMPORTANT: As we write in mid-1998, using an AITD as a way to delay paying taxes when you have "excess mortgage over basis" is contrary to a ***temporary*** IRS regulation. However, the Tax Court has held the temporary regulation to be **invalid** and the IRS has acquiesced. (IRS publications still advise taxpayers to follow the temporary regulation.) Please consult with your tax advisor on this issue.

Another Alternative: Sam could rent the house for a period of time, which would convert it to an investment property. At some time in the future he could exchange it for other investment property under IRC Sec.1031. A properly-done Sec. 1031 exchange can also postpone the problem of "excess mortgage over basis."

OTHER RISKS TO CONSIDER WHEN YOU ARE ASKED TO CARRY A NOTE:

SELLING "SUBJECT TO" A FIRST LOAN WITH A "DUE ON SALE" CLAUSE
Bob Buyer wants to buy Sam Seller's property "subject to" the existing loan with Insecurity Bank which has a due-on-sale provision. Bob wants to give Sam a down payment and have Sam carry a 2nd Mortgage for the difference. This could be a dangerous move for Sam because Insecurity Bank could exercise its due on sale provision and start a foreclosure which, if Sam could not step in and cure the default, and foreclose on his 2nd, would cause him to be wiped out by the Bank's foreclosure action.

SELLER BEWARE: THE "SILENT SECOND"
Suppose Bob Buyer offered to buy Sam Seller's Park Ave. house for $100,000 on the following terms: Bob to pay Sam $2,000 cash down, take out a new loan at Insecurity Bank for $80,000 and give Sam a note for $18,000 secured by a second deed of trust on Park Ave. Bob suggests that the escrow instructions reflect only the new loan and that Sam received $20,000 outside of escrow. He asks Sam to hold the $18,000 note and 2nd deed of trust for several months "unrecorded" (THAT'S THE SILENT PART) so Insecurity Bank won't notice. Is anything wrong with this proposal?

YES!!! At least THREE things:

1. The very thin cash down payment. We will discuss that more thoroughly in Chapter 8.
2. As long as Sam holds a deed of trust unrecorded, he is vulnerable to Bob further encumbering the Park Ave. property without his knowledge. Or, a lien might attach to the property and have priority over Sam's unrecorded second deed of trust.
3. **THE SCHEME IS ILLEGAL.** Bob is withholding financial information from Insecurity Bank, which, if it knew about it, would not make the $80,000 loan. If Sam were to go along with this scheme, he would be participating in a conspiracy some people might call "defrauding the lender." This scheme is not much different from falsifying a loan application, another NO! NO! Defrauding a lender is serious business. The penalties are severe. No seller, buyer or agent should try this scheme. Sam's response should be a firm, "NO, THANK YOU!"

A variation of this skullduggery would be for Bob to borrow the $18,000 down payment from Sam, pass the cash through the escrow, take out a new 1st loan with Insecurity Bank, close and give Sam a note for $18,000 with a second T/D to be recorded at a later date. All variations of the SILENT SECOND scheme are basically illegal and should be avoided.

CAUTION TO NOTE BUYERS: A second deed of trust that is recorded a few days to a few months after the closing date (not shown on the title policy or closing statement and uninsured) is usually suspect. Be careful, no deal is worth the potential hassle of getting involved with a SILENT or UNRECORDED LOAN.

TRANSFERRING PROPERTY TITLE "SUBJECT TO"
Occasionally a buyer will purchase property "subject to" the existing loan(s). "Subject to" means taking title without assuming the existing loan(s). Usually the existing financing is a first loan made by a financial institution, which contains a due-on-sale clause. Escrow or closing attorneys are instructed not to contact the lender as the parties do not want the lender to know of the title transfer. Without the lender's waiver of its right to accelerate the due date of the loan, the lender has the right to call the entire loan due and payable upon learning of the transfer of title.

Suppose the seller carries back a note secured by a second mortgage for a buyer who takes title "subject to" the first loan. Both buyer and seller are then vulnerable for the term of both the first and second loans. Should the first lender call its loan due and payable and the new payor cannot payoff the loan, the lender may start foreclosure on the first. The holder of the second could then foreclose on his note but would have to assume or pay off the first loan ahead of him.

Such an experience may be very costly and frustrating to both buyer and seller.

ANOTHER RISK:
Not often discussed or even realized by a seller is that for the seller to be properly secured, separate security agreements may be required for different parts of the property (both real and personal).

MIXED COLLATERAL: REAL & PERSONAL PROPERTY

An example: Sam Seller owns vacant land and puts a mobile home on it. Later he decides to sell both the land and the mobile home together. The land is real property but the mobile home may be personal property. In California a note and deed of trust are used to secure the debt on real property and a note and security agreement are used to secure the debt on personal property, such as a Mobile home which has not been converted into real property. In California mobile home titles are registered and transferred through the State Department of Housing and Community Development, which has regional offices through the state.

These regional offices have a statewide computer network. For a reasonable fee you can obtain an instant title report on a California registered mobile home.

In Arizona the owner may file an AFFIDAVIT OF AFFIXTURE which in effect declares the mobile home to be real property. If this AFFIDAVIT is filed, then a deed of trust would be sufficient to pledge the land and the mobile home as security for the note. Many states including California allow the mobile home and land to be combined, thereby converting the mobile home to real property. Be sure to check the laws in your state on how to properly secure note(s) with mixed collateral. Too many transactions of this type are improperly documented and the seller may not be properly secured.

A common type of mixed collateral transaction is the sale of a business that includes real estate. Problems are particularly acute in the sale of a motel or hotel where there are large amounts of personal property.

Mixed collateral can involve real challenges when a default and foreclosure action is necessary. Consult an attorney with experience in this subject.

Now that we have covered the elements of a note and looked at four alternative financing structures, let's look more closely at one critical aspect of a seller's carryback note - the balloon payment. Balloon payments get many buyers in trouble and leave the sellers with an undesirable situation. This subject is <u>very</u> <u>important</u> and deserves its own chapter.

CHAPTER 5

BALLOON PAYMENTS

In California a "balloon payment loan" is a loan which provides for a final payment as originally scheduled which is more than twice the amount of any of the immediately preceding six regularly scheduled payments or which contains a call provision. Should the lender not call for payment of the loan when it is due, then the loan does not have a balloon payment (CA Civil Code §2924i(d)(1)).

California's definition is NOT the common definition. Nationwide, the term "balloon payment" generally means the principal balance due and payable (full payoff) at some specified time in the future.

<u>Balloon payment advantages:</u>

1. When Sam Seller agrees to carry a note with a balloon payment, he understands that Bob Buyer can't afford a high payment, which would amortize the note in a short time period. Instead, Sam accepts a lower payment and puts a due date three, five, ten, fifteen, or more years from the date the sale closed and interest begins. Sam's <u>primary objective</u> is getting Bob Buyer committed to buy Sam's property. The term of the balloon is of secondary importance to Sam.
2. A balloon payment is one way for Sam Seller to keep pace with changing interest rates. Suppose that when Sam's balloon payment is due in ten years, interest rates have risen. When the note was written, a competitive rate was 9%. Current rates may be 11-1/2%. If Sam has no better use for the money, he and Sally could agree to modify the note to 11% interest and to extend the due date for another three years. At the end of that time the Buyers could pay it off or the parties may agree to modify and extend again.
3. Bob Buyer also benefits. He hopes to have more income as time passes and be able to qualify for a new loan with Insecurity Bank to pay off the balloon when due.

<u>Balloon payment disadvantages:</u>

<u>Disadvantages for Bob Buyer:</u> If he doesn't have the cash or borrowing power now and does not improve financially, he may not have the money later. He could lose the property by not paying the balloon payment when it is due.

<u>Sam Seller's disadvantage</u> arises if he wants to sell the note. The further out the balloon payment, the less the note is worth in cash today. For example, a $10,000 note amortized for 15 years @ 10% all due in 8 years is worth <u>less</u> than a note with

the same interest and payment that is all due in 5 years. This is another example of the "MORE SOONER IS BETTER" idea.

Calculation of balloon

Problem: What is the balance of the $10,000 loan after 6 years? For those with curious minds and financial calculators, here are two methods you can use to calculate the balloon payment.

METHOD #1. Calculation using months remaining on the loan:

We strongly suggest that if you are using a financial calculator, begin the habit of thinking of, then writing, these symbols in the following order, **N, I, PV, PMT, FV** (the same as on the calculator) whenever a note calculation is to be done. These symbols mean:

N = Time   **I** = Interest Rate   **PV** = Present Value   **PMT** = Payment   **FV** = Future Value

First enter each value where applicable and solve for the unknown. You can solve only for one missing element at a time. A financial calculator requires 3 known items to solve for a 4th or 4 known items to solve for a 5th.

For "N" use the number of months left if the loan were to be amortized in full. If the full term is ten years and the balloon is due in six years, then four years are left (4 yrs. x 12 mos.= 48 months).

N   = 48 months
I   = 10% divided by 12 months (as we are paying interest monthly)
PMT= $132.15 (per month)

Solving for Present Value, or PV, the amount of the balloon payment is $5,210.

METHOD #2. Calculation using the Future Value (FV) button on the financial calculator:

In this alternate calculation, first verify the payment amount:

N	**I**	**PV**	**PMT**	**FV**
120 (10 years)	.833/month (10%)	10,000	solve for PMT	0

After finding the payment amount is 132.15, change N to the number of payments until the balloon payment is due:

N	**I**	**PV**	**PMT**	**FV**
72 (6 years)	.833/month (10%)	10,000	132.15	solve for FV

The balloon payment shows in Future Value (FV) as $5,210, as we calculated in our first example.

IMPORTANT IN CALIFORNIA: State law requires that for residential property 1-4 units notice be given before a balloon payment is due. For balloon payments secured by a deed of trust on owner-occupied residential property (1-4 units), notice is required under CC §2924i. When the property is not owner occupied (1-4 units), notice is required by CC §2966 when there is a seller carryback note; also, a provision regarding notice when the balloon payment becomes due must be inserted in the note.

EX #13: NOTICE OF BALLOON PAYMENT DUE. See sample notice form on page 68.

Failure to notify the payor can delay foreclosure until the proper notice is given.

Following is sample wording that (in California) <u>must</u> be included in a seller carryback note containing a balloon payment and secured by residential property (1 to 4 units):

THIS NOTE IS SUBJECT TO SECTION 2966 OF THE CIVIL CODE, WHICH PROVIDES THAT THE HOLDER OF THIS NOTE SHALL GIVE WRITTEN NOTICE TO THE TRUSTOR, OR HIS SUCCESSOR IN INTEREST, OF PRESCRIBED INFORMATION AT LEAST 90 AND NOT MORE THAN 150 DAYS BEFORE ANY BALLOON PAYMENT IS DUE.

Even in states that do not require notice of a balloon payment, a Beneficiary/Mortgagee can attempt to ensure prompt payment and avoid hard feelings by sending a reminder letter to the payor at least 60 days in advance of the due date of the balloon payment. This will provide time to arrange a new loan.

When the time comes for Bob Buyer to pay his balloon payment, Insecurity Bank may not refinance his loan for enough to pay off the balloon payment when due. Bob faces possible uncertainties of high interest rates, a "no loan" lender policy, or an institution's refusal to extend him credit. Without a protective clause giving him a way out of paying the balloon, any or all of these uncertainties could cause him to default on the balloon payment and possibly to lose his property.

A good solution for Bob Buyer:

When offering to purchase Sam's property, Bob Buyer should try to negotiate a protective clause into the note. The wording would permit him to extend the due date in the event he cannot pay the balloon payment. When the balloon comes due, Bob could have the right to extend the note for a specific period of time by giving Sam any of the following, either individually or in combination.

1. Higher interest rate
   Buyer shall have the right to extend the due date for one year by increasing the rate of interest to 12%, or by establishing the new fixed rate with a simple formula, such as so many points above a known index, like the current prime rate.
2. Larger monthly payments
   By increasing the monthly payment to $160 per month, buyer shall have the right to extend the due date 2 years beyond the original due date on the note.
3. Paying part of the balloon payment
   If buyer makes a one time principal payment of $3,000 on or before the due date,

EXHIBIT 13

NOTICE OF BALLOON PAYMENT DUE

TO: <u>Bob and Betty Buyer</u>　　　　DATE: <u>June 15, 2002</u>

　　<u>999 Main Street</u>　　　　　　CERTIFIED MAIL NO.
　　　　　　　　　　　　　　　　　　　1 23 567 89
　　<u>Anytown, CA 99999</u>

As the owner of the real estate securing a promissory note dated <u>October 1</u>, 19<u>92</u>, in the original amount of $<u>82,000.00</u>, in conformance with current California law, you are hereby notified that you will have a balloon payment due as follows:

DATE DUE: <u>October 1, 2002</u>

ESTIMATE OF AMOUNT DUE:

　　Principal $<u>73,401.41</u>　(after payment due <u>September 1, 2002</u>)

　　Interest　<u>550.51</u>　(accrued to <u>October 1, 2002</u>　)

　　Total Due $<u>73,951.92</u>　on <u>October 1, 2002</u>

Payment is to be made to:

　　　　<u>Sam and Sally Seller</u>

　　　　<u>123 Elm Street</u>

　　　　<u>Anytown, CA 99999</u>

Between <u>October 1, 2002</u> and the date of final payment interest will accrue at $<u>18.10</u> per day.

We are ____ are not ____ interested in refinancing or extending this note.

After you receive your original Note and Deed of Trust, we recommend you deliver it to the Trustee as soon as possible and obtain a full reconveyance.

　　　　　　By: _____
　　　　　　　　Sam Seller　　　　　Beneficiary

　　　　　　By: _____
　　　　　　　　Sally Seller　　　　Beneficiary

Balloon Battering
by Lorelei Stevens, Pres.
Wall Street Brokers, Seattle, WA   (reproduced with author's permission)

When seller-financing a home, sellers and real estate agents must be aware of the "Balloon Battering" law in Chapter 13 Bankruptcy. A final balloon payment can be delayed by the buyer of the home for up to five years! If the buyer files Chapter 13 Bankruptcy, the seller's note is secured by the buyer's principal residence, and the seller has a "cash out balloon" due by the home buyer, the seller might have to wait and wait for the money.

In October of 1994, Bankruptcy Code Section 1322(c)(2) went into effect. It allows the buyer to subject the seller's rights to a balloon payment to rough treatment and heavy blows. The balloon could be delayed for up to five years. Prior to this date, balloons were normally unalterable. For example, if a seller sells a home with a payment in full provision due in 3 years, the buyer's Chapter 13 Bankruptcy plan could stretch that balloon to 8 years.

How would the seller be affected?

The seller's expectations of cash could be tied up for an extra 5 years, which may hinder the seller's plans for liquidity. A portion of this Bankruptcy code states "...in a case in which the last payment (seller's balloon) on the original payment schedule for a claim secured only by a security interest in real property that is the debtor's (home buyer's) residence is due before the date on which the final payment under the plan is due, the plan may provide for the payment of the claim as modified..." Bankruptcy Code Section 1322(d) states: "The plan may not provide for payments over a period that is longer than three years, unless the court, for cause, approves a longer period, but the court may not approve a period that is longer than five years."

Sellers may decide to shy away from selling a home and accepting a note from the home buyer with a large balloon payment provision, if liquidity at the time the balloon is due is important. Or, sellers can accept the chance that the home buyer may file Chapter 13 Bankruptcy, causing delays in receiving the balloon payment. Some due diligence involving the buyer's creditworthiness and financial status can reduce this risk.

Sellers and real estate agents are advised to consult a bankruptcy attorney of their choice prior to seller-financing a balloon.

seller agrees to extend the due date 2 years beyond the original due date of the note.

Combining all three of the above

If buyer makes a one time principal reduction of $3,000 on or before the due date of this note and buyer increases the monthly payment to $160 and the interest rate to 12%, then the seller agrees to extend the due date for 3 years beyond the original due date of the note.

A better solution for Bob Buyer: No balloon

Use a step-up in payments to defuse the balloon. Stepped payments are increases in the monthly payment each year. For example, on a $10,000 note, if Bob stepped up his monthly payment by $30 from $132.15 for the first year to $162.15 for the second year, to $192.15 for the third year, and so on, the loan would amortize in 5 years 8 months. The payoff schedule would look like this.

$30 per month increase in payment annually

Year	N	I	PV	PMT	FV
1	12	.833/mo. (10%)	10000.00	132.15	9386.59
2	12	.833/mo. (10%)	9386.59	162.15	8331.98
3	12	.833/mo. (10%)	8331.98	192.15	6789.97
4	12	.833/mo. (10%)	6789.97	222.15	4709.53
5	12	.833/mo. (10%)	4709.53	252.15	2034.28
6	8	.833/mo. (10%)	2034.28	282.15	0

If an annual increase of $30 per month is too much for the Buyer's budget, see if a smaller increase will work for both parties.

$10 per month increase in payment annually

Year	N	I	PV	PMT	FV
1	12	.833/mo. (10%)	10000.00	132.15	9386.59
2	12	.833/mo. (10%)	9386.59	142.15	8583.29
3	12	.833/mo. (10%)	8583.29	152.15	7570.22
4	12	.833/mo. (10%)	7570.22	162.15	6325.42
5	12	.833/mo. (10%)	6325.42	172.15	4824.61
6	12	.833/mo. (10%)	4824.61	182.15	3040.99
7	12	.833/mo. (10%)	3040.99	192.15	944.95
8	5	.833/mo. (10%)	944.95	202.15	0

Stepped Payment Language for Promissory Note.

One year after close of escrow, and annually thereafter until the note is paid in full the amount of the monthly installment shall be increased $_____ per month above the amount paid during the previous year.

or

One year after close of escrow, and annually thereafter until the note is paid in full the amount of the monthly installment shall be increased ____ percent above the amount paid during the previous year.

Another suggestion: As part of his negotiations for the property, Bob Buyer could offer Sam Seller a fully amortized 8 year note (no balloon) instead of a 10 year loan all due in 6 years.

N	I	PV	PMT	FV
96	.833/mo.(10%)	10,000	$151.74	0

MORE IDEAS:

Offering a lower interest rate in the early payment years would help pay off the loan more rapidly. The reason is that with a lower interest rate, more of the total payment would be applied to principal.

The more of the payment that applies to principal, the faster the loan balance will decrease.

A **combination of a lower interest rate** in the early years and an increased interest rate in the later years, **combined with stepped payments,** would give Bob Buyer dramatic results. Sam Seller may go along with the idea if it meant getting his loan paid off sooner. An escalating interest rate may appeal to Sam and might encourage Bob to pay the note off sooner. You never know until you ask. The "MORE SOONER, IS BETTER" for Sam.

Increasing or stepped payments from a seller's viewpoint can be beneficial in keeping pace with inflation. The seller will have more dollars to spend as time goes on.

Incidentally, in California using stepped payments **is not** considered a variable interest rate loan.

Here is how Sam Seller's first example on page 36 would look using stepped payments on his first trust deed note to shorten a 30 year amortization to 14 years **without** a balloon payment. We increased the monthly payment 5% each year over the life of the loan. This gives the seller, who holds the note, more cash flow each year. A buyer will avoid the uncertainty of a balloon payment that may be difficult to pay coming due.

Loan balance: $82,000.00   Interest Rate 9%   30 Year Loan

Year	Mo. Pmt.	Ttl. Pmt.	Ttl. Int. Pd.	Ttl. Princ. Pd.	Balance
1993	$ 659.79	7917.48	7357.24	560.24	81,439.76
1994	$ 692.78	8313.36	7287.98	1025.38	80,414.38
1995	$ 727.42	8729.04	7174.21	1554.83	78,859.55
1996	$ 763.79	9165.48	7009.88	2155.60	76,703.95
1997	$ 801.98	9623.76	6788.29	2835.47	73,868.48
1998	$ 842.08	10104.96	6501.95	3603.01	70,265.47
1999	$ 884.18	10610.16	6142.56	4467.60	65,797.87
2000	$ 928.39	11140.68	5701.05	5439.63	60,358.24
2001	$ 974.81	11697.72	5167.23	6530.49	53,827.75
2002	$1023.55	12282.60	4529.89	7752.71	46,075.04
2003	$1074.73	12896.76	3776.63	9120.13	36,954.91
2004	$1128.46	13541.52	2893.83	10647.69	26,307.22
2005	$1184.89	14218.68	1866.35	12352.33	13,954.89
2006	$1244.13	14632.46	677.57	13954.89	0.00

Bob, we recall, wanted the balloon so his monthly payments would be less. Using stepped payments would definitely not help him with his cash flow. However, he may sleep better at night not worrying about a future balloon payment. Bob could view the stepped payment idea as a forced savings plan and a way to get his mortgage paid off without a balloon payment.

Remember: **ALL TERMS ARE NEGOTIABLE**

Bi-Weekly Loans
Another way to shorten the loan term and to save a large amount of interest is to pay the monthly payment in two equal parts, one every other week. This type of payment schedule is called a Bi-Weekly Plan. It results in the lender receiving one extra monthly payment each year. The reason is that on a monthly basis there are 12 payments made, one each month. Each year has 52 weeks. Using the Bi-Weekly format, 26 payments are made during a year, which results in the equivalent of one more monthly payment. The following table compares three amortization schedules:

A standard (30 year) one payment per month, a Bi-Weekly payment plan, and a plan that doubles the 12th payment regularly once each year. We are using the previous example of an $82,000 loan with payments amortized over 30 years including 9% interest.

Note that $49,534 interest is saved by using the Bi-Weekly payment plan. Compared to a more traditional 30 year loan, the Bi-Weekly loan will be paid in full almost eight years sooner.

Bi-Weekly loans must either be originated as such or an existing loan calling for a monthly payment **would have to be modified with the consent of the lender.** The computer systems of many lenders are not set up to handle Bi-Weekly payments.

To overcome this hindrance financial service intermediaries are available. Through direct wire transfer withdrawal from your checking account the intermediary will accumulate two (bi-weekly) payments and then make the regular monthly payment to your lender as required by your loan documents. There is usually a one time setup fee of several hundred dollars and then a per transaction charge of several dollars on each transfer. The long term savings can be well worth the cost. Suppose you followed through with a bi-weekly program. Your mortgage would be paid in full at the end of 21 years, 11 months. By then your budget would be used to a bi-weekly payment of $329.90. If you then directed that same $329.90 bi-weekly payment to go into the purchase of an annuity for the next eight years and one month, at the end of 97 months at an earning rate of less than 6% (very achievable) you would have accumulated over $82,000, the original amount of your mortgage. If you were ready to retire at that point you could start receiving a monthly income stream that could last a lifetime and supplement your Social Security and pension benefits. These results are readily achievable, even for people who don't consider themselves financial experts.

Alternative: If the lender will not accept bi-weekly payments, you may have an alternative. Provided your loan permits additional principal payments, you may make one extra full payment at the end of each year. This is called "double the 12th". Be sure that your lender gives you current reduction on your principal balance.

By using the plan to double every 12th payment, the following results are obtained in the above loan: $47,294 interest is saved over the loan term compared to the more traditional 30 year loan. The loan is paid in full a little less than eight years sooner.

The double the 12th payment procedure gets results that are almost comparable to a bi-weekly program with no intermediary or cost involved. Unfortunately statistics indicate that only a tiny fraction of consumers (about 1%) ever take advantage of this money saving concept.

THESE ACCELERATING PAYMENT PROGRAMS ARE BENEFICIAL EVEN IF YOU ARE ONE OF THOSE FAMILIES THAT MOVE ABOUT EVERY SEVEN YEARS. THERE IS STILL **$6,400** M/L IN ADDITIONAL PRINCIPAL REDUCTION ON YOUR MORTGAGE. STUDY THE LOAN COMPARISON CHART AND PROVE IT TO YOURSELF.

LOAN COMPARISON ANALYSIS

	STANDARD PLAN	BI-WEEKLY	DOUBLE 12TH
Term of Loan	30 yr/0 mo	21 yr/11 mo	22 yr/3 mo
Principal Paid	82,000.00	82,000.00	82,000.00
Interest Paid	155,510.22	105,976.16	108,216.30
Total Payments	237,510.22	187,976.16	190,216.30
Interest Difference	0	-49,534.06	-47,293.92
Payment Amount	659.80	329.90	659.80
A.P.R.	N/A	N/A	N/A
Finance Charge	N/A	N/A	N/A

Comparison of Principal Balance (Year End)

		STANDARD PLAN	BI-WEEKLY	DOUBLE 12TH
	1998	81,439.64	80,749.35	80,779.84
	1999	80,826.75	79,381.11	79,445.26
	2000	80,156.34	77,884.27	77,985.48
	2001	79,423.02	76,246.70	76,388.75
end 5th yr	2002	78,620.94	74,455.19	74,642.23
	2003	77,743.64	72,495.28	72,731.88
	2004	76,784.02	70,351.13	70,642.34
	2005	75,734.38	68,005.39	68,356.77
	2006	74,586.28	65,439.17	65,856.80
end 10th yr	2007	73,330.49	62,631.68	63,122.33
	2008	71,956.90	59,560.31	60,131.33
	2009	70,454.46	56,200.22	56,859.75
	2010	68,811.05	52,524.25	53,281.29
	2011	67,013.48	48,502.71	49,367.14
end 15th yr	2012	65,047.30	43,103.15	45,085.81
	2013	62,896.68	39,290.03	40,402.85
	2014	60,544.31	34,024.43	35,280.60
	2015	57,971.27	28,263.84	29,677.83
	2016	55,156.87	21,961.74	23,549.50
end 20th yr	2017	52,078.47	15,067.24	16,846.32
	2018	48,711.29	7,220.76	9,514.32
	2019	45,028.24	0.00	1,494.52
	2020	40,999.69		0.00
	2021	36,593.25		
end 25th yr	2022	31,773.44		
	2023	26,501.50		
	2024	20,735.01		
	2025	14,427.58		
	2026	7,528.48		
end 30th yr	2027	0.00		

Note: The last two alternatives prove the economic concept that the rate of interest on a loan is not as important as the total amount of interest paid over the life of the loan. More people than ever before are considering 15 year loans or some type of accelerated pay-down on their home mortgages.

IMPORTANT: Think of an agreement to buy real estate on terms as a contract to save just so much money, just so often.

The subject of saving money by purchasing real estate brings us to the concept of equity. What is equity? An owner's equity in a property is the difference between the value of the property and its total debt. Whose value? Good question. Without a buyer, equity is in the eye of the owner. The ultimate test of equity is what a ready, willing and able buyer will pay for the property.

EQUITY PERSPECTIVES: There are three categories of equity: **Gross Equity**, **Net Equity**, and **Protective Equity.**

Gross Equity: The fair market value of a property less the total loans against it.

Net Equity: Gross equity less costs of selling the property.

Protective Equity: Gross equity from a lender or note holder's perspective. Let's examine these concepts in greater detail.

Here again is our first example of seller carryback financing:

Price: Seller's home on Park Ave	$100,000
Cash down payment by Buyer	$ 18,000
Seller to carry back a note secured by a first trust deed on their property for	$ 82,000

Sam Seller's house appraised for $100,000 and has no debt. Sam's **GROSS EQUITY** is $100,000. Sam's **NET EQUITY** would be less. Net equity is the seller's equity after deducting expenses incurred when selling his property. Here is a list of typical Seller expense categories. See **EX #14, pg 77:** Seller's Net Sheet.

Sam may employ Arthur Agent, a local real estate agent, to organize and implement the marketing effort. If so, a brokerage fee will usually be the largest expense. Listing with Arthur (or any agent) *does not* justify a higher-than-market asking price for the property.

Sellers who sell their own property are trying to save the commission. Buyers who buy "For Sale By Owner" (FSBO) property are trying to save the commission. **Both** buyer and seller cannot win at that game. **One must lose.**

Arthur Agent earns his commission by providing the knowledge, time, effort and expense to get the property sold. If Sam Seller feels he can market the property himself, he will EARN (not save) the commission for having devoted the knowledge, time, effort and expense to getting his property sold.

Employing the "right" agent to list and market your property can be profitable. A knowledgeable, experienced agent will make suggestions to enhance the value of your property. The agent earns his/her commission by benefiting and protecting you, the client, throughout the transaction.

Bob Buyer's gross equity after closing is $18,000, the difference between the selling price and the loan balance. From the Seller's viewpoint (after the sale) the Seller has $18,000 **protective equity** behind his $82,000 note. The only protection for a note holder is **protective equity. Protective equity** is the <u>margin of safety</u>. From a seller's/note holder's perspective **THERE IS NO SUBSTITUTE FOR PROTECTIVE EQUITY.**

REMEMBER: Real Estate values fluctuate up and down over time, even in good areas. **PROTECTIVE EQUITY** also changes with the times (up and down).

If we assume that over time real estate generally either holds or increases in value, then the principal payments on a real estate loan reduce its balance and increase the owner's equity. Take a second look at our chart from page 33.

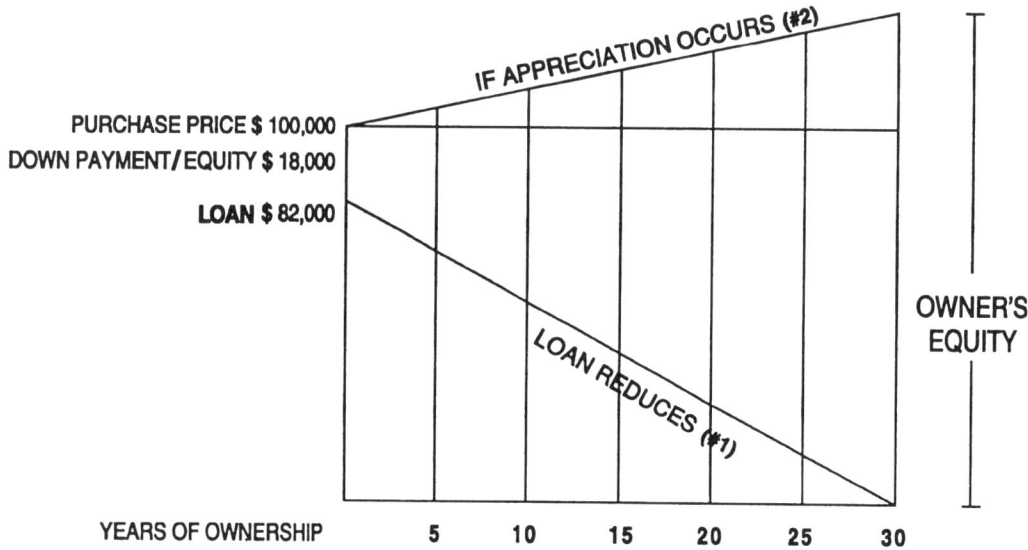

The above graph illustrates how an owner's equity may expand from the date of purchase as a result of two things:

#1. Principal reduction on their loan, and
#2. If there is appreciation in property value.

EXHIBIT 14

SELLER'S NET SHEET

ESTIMATED PROCEEDS ON SALE OR EXCHANGE OF PROPERTY

The amounts estimated in this net sheet are for the following agreement:

☐ Purchase agreement
☐ Counteroffer
☐ Exchange agreement
☐ Seller's listing agreement
☐ Escrow instructions

Dated: _____ ,19____

Entered into by _____

Prepared for_____

Prepared by _____

Date prepared _____ ,19___

Closing date anticipated _____ , 19___

Property Sold/Exchanged _____

_____

SALES PRICE:

1. Price Received . . . . ADD: $_____

ENCUMBRANCES:

2. First Trust Deed . . . . $_____
3. Second Trust Deed . . . . $_____
4. Other Encumbrances/Liens/UCC-1 . . . . . $_____

5. TOTAL ENCUMBRANCES . . . . . DEDUCT: $_____

SALES EXPENSES AND CHARGES:

6. Title Insurance Premium . . . . $_____
7. Escrow Fees . . . . $_____
8. Notary Fees . . . . $_____
9. Document Preparation Fee . . . . $_____
10. Documentary Transfer Taxes . . . . $_____
11. Recording Fees . . . . $_____
12. Home Warranty Premium . . . . $_____
13. Homeowner's Statement Fee . . . . $_____
14. Pest Control Report . . . . $_____
15. Pest Control Repairs (Approx.) . . . . $_____
16. Prepayment Penalties . . . . $_____
17. Smoke Detector . . . . $_____
18. Reconveyance Fees . . . . $_____
19. Beneficiary Statement Fee ($60) . . . . . . $_____
20. FHA-VA Loan Appraisal Fee . . . . $_____
21. FHA-VA Points (Approx. _____%) . . . . . $_____
22. Repairs Required by Lender (Approx.) . . . . $_____
23. Brokerage Fee . . . . $_____
24. Attorney's Fee . . . . $_____
25. Accountant's Fee . . . . $_____

26. TOTAL EXPENSES AND CHARGES . DEDUCT: $_____

27. ESTIMATED NET EQUITY . . . . $_____

ADJUSTMENTS TO NET EQUITY FOR PRORATES

27. ESTIMATED NET EQUITY (Carried forward) . . $_____

PRORATES DUE BUYER:

28. Rent Collected and Unearned at Close . . . $_____
29. Tenant Deposits . . . . $_____
30. Unpaid Property Taxes . . . . $_____
31. Accrued Interest Unpaid . . . . $_____

32. TOTAL Prorates Due Buyer . . . . . DEDUCT: $_____

PRORATES DUE SELLER:

33. Prepaid Property Taxes . . . . $_____
34. Prepaid Insurance Premiums . . . . $_____
35. Impound Account Balance . . . . $_____
36. Prepaid Homeowner's Assessment . . . . . $_____
37. Prepaid Ground Lease . . . . $_____
38. Prepaid Equipment Lease . . . . $_____

39. TOTAL Prorations Due Seller: . . . . . . ADD: $_____

40. ESTIMATED PROCEEDS AT CLOSING . . . . $_____

The net proceeds from sale/exchange will be in the form of:
$_____Cash.

$_____Note secured by carryback trust deed.

$_____Other:_____.

This form is prepared and presented by the seller's broker when advising seller on an offer or counteroffer to buy, sell or exchange.

This net sheet assists the seller to anticipate net proceeds at close and in what form these proceeds will be received.

The figures estimated in this net sheet may vary and thus cannot be guaranteed because of daily changes in lender demands, escrow fees, other charges and prorates.

Tax consequences are not included in this form. If disposing of IRC §1031 property, use a §1031 Recapitulation Form to compute tax consequences. [Form 354]

Seller's Broker: _____

Agent: _____

Address: _____

_____Phone (____) _____

Date:_____, 19 _____

Agent's Signature: _____

Broker's Approval: _____ __/__/__

I have received and read a copy of this estimate of net proceeds.

Seller's Name: _____

Address: _____

_____Phone (____) _____

Seller's Signature:_____

Seller's Signature:_____

Date: _____ , 19_____

FORM 310   09-96   ©1996 **first tuesday**, P.O. BOX 20069, Riverside, CA 92516 (909)781-7300

SPECIAL NOTE: THOSE PEOPLE WHO STRUCTURE, BUY, SELL, BROKER, AND/OR INVEST IN NOTES MUST RECOGNIZE THE IMPORTANCE OF PROTECTIVE EQUITY. IT IS FREQUENTLY UNDEREMPHASIZED OR OVERSHADOWED BY THE "YIELD" GOAL. WITHOUT ADEQUATE PROTECTIVE EQUITY THE NOTE HOLDER'S CAPITAL IS AT GREAT RISK. WE WILL GIVE THIS CONCEPT EVEN MORE ATTENTION IN THE NEXT CHAPTER.

Once the sale is closed and Sam Seller has a carryback note and trust deed or mortgage, what alternatives does Sam Seller have?

CHAPTER 6

TO KEEP, SELL, EXCHANGE OR BORROW? THAT IS <u>THE</u> QUESTION

#1. <u>Keep the note</u>

As we discussed earlier, Sam Seller realizes important benefits by keeping his carryback note.

Two compelling reasons are:
1. Reliable income secured by a known property.
2. A higher interest rate than may be available from a savings account, Certificate of Deposit (CD) or money market fund.

Sam should keep the original note in a safe place, preferably a fireproof safe or in a safe deposit box in a financial institution. Where a deed of trust is used to secure a note, the Trustee will require Sam to deliver (after payoff) the original note with a Request for Full Reconveyance **(EX #15, pg 80)** before the Trustee will issue a Full Reconveyance clearing the title for Bob Buyer. If Sam loses the note or it is destroyed in a fire or blown away in a tornado or Sam accidentally throws it out with the trash, then Sam's life gets complicated. The Trustee could require Sam to produce a lost instrument bond from a reputable casualty insurance company for a fee of 2% to 5% of the original face value of the note. The Bond may have to be $1^1/_2$ to 2 times the original amount of the note. Lost instrument bonds are not easy to get and are fairly expensive. Keeping the original note in a safe deposit box is cheaper.

Sam should keep an accurate record of payments received from Bob. He'll need this for income tax reporting purposes. Also, the payment history will be valuable if he ever decides to sell the note.

<u>Calculating interest and the new balance due</u>

Interest normally is paid in arrears. A note payment due on May 1 covers interest for the period from April 1 through April 30. When the payment due on May 1 is received, then the date that interest is paid to is May 1. Interest on real estate notes is usually calculated on a 360 day basis. We saw that in our calculations when we divided 12 months into the annual interest payment to get a monthly interest payment. Unless a note specifically calls for interest calculations using 365 days, a 30 day month is used. Using a 30 day month, February as well as March are each assumed to have 30 days for interest calculation purposes.

Suppose Sam carried back a $10,000 note secured by a trust deed or mortgage bearing interest at 10% per annum. The monthly payment is $132.15 P & I (Principal & Interest). If he keeps the note, Sam should know how to calculate interest received and his principal balance. He may do this several ways.

EXHIBIT #15

REQUEST FOR FULL RECONVEYANCE

A reconveyance will be issued only upon presentation of this notice properly signed and accompanied by the reconveyance fee, and surrender of the Deed of Trust and the original note or notes secured thereby.

To FIRST AMERICAN TITLE INSURANCE COMPANY, TRUSTEE:

You are hereby notified that the undersigned __Sam & Sally Seller__ the legal owner__s__ of the _____ promissory note__ for the sum of $__82,000.00__ _____,

with interest, secured by that certain Deed of Trust, dated the __1st__ day of __October__, 19__92__,

executed by __Bob Buyer and Betty Buyer, husband and wife as joint__ _____ __tenants__ _____

to FIRST AMERICAN TITLE INSURANCE COMPANY, Trustee, which said Deed of Trust was recorded in the office of the County Recorder of the County of__San Luis Obispo__, State of California, on the _____10th_____ day of __October__, 19__92__, in Book__4321__,

Page_____420_____ et seq. of Official Records, as Instrument Number__98765__

That said note__, together with all other sums and indebtedness secured by said Deed of Trust, ha__s__ been fully paid and satisfied; and you are hereby directed and ordered, upon presentation to you of said Deed of Trust and the note or notes secured thereby, and on cancellation by you of said note or notes, and payment to you of any sums owing to you under the terms of said Deed of Trust, to release and reconvey, without warranty, all the estate in the premises in said Deed of Trust to you by said instrument granted, or so much thereof as is now held by you, unto the parties designated by the terms of said Deed of Trust, at their request and cost, as provided in said Deed of Trust.

Dated this_____21st_____ day of_____November_____, 19__94__.

_____Sam Seller_____

_____Sally Seller_____

_____

1. With pencil and paper. Calculate the monthly interest payment by multiplying the annual interest rate times the principal balance. Then divide that annual amount by 12 months to get monthly interest. For example, the first interest payment on the $10,000 loan would be 10% x $10,000 or $1,000, divided by 12 months. The first monthly interest payment is $83.33.

The difference between total monthly payment of principal and interest (P & I) and the interest payment is the principal payment. Subtract $83.33 interest from the $132.15 payment = $48.82 principal. Subtracting the principal part of the payment from the current principal balance gives the new principal balance ($10,000 - $48.82 = $9,951.18). This new balance is then used to calculate the next month's interest.

2. Sam can do the same calculation on a hand-held, not necessarily a financial, calculator. After calculating the monthly interest amount, enter total payment as a minus number. The principal payment will then be negative. Next, enter the old principal balance as a plus amount and the new positive principal balance will appear.

3. Financial calculators that include the symbols **N, I, PV, PMT, & FV,** are now available for less than $30. Texas Instruments and Hewlett Packard are popular models that are readily available nationwide. They may cost more.

4. Computer software programs are available that also print schedules which break down payments into interest and principal. Some also give year end totals. Having such a printout is handy at tax time. More sophisticated and expensive programs can track impounds that are being collected for taxes and insurance and can account for late charges. They can also complete the 1098 & 1099 reporting forms required by the IRS.

REPORTING INTEREST RECEIVED:
If you hold many notes and are perceived as being in the lending business, you may be required to file Internal Revenue Code (IRC) forms 1098 & 1099 (**EX #16, pg 82**). Ask your accountant if you are required to file either form.

A Dynamite Idea for Note Holders!
Interest First – Then Principal

Many notes state, "Each payment shall be credited first to the interest then due and the remainder on the principal sum". If that language appears, then the payee has the right to charge "daily" interest from the date interest is paid to until the date the current payment is made (usually determined by the postmark on the envelope). When the payor frequently pays late and no late charge provision is in the note, then interest may be applied according to the terms of the note. The payor could find that the note's principal balance is increasing rather than decreasing.

For example: Bob Buyer signed an $82,000 note payable to Sam Seller $660 or more per month including 9% interest. A normal 30 day calculation of interest on the 1st payment would be $615 interest and $45 principal. Dividing $615 by 30 days = $20.50 interest per day. If the note's language permits and if the payment (due on the 1st of the month) is not paid until the 10th day of the month, then the interest

EXHIBIT #16

The I.R.S. requires that interest paid in the course of a taxpayer's investment or trade or business activities (including property rental) be reported annually on form 1099. Reporting is required if the payments exceed $600 in a calendar year and are made to an individual, partnership or unincorporated business.

9292 ☐ VOID ☐ CORRECTED

PAYER'S name, street address, city, state, ZIP code, and telephone no.	Payer's RTN (optional)	OMB No. 1545-0112 **1997** Form **1099-INT**	**Interest Income**
PAYER'S Federal identification number	RECIPIENT'S identification number	**1** Interest income not included in box 3 $	**Copy A** For **Internal Revenue Service Center** File with Form 1096.
RECIPIENT'S name		**2** Early withdrawal penalty $	**3** Interest on U.S. Savings Bonds and Treas. obligations $
Street address (including apt. no.)		**4** Federal income tax withheld $	For Paperwork Reduction Act Notice and instructions for completing this form,
City, state, and ZIP code		**5** Foreign tax paid	**6** Foreign country or U.S. possession
Account number (optional)	2nd TIN Not. ☐	$	see **Instructions for Forms 1099, 1098, 5498, and W-2G.**

Form **1099-INT**   Cat. No. 14410K   Department of the Treasury - Internal Revenue Service

If mortgage interest related to your Trade or Business or to investment property is received from an individual and it exceeds $600 in a calendar year, a form 1098 must be filed with the I.R.S.

8181 ☐ VOID ☐ CORRECTED

RECIPIENT'S/LENDER'S name, address, and telephone number	OMB No. 1545-0901 **1997** Form **1098**	**Mortgage Interest Statement**
RECIPIENT'S Federal identification no.	PAYER'S social security number	**1** Mortgage interest received from payer(s)/borrower(s) $	**Copy A** For **Internal Revenue Service Center** File with Form 1096.
PAYER'S/BORROWER'S name		**2** Points paid on purchase of principal residence $	For Paperwork Reduction Act Notice and instructions for
Street address (including apt. no.)		**3** Refund of overpaid interest $	completing this form,
City, state, and ZIP code		**4**	see **Instructions for Forms 1099, 1098, 5498, and W-2G.**
Account number (optional)			

Form **1098**   Cat. No. 14402K   Department of the Treasury - Internal Revenue Service

For due date and further filing requirements, please consult with your tax advisor.

FAILURE TO FILE THE ABOVE FORMS IN A TIMELY FASHION CAN RESULT IN PENALTIES!

THE I.R.S. HAS A BOOKLET ....
"INSTRUCTIONS TO FILERS OF FORMS 1098,1099,5498 AND W-2G".

charge would be 40 days x $20.50 or $820 less the $660 payment received. This leaves a $160 shortage in interest, which adds to the principal.

The principal balance on which interest will be calculated the following month will be $82,160. Many payees find it easier to just follow an amortization schedule and credit the monthly payment rather than go to the extra effort to compute and apply the interest as shown above. A few prudent and savvy payees find this calculation of daily interest well worth the effort.

Note Collection and Servicing:

Because of IRS reporting requirements, some sellers who carry back notes place them with a financial institution's note servicing (collection) department or with a private note servicing (collection) company.

In Arizona and New Mexico many firms provide note servicing for seller carryback paper. In California such servicing firms are less common. In Arizona and New Mexico servicing firms usually hold the original documents (note and deed of trust). In California they usually hold copies of the documents and the note holder keeps the originals.

ADVANTAGE: For a monthly fee a collection service will receive the payment, calculate the principal and interest due, calculate the new principal balance, and issue the proper year-end reporting form (1098 and or 1099s).

DISADVANTAGE: If they do <u>not</u> receive the payment, some loan servicers may not notify you, or, they will charge more if you want notification. Only a few will send a letter to the payor reminding the payor that he/she is delinquent. Before setting up a collection account, ask what services the collection agent will provide. Very few are set up or willing to handle a foreclosure in the event that such action becomes necessary. As a note holder, you should be prepared to follow up with late charge notices and/or Notice of Default for foreclosure. Depending on where you live, your state may permit real estate attorneys, private title insurance companies, or private foreclosure companies to initiate foreclosure proceedings. Foreclosures can be complex. Seek competent counsel!

Caveat: You should always deal with a "BONDED" collection service.

#2. <u>Sell the note</u>

There are more cash buyers for privately held notes secured by real estate than ever before in our history. Many note holders do not realize they can raise cash by selling all or a portion of their note. Here are several alternatives.
1. Sell the entire note.
2. Sell only a series of payments. In note brokers jargon this is called "selling a partial" Here is an example:
   Suppose Sam Seller holds a note from Bob Buyer with a current balance due of $30,000 and 180 payments remaining. The monthly payment is $304.28 including 9% interest. Rather than sell the entire note, Sam employs Ned Notebroker to sell

EXHIBIT #17

Order No.
Escrow No.
Loan No.

WHEN RECORDED MAIL TO:

Norman Noteholder
58 Park Place
Anytown, CA 99999

APN 151-020-008

ASSIGNMENT OF DEED OF TRUST

FOR VALUE RECEIVED, the undersigned grants, assigns and transfers to:

Norman Noteholder, a single man

all beneficial interest under that certain Deed of Trust dated October 1, 1992
executed by Bob Buyer and Betty Buyer, husband and wife

, Trustor,

to First American Title Insurance Co., a California Corporation   , Trustee
and recorded October 10, 1992 as document No. 98765   , in Book 4321 , Page 420   ,
of Official Records in the office of the County Recorder of San Luis Obispo   County, California,
describing land therein as:

Lot 3 of Tract No. 890, Whispering Pines Subdivision in the
County of SLO, State of California as per map recorded in Book
12, Pages 4 and 5 of Maps, in the office of the County Recorder
of said County.

TOGETHER with the note or notes therein described or referred to, the money due and to become due thereon with interest,
and all rights accrued or to accrue under said Deed of Trust.

Dated December 15, 1992

STATE OF CALIFORNIA   }
COUNTY OF _____ }ss.
                          }

On _____ before me,

_____ ,

personally appeared_____

_____

personally known to me (or proved to me on the basis of satisfactory

evidence) to be the person(s) whose name(s) is/are subscribed to the

within instrument and acknowledged to me that he/she/they executed the

same in his/her/their authorized capacity(ies), and that by his/her/their

signature(s) on the instrument the person(s) or the entity upon behalf of

which the person(s) acted, executed the instrument.

WITNESS my hand and official seal.

Signature _____

_____
Sam Seller

_____
Sally Seller

CARRYBACK DEED OF TRUST ON

PAGE **39**

(This area for official notarial seal)

a partial. Sam needs $12,000. Ned arranges a sale of the next 60 payments to Norman Noteholder and Sam receives $12,000 after costs (including Ned's commission). Sam assigns the note and mortgage to Norman. After Norman receives the 60th payment he will assign the note and mortgage back to Sam Seller. At that time the current balance due should be $24,020. Sam will then be entitled to receive the remaining 120 payments of $304.28 per month from the payor, Bob Buyer.

3. Sell only a portion of each payment.
4. Sell only the future balloon payment and keep receiving the regular payments until the balloon is due and payable.

TRANSFER OF EXISTING NOTE BY ASSIGNMENT

When an existing note is sold, the purchaser will want to have the original note transferred to him. Notes are commonly transferred by assignment language typed either on the back of the original note or on a separate sheet of paper and stapled to the back of the original note. For example:

Assignment of Promissory Note

Date: _____

For value received, Sam Seller and Sally Seller hereby assign, transfer, and deliver all of their right, title and interest in the promissory note dated October 1, 1992 in the face amount of $82,000, executed by Bob Buyer and Betty Buyer, secured by a deed of trust dated October 1, 1992, to Norman Noteholder, a single man or order to:

_____   _____
Sam Seller   Assignee

_____   _____
Sally Seller   Original T/D recording reference

The proper transfer of a note secured by a deed of trust involves two steps.
1. Transfer of the note using "endorsement or assignment language" which should be typed on the back of the original promissory note and signed by the assignors.
2. Transfer of the note and deed of trust (the security for the note) is evidenced by recording an "Assignment of Deed of Trust form" **(EX #17, pg 84)**. The Assignor(s) signature(s) must be notarized.

The authors prefer using an endorsement when acquiring a note to transfer ownership of the note.

TRANSFER OF EXISTING NOTE BY ENDORSEMENT

When an existing note is sold, using an endorsement is a better way for the new payee to receive ownership. A transfer by endorsement can be accomplished by having the holder of the note type or write on the back of the note the following words: Pay to the order of (buyer's name) followed by the holder's signature.

For example, Sam & Sally Seller decide to sell their $82,000 note to Norman Noteholder.

This is how the endorsement on the back of the note would look.

April 15, 1998
Pay to the order of Norman Noteholder, a single man.

_____   _____
Sam Seller   Sally Seller

The endorsement is essentially the same as a check endorsement.

When a note is endorsed instead of assigned, the former holder, Sam Seller (seller of the note), may retain liability for payment of the note as a guarantor. If Sam does not want to be a guarantor, he should add the words "without recourse" to the endorsement. The endorsement line would then read:

April 15, 1998
WITHOUT RECOURSE, pay to the order of Norman Noteholder, a single man.

_____   _____
Sam Seller   Sally Seller

When a note is endorsed, instead of being assigned, the buyer of the note (Norman Noteholder) is a "holder in due course." If the maker (payor, Bob Buyer) of a note is sued for payment, Bob cannot assert against a holder in due course (Norman) certain legal defenses against payment. Those legal defenses would be available to Bob against the original holder of the note (Sam Seller).

Legalese translation: For example, suppose Bob Buyer was persuaded to sign the note because of misrepresentations made to him by Sam Seller. Bob stops paying. Bob can use the misrepresentations as a defense if he is sued by Sam Seller who made the misrepresentations. Bob could not use Sam's misrepresentations as a defense if he is sued by Norman Noteholder, a holder in due course, who had no knowledge of the misrepresentations.

The laws governing endorsement and the rights of a holder in due course vary from state to state and are complex. The purpose of this brief discussion is to make you aware of the topic. You should always consult with an attorney to have your legal questions answered.

FINDING A BUYER:
Should Sam Seller decide to sell his note, he will find the marketplace is difficult to locate and tough to understand. Each trust deed and mortgage is unique. Unlike the few securities markets where bid and ask prices are quoted and where market specialists in each security stand ready to buy in order to maintain an orderly market, the note seller guesses. Should I sell to John who offers X dollars for my note or to Harry who offers Y dollars for my note? Chances are that unless Sam Seller tells each of them, John and Harry will not know what the other bid. Should Sam Seller wait for another offer? Just as this lack of a structured market may work against a note seller, it can work for a note buyer.

Note Buyers and Note Holders

There are two types of note buyers: Individuals and Institutions. Individuals, such as Nancy Notebuyer, often function as a middle person between the note seller and note buyer.

Individual buyers and investors

Nancy Notebuyer has her own business. She buys privately held notes and then sells them at a higher price to institutions and/or private investors. She has no one to account to if she either makes a mistake or gets a great buy. Nancy alone is responsible. Individual investors like Norman Noteholder buy notes and hold them for income. Such notes traditionally offer higher rates of return than savings accounts, certificates of deposit (CDs) or money market funds.

If Nancy Notebuyer can buy a note at a wholesale price, she may then try to sell the note to Norman Noteholder at a higher retail price and keep the profit. For example, if she can buy a note at a 19% yield and sell it to Norman at a 14% yield, she keeps the 5% difference (spread) as profit. It takes time, skill and money to be in the note business. Nancy must be able to pay her overhead and make a profit to stay in business.

Norman is not in the note business. He is a passive investor in notes. He doesn't mind Nancy making a profit. She earns it by providing him with a valuable service, offering him notes to buy that fit his economic objectives and personal comfort level (risk tolerance). Nancy is a principal and closes deals <u>with her own money</u>. She is neither Norman's agent nor Sam Seller's agent. Norman still makes an attractive return compared to other investment alternatives.

Institutional buyers

When we write about institutional buyers, we are not talking about your local bank or savings and loan association. Most banks or savings and loans won't buy or make loans secured by seller carryback trust deeds and mortgages. Institutional buyers are few. They include, but are not limited to, a few mortgage lenders, finance companies, and <u>an occasional</u> small bank or insurance company. People in the note business sometimes refer to these institutional buyers as "Corporate America". "Corporate America" is a generic term that includes the large institutional buyers of privately held mortgages. Corporate America buys most of its notes through independent note brokers. Owner-directed Pension or Profit Sharing Plans are not institutions, but occasionally buy notes.

Each buyer has its own standards for buying notes. First, they consider the type of property (house, land, office building, farm) that secures the note and where the property is located. If satisfactory, then they apply their own criteria of **protective equity** and loan-to-value ratios to establish that the note is or is not a candidate for purchase. Their loan-to-value ratios are set according to the type of property that secures the note.

The Loan-To-Value (LTV) ratio is the amount of debt on a property expressed as a percentage of the Fair Market Value (FMV) of the property.

Example: A property valued at $100,000 has a first loan of $50,000 and a second loan of $20,000. The $70,000 total debt divided by $100,000 Fair Market Value (FMV) = 70% LTV. The lower the loan-to-value percentage, the more equity an owner has. For example, with only $50,000 debt, the same property would have a LTV ratio of 50%.

Some typical Loan-To-Value (LTV) Ranges required by note buyers:

TYPE OF PROPERTY SECURING NOTE	LTV RANGE
Owner-occupied single family home	70% to 80%
Non-owner-occupied single family house	60% to 70%
Owner-occupied condo	50% to 70%
Mobile homes	50% to 70%
Multi-family apartments	50% to 70%
Commercial property	60% or less
Urban land with utilities (to the property)	50% more or less
Rural land (non farm)	50% or less

Two things may be learned from this list:

1. The type of notes preferred by note buyers. Owner-occupied homes are the most desirable. History has proven them to be the most stable. Notes secured by land usually have the greatest risk and justify a lower loan to value ratio (LTV).
2. Real estate values fluctuate both up and down over time, even in good areas. A note holder's best protection against loss is **protective equity** established at the time he acquires a note. An owner with a substantial equity who is paying on a note will be motivated to protect his/her equity position.

Discounting

Suppose, when selling his property to Bob Buyer, Sam Seller carried back a $20,000 note amortized at 10% interest, in equal monthly installments of principal and interest for a period of 10 years. Once the sale closed, those terms are pretty much set in concrete. Even though Bob improves the property, which enhances the loan to value ratio, this will not alter the terms of the note. Regardless of any second thoughts or subsequent change in circumstances that Sam may have, Bob is under NO OBLIGATION to change the terms of the note. If Sam offers to change the terms and modify the note, Bob has the choice to accept or not accept Sam's offer.

If Sam wants to sell his note, he may call Nancy Notebuyer for a quote on the 10 year note he holds from Bob. He is asking Nancy to put a dollar value today on that series of payments to be received in the future. As we explained in Chapter 2 about the Time Value of Money, each payment has a different value depending upon when it is received. The payments to be received during the early years on this note are much more valuable than the payments to be received during the later years of this note. **A dollar to be received in the future is worth less than a dollar received today.** Most note buyers will discount each future payment to its present value.

As Sam carried back the above note at 10%, that is the face interest or yield to Sam. Nancy Notebuyer will not be willing to invest her money at 10%. She must buy at a wholesale yield (higher here than 10%), then sell at a retail yield and keep the difference in order to stay in business. So, Sam's note must be discounted to give a higher yield that Nancy will accept.

To understand how discounting works, let's review what we learned in Chapter 5 on Balloon Payments.

Think in these terms: <u>**N**</u> <u>**I**</u> <u>**PV**</u> <u>**PMT**</u> <u>**FV**</u>

Time: Expressed in months or years (Calculator symbol **N**)

Interest: The rate of interest or yield desired usually expressed per month or per year (Calculator symbol **I**). The annual interest rate must be divided by the number of payments that the note requires during the year. Monthly, ÷ by 12; quarterly, ÷ by 4; semi-annually, ÷ by 2; semi-monthly, ÷ by 24; bi-weekly, ÷ by 26; etc.

Present Value: The dollar value today of dollars (principal) to be received in the future. (**PV** is the symbol.)

Payment: The amount of money paid periodically on the note. In the above example, payment includes principal and interest. (Payment is the **PMT** symbol on a financial calculator.)

Future Value: As Sam carried back a note fully amortized over 10 years, the future value (**FV** on the financial calculator) would be zero. Suppose a note has a balloon payment due before it fully amortizes. If you are solving for **PV**, you must first calculate the amount of the balloon or the **F**uture **V**alue (**FV**) before you can calculate or solve for the discounted **PV** value. We suggest you review Chapter 5 to see the mechanics of doing this.

Note buyers think in terms of a percentage yield or return on their money. The yield required determines the discount. The dollar amount they offer for a note may, of course, be translated into a discount from the note's current balance. However, informed note buyers do not buy in terms of an arbitrary 20% to 25% discount. Discounts on performing notes frequently range from about 10% on the low end to over 60% on the high end. The discounts may be even larger on non-performing notes if they have a high probability for foreclosure. Numerous risk factors listed below determine the yield or return required by each individual note buyer. In turn that yield determines the discount on a given note. Obviously then,

THERE IS <u>NO</u> "STANDARD DISCOUNT!"

We emphasize this fact for the benefit of those who want to sell a note and may ask an unqualified friend (the barber, supermarket checker, or real estate agent) what the "going discount rate" is for notes these days, as if there were such a thing as a "standard discount." Anyone who tells you that the "standard discount" on notes is a certain percentage is an UNINFORMED AMATEUR. When a note buyer is given no other information about a note and the note seller asks, "What's the discount?" the only correct answer is, "It depends." On what does the discount depend?

Other factors which influence the size of the discount and affect the potential yield include but are not limited to:

- type of property
- amount of **protective equity**
- location of the property
- priority of the note being considered (1st, 2nd or 3rd position)
- cost of protecting cash invested in the event of default and foreclosure
- payment history, credit standing and financial strength of the payor
- trends in the local real estate market or neighborhood where the security is located
- trends in the state and national economy

Each note buyer's interpretation of these facts may be DIFFERENT (and it frequently is).

The yield or return required influences the discount and will vary depending on each note buyer's analysis and perception of the risks involved.

Let's take a closer look at yield.

For those with a financial calculator, here is a yield calculation:

You may recall the example we used of a $10,000 note for 10 years @ 10% with monthly payments of $132.15. The loan balance is due and payable in full in 6 years. The balloon payment is $5,210.

We wrote about notes with balloon payments earlier in Chapter 5. Following is the calculation for a note buyer who wants to buy a note that will return 15% on the cash invested. Using a 15% yield, the above $10,000 note would be worth:

N	**I**	**PV**	**PMT**	**FV**
72 (6 years)	1.25/month (15%)	solve for PV	132.15	5,210

PV(Present Value) = $8,380. That amount can be broken down to two parts:

1. The balloon payment

N	**I**	**PV**	**PMT**	**FV**
72 (6 years)	1.25/month (15%)	solve for PV	0	5,210

PV (Present Value) of the balloon = **$2,130**, and,

2. The total of all note payments (72 payments x $132.15 = $9,544) not including the balloon

N	**I**	**PV**	**PMT**	**FV**
72 (6 years)	1.25/month (15%)	solve for PV	132.15	0

(PV) Present Value of the 72 monthly payments = **$6,250**

Together those two parts **($2,130 + $6,250)** add up to **$8,380**, the PV of the entire note.

Suppose Sam sells the entire note (the balloon payment and the stream of note payments at the same time). Sam will lose the difference between the face amount of the note, $10,000, and $8,380 (the note's discounted value to yield 15%). Any costs (title insurance, escrow, attorney's fees, brokerage fee) paid by Sam to sell the note will also be deducted from the $8,380 paid by the note buyer.

The difference, or loss in value on the house sale would be $1,620 ($10,000 - $8,380) less costs to sell the note. This is equivalent to Sam Seller selling his home for $98,380 CASH ($100,000 less the $1,620 discount) less any costs of selling the note.

Note buyers and investors try to minimize risk while making the highest return. Balancing risk and return translates into having the most **protective equity** possible. People like Norman Noteholder invest in trust deed and mortgage notes for the income the notes produce. Norman's objective is a steady, secure income stream. He looks upon foreclosure ONLY as a <u>last resort</u> to protect his investment. Should he have to foreclose, he hopes to be bought out FOR CASH at the foreclosure sale. He does not want to own and manage property. His primary insulation against loss is a **strong protective equity** position. Earlier we said that real estate values fluctuate both up and down over time, even in good areas. For that reason, believe us when we say

THERE IS NO SUBSTITUTE FOR PROTECTIVE EQUITY!

Actual Yield vs Potential Yield

Actual yield can only be measured in hindsight, after a note has been paid off. Potential yield is what a note buyer/investor hopes to earn on his/her invested capital when s/he buys a note at a discount. The assumption (hoped for end result) is that all payments will be received in a timely manner (or sooner) according to the terms of the note.

INVESTMENT-TO-VALUE (ITV)

Another concept we introduced earlier (on page 53 in Chapter 4) is Investment-to-Value (ITV). Investment-to-Value means the price the note buyer is paying divided by the property's value. Suppose a $10,000 note that Sam Seller owns is secured by a lot valued at $15,000. If Norman Noteholder wanted a return or yield of 18%, he would offer Sam $7,334 for his $10,000 note. Norman's Investment-to-Value ratio (ITV), $7,334 to $15,000, would be approximately 49%. Norman Noteholder, you remember, buys and holds notes for income.

If Nancy Notebuyer, who buys and sells notes, looking at the same facts did not feel comfortable with even a 50% ITV, she could ask Sam Seller how much money he really needs. If Sam needs only two thousand dollars, he has alternatives other than selling the entire note.

For example, Nancy Notebuyer could buy the next 18 months of payments. This is commonly referred to as buying a "partial," meaning only a part of the income stream is purchased. Use a financial calculator where

N	**I**	**PV**	**PMT**	**FV**
18	1.5%/month (18% yr.) (the yield Nancy requires)	?	$132.15	0

Solving for PV, she would offer $2,071 (less costs) for 18 payments of $132.15 (18 x $132.15 = $2,378). Her Investment-to-Value ($2,071 ÷ $15,000) ratio is now 14%, leaving her with 86% **protective equity**, a very secure position.

What are the tax consequences when buying and selling some payments?

To Nancy:
The difference between what Nancy pays for the payments ($2,071) and the total ($2,378) of those 18 payments, $307, is interest income to Nancy. Each month she must recognize that month's income just as if she had made a loan of $2,071 @18% payable in 18 installments.

To Sam:
Due to the discount, Sam Seller needs to recalculate the amount of gain in his note. Receipt of the $2,071 is treated as a payment on the note. Income tax he pays on that money depends on his recalculated gain. If you are in Sam Seller's situation, see your accountant and inquire about your new gross profit percentage.

When Nancy Notebuyer paid $2,071 for 18 payments on a lot valued at $15,000, we said her Investment-to-Value (ITV) ratio was 14%. Let's see how the ITV concept applies to another situation.

If there is a senior loan, then add that amount to the price you are paying for the junior loan, divide by the property value and that will give you the Investment-to-Value ratio.

For example, when there is a note secured by a 2nd deed of trust as in the example on page 52 of Chapter 4, the ITV would be calculated as follows:

Property Value		$100,000
1st loan	$60,000	
2nd loan	$22,000	
Total Debt		$ 82,000
The **Protective Equity** is		$ 18,000 (18%)

If Norman Noteholder buys this $22,000 2nd for $15,000 cash, then the Investment-to-Value is $60,000 + $15,000 = $75,000 ÷ $100,000 or an ITV ratio of 75%. The lower the Investment-to-Value ratio (ITV), the more **protective equity** you will have.

Restructuring a note to increase yield.

THIS CONCEPT APPLIES ONLY TO NOTES PURCHASED AT A DISCOUNT!

Suppose Nancy Notebuyer bought Sam Seller's $10,000 note for $7,334 (discounted to yield 18% where N = 120 (10 yrs.), I = 1.5 (18%), and PMT = $132.15). Nancy would calculate a PV of $7,334. She may want to encourage Bob Buyer to pay off the note sooner. Nancy's reason? "MORE SOONER IS BETTER!" for her.

If Nancy Notebuyer can get Bob Buyer (now the payor) to pay not $132.15 per month, but $200 per month instead, Nancy could offer Bob a lower interest rate, one reduced from 10% to perhaps 6%. Suppose Bob paid $200 per month including 6% interest on his $10,000 note. The note would be repaid in 58 months, not quite 5 years. As Nancy had paid $7,334 for the note, her rate of return would increase to 20.4% (N = 58, PV = $7,334, PMT = $200 and solve for I). This is a win-win situation for both Bob and Nancy.

To carry that line of reasoning to its ultimate conclusion, Nancy could forget interest entirely if she could negotiate a high enough monthly payment with Bob. For example, with a payment of $400 per month and NO interest, Nancy would be paid off in 25 months ($10,000 divided by $400). Nancy's rate of return would increase to 30.5% (N=25, PV= $7,334, PMT = $400 and solve for I). "MORE SOONER IS BETTER" is indeed GOOD BUSINESS for Nancy. If Bob can handle the higher payments, it is a good deal for him too, as he may save a large amount of interest.

Restructuring a note to increase its cash value.

A home seller who carried back a note and later decides to sell it may use the same techniques referenced above. Having the buyer agree to change the note's terms, such as increasing the payment and decreasing the interest rate, or shortening the due date, the note holder CAN INCREASE THE CASH VALUE **BUT NOT THE YIELD** of a carryback note. Normally, the yield to the Seller, who carried the note, will remain the same. "MORE SOONER IS BETTER" applies here to increase the cash value of the note.

IMPORTANT: Modifying or restructuring a note bought at a discount can be profitable, but only when properly done. Consult a real estate-oriented attorney with experience in the loan/note field. Consult a real estate-oriented CPA for any tax impact. You may need to call several before you find the right one. They are not easy to find. Or, an experienced mortgage loan broker or real estate consultant who regularly deals in private money financing may be able to help you.

NORMAL EXTENSION AND/OR MODIFICATION

In our first example, in Chapter 2, Sam Seller sold his Park Avenue house to Bob and Betty Buyer and carried back a note secured by a 1st deed of trust for $82,000 payable $660 or more per month including 9% interest, all due in 10 years.

Suppose that 9¹/₂ years have passed and the balloon payment of $73,292 will be due in six months. The Buyers have a good payment history with Sam Seller. The Sellers don't need the cash but could use a higher payment. Assume that interest rates at Insecurity Bank are currently 11¹/₂% on real estate loans. After some discussion, the Buyers and Sellers agree to extend the note for three more years at a monthly payment of $730 or more per month including 11% interest. The Note Modification and Extension Agreement would look like this: see **EX #18, pg 95.**

Potential Tax Trap:

A seller takes back a note for a portion of the purchase price. The note calls for a balloon payment. The seller may decide to extend or renew the note. In Saint Claire Corp., TC Memo 1997-171 the Tax Court concluded that the extension of a note <u>after</u> it became due and payable resulted in the sellers being in "constructive receipt" of the note principal. To avoid this problem with its adverse tax consequences, complete any extension or renewal before the note or balloon payment becomes due and payable.

Suppose you are modifying or extending a note you purchased that does not have a due-on-sale, late charge or other such important provision(s). Such items could now be included in the modification .

A modification and/or extension agreement should be in writing and signed by all parties <u>including junior lien holders</u>. For the Seller's protection the Buyers should provide an endorsement to the original title insurance policy held by the Seller/note holder insuring the priority of his note. If this is not done and there was a junior lien (loan) holder who did not agree (in writing) to the modification and extension, the Sellers could lose their senior lien position.

NOTE: The security instrument (trust deed or mortgage) is normally recorded. In most cases the original note is not recorded and the world is not aware of its specific terms. The precise terms of the modification and extension can be kept confidential by recording a Memorandum of Modification as shown in **EX #19, pg 96**. What a great way to keep your business confidential!

Modifying the interest rate on a note may have usury potential and may require state and federal loan disclosure documentation. Seek appropriate counsel to prevent this problem. See page 46 for our discussion of usury.

DEBT COVERAGE RATIO

Except where the note is secured by a single family house, institutions and experienced investors seldom buy a secured junior note when the possibility of taking on a larger senior debt payment (in the event of foreclosure) is not supported by a property's cash flow. For example, buying a $30,000 second loan behind a $200,000 first would mean that if the note buyer is to avoid paying from his own income, then the property's net operating income (NOI), the income left after a vacancy allowance and paying all operating expenses, would need to cover at least the payments on the

EXHIBIT #18

MODIFICATION OF PROMISSORY NOTE

1. __PARTIES__ .The Parties to this Agreement are ___Sam Seller and Sally Seller___ , ___husband and wife as joint tenants___ ,hereinafter referred to as "Beneficiary," and ___Bob Buyer and Betty Buyer, husband and wife___ hereinafter referred to as "Owner."

2. <u>Note Secured by Deed of Trust</u>. Owner is the owner of real property described in a Deed of Trust recorded ___October 10, 1992___ , as Instrument No. ___98765___ in Volume/Book ___4321___ , Page ___420___ ,of the Official Records of ___SLO___ _____ County, California. The Deed of Trust secures payment of a Promissory Note in the original amount of $___82,000.00___ , which was signed by ___Bob Buyer and Betty Buyer, husband and wife___ , in favor of ___Sam Seller and Sally Seller, husband and wife as joint tenants___ .

3. <u>Modification of Note</u>. The parties agree to the following modification of the payment terms of the Note:

> Beneficiary agrees to extend the due date on the above referenced note to October 1, 2005. The interest rate shall be 11% on the unpaid balance and the monthly payment shall be $730.00 or more per month.

4. Broker Arranging the Modification. This Modification Agreement was arranged by ___ABC, Inc.___ ,which has its principal office at___590 Palm Avenue___ (City)___Anytown___ (State) _____ .

5. Other .

> All parties agree that the unpaid balance on this note on October 2, 2002 is $73,291.86.

6. Binding Effect . This Modification Agreement is binding upon the successors and assigns of the parties.

7. Effective Date . The effective date of this Modification is ___October 2, 2002___ , or the date the 110.6 endorsement referred to in paragraph 5 above is effective, whichever date occurs last.

Date_____   Date_____

OWNER/TRUSTOR   BENEFICIARY

_____   _____
Bob Buyer   Sam Seller

_____   _____
Betty Buyer   Sally Seller

EXHIBIT #19

MEMORANDUM OF MODIFICATION OF NOTE
SECURED BY TD

Recording Requested By:

When Recorded Return To:

Mr. and Mrs. Sam Seller
123 Elm Street
Anytown, CA 99999

APN # 760-895-653

MEMORANDUM OF MODIFICATION OF NOTE SECURED BY DEED OF TRUST

On <u>October 10, 1992</u> a Deed of Trust was recorded as Document No. <u>98765</u> in Vol/Book <u>4321</u> at Page <u>420</u> of the official records of <u>S L O County</u>, State of <u>California</u>, for the purpose of securing payment of a promissory note signed by <u>Bob Buyer and Betty Buyer</u>, <u>Husband and Wife as Joint Tenants</u>, hereafter referred to as "Trustor," in favor of <u>Sam Seller</u> and <u>Sally Seller</u>, <u>Husband and Wife as Joint Tenants</u>, in the original amount of <u>$82,000.00.</u> The present holder of the promissory note is <u>Sam Seller and Sally Seller</u>. Trustor and <u>Sam Seller and Sally Seller</u> have agreed to modify the terms of the promissory note secured by said Deed of Trust, and the modification provisions have been attached to the original promissory note.

Date: September 12, 2002   Date: September 26, 2002

<u>TRUSTOR</u>   <u>BENEFICIARY</u>

_____   _____
Bob Buyer   Sam Seller

_____   _____
Betty Buyer   Sally Seller

first loan. If the net operating income does not cover the first loan payment, foreclosing on the second and making payments on the first could be an out-of-pocket experience. To illustrate the point, let's use some numbers.

Value of apartment building		$330,000	
1st loan	$200,000		Payable $2,000/mo. P & I
2nd loan	$ 30,000		Payable $ 500/mo. P & I
Total loans		$230,000	
Equity		$100,000	

Suppose that last year's income and expense records on the building showed:

Total (Gross) Income received	$ 39,000
Less: Operating Expenses	$ 16,200
Net Operating Income	$ 22,800 (available to pay loans)

If the annual loan payment on the $200,000 lst loan is $24,000 ($2,000 per month), we see that the entire Net Operating Income plus $1,200 is required to make the payments on the lst loan. The property's owner, the payor on both loans, is making the $500/month payments on the $30,000 2nd plus the $100/month shortage on the first loan from his or her other income, not from income generated by this apartment building. Buying such a note when the property's income will not at least cover the payments on the first loan could be dangerous. Carrying back a note where the property's income will not make the payments means the note will be less desirable to a note buyer. This translates into a larger discount for the note Seller and higher yield for the note Buyer to compensate for more risk.

Additional insights on selling notes:

Sam Seller decides to sell his note and contacts Nancy Notebuyer. Nancy, a person in the business of buying notes, may sell notes she has bought to institutions. She must, of course, comply with their paperwork requirements. She must get the necessary information and documentation from Sam Seller.

Required documentation is somewhat standardized. Usually a committee reviews proposed purchases. Most institutional buyers (Corporate America) are accountable to shareholders, and management must show "due diligence" (fact finding). Note brokers representing buyers and sellers have similar responsibilities. Note buyers feel such information includes but is not limited to:

1. Copy of the promissory note. **Always know where your original note is.**
2. Copy of trust deed or mortgage. If the original was recorded and you can't find it, you can get a copy from the County Recorder's office in the county where the property is located.
3. Copy of the closing statement of the transaction when the note was originated.
4. Copy of title insurance policy issued on the sale where the trust deed or mortgage is referenced. Was the T/D or mortgage insured as to seniority when it was originated? The vast majority of states (CA is an exception) require a separate Mortgagee policy of Title Insurance to insure the noteholder. It should be obtained

and is cheapest if purchased concurrently with the closing of the sale transaction in which the Deed of Trust or Mortgage is originated. If the note and mortgage are sold in the future, many times a note buyer can obtain an assignee's endorsement to that Mortagee policy at a very reasonable cost. This endorsement usually insures the Assignee as to the validity of the assignment and the priority of the lien.

5. Copy of either or both the escrow instructions or Purchase Agreement.
6. Current Market Value Appraisal.
7. Photos of property.
8. If the note is a 2nd or 3rd, copies of the senior loan documents and written confirmation by the payees as to the current balance due. Compare this with what the payor tells you. A property seller who carries back a junior lien should get this information on the buyer's first loan when the closing takes place on the sale. This information should be kept with the original note in the event the note holder decides to sell their note at some time in the future.
9. Name, mailing address and social security number of the payor/trustor/mortgagor.
10. Credit report on the payor/trustor/mortgagor.
11. Offset Statement, Statement of Balance Due or Estoppel letter (all mean about the same). This is a document signed by the payor/trustor/mortgagor confirming the balance they owe.
12. Payment history on the note (records of when payments were received).

Some institutions buy notes that are only above a certain balance, perhaps $20,000. Other institutions have a minimum discount. An example of a minimum discount would be a note buyer who will discount a loan by at least 10% or by $3,500, whichever is greater.

Note buyers who successfully broker notes to institutions tend to concentrate on notes over $20,000. TIME IS MONEY! The same amount of time, knowledge and effort is required to market larger notes as smaller notes. Several years ago one successful note broker we know began brokering notes with a $20,000 minimum balance and today brokers only notes of $40,000 or more. Considerable knowledge, homework and due diligence are required to broker notes properly.

Some individuals make their living by brokering notes. Each state has its requirements regarding what you as an individual must do to engage in this activity. You may be required to have a mortgage broker's license or a real estate license. Best to check with your state's Department of Corporations, Department of Banking, and with your state's Department of Real Estate. One or more may claim jurisdiction over such activities. Jurisdiction varies from state to state. California has the most comprehensive laws for buying and selling notes in the US. Some states do not regulate people who buy and sell existing notes secured by real estate. The definite trend is toward state licensing of people involved in buying and reselling notes. When notes are bought and sold interstate, then Federal security regulations may apply.

#3. **Exchange the note**

> **The number of cash buyers for notes is far less than those who would exchange their equity in real estate or personal property for a note. More takers with equity are ALWAYS available in the real estate marketplace than cash buyers. IMPORTANT - Turn now to illustration on page 104.**

Some property sellers may accept either existing or created notes (where the buyer writes a note and secures it with his own property) for the equity in the seller's property. More details in Chapter 9. The terms of a created note are whatever the parties agree to. As we emphasized in Chapter 2, ALL TERMS ARE NEGOTIABLE when seller carryback financing is involved. Some note holders would accept property if they could avoid a discount and receive face value for their note. Often property sellers don't realize that a note holder (buyer) would accept a property equity in exchange for their note.

Both parties, those who own equities and those who own notes, should understand that each may be able to help the other. Real estate agents can be a catalyst in this process, but the majority of agents are not familiar with these marketing concepts. **Ask around**. Try to locate an agent who has documented experience in creative marketing, owner financing and exchanging. The brochure, *What Every Seller (and Agent) Should Understand About Marketing Real Estate,* **(EX #20, pgs 190-193)** was developed in the mid '80s by the authors of this book to assist agents in this educational process. For your reference we have reproduced the brochure in the back of this book.

Here is an example of exchanging a note (personal property) for real estate.

Evelyn Exchangor owns a $100,000 trust deed note. Real estate is appreciating in her area. She is experienced in managing rental property. Evelyn spots an apartment house offered for sale by Friendly Realty. While talking to the listing agent, she learns that the owner wants to retire and move to Florida. The asking price on the apartments is $318,000. There is an existing, assumable loan of $200,000. Evelyn offers to exchange her $100,000 note plus $18,000 cash for the equity in the apartments.

Benefits to Evelyn:
She converts her note, which will not grow in value, to a real estate equity that may later appreciate in value. She may sacrifice cash flow in the short run. But, by putting her management skills to work, she may end up with a greater cash flow from the apartments in years to come than if she kept the note. The apartment house may increase in value, her note will not.

Benefits to apartment seller:
Taking Evelyn's note facilitates the sale of the apartments so the seller can get on with his life. He receives enough cash to pay his broker, pay other transaction costs, and move to sunny Florida. The trust deed note requires much less management than his apartments and will provide him with income to supplement his Social

Security and pension. He now has time to fish, play golf and travel.

Another Investment Strategy
Steve Speculator, a real estate dealer, buys notes at steep discounts for cash and then trades them at face value for real estate. For example, Steve buys a $100,000 note secured by real estate for $65,000 cash. Then he trades the $100,000 note for Sam Seller's free and clear house priced at $100,000. Steve next goes to Insecurity Bank and gets a new loan on the home for $70,000. He rents the house and a few months later trades his $30,000 remaining equity in the house for a $20,000 lot and a $10,000 note secured by other real property.

An indirect path to cash....
Note holders may not see a path to cash by exchanging a note for equity. There is a way. Here is an example.

With his agent's help Sam Seller could find a home seller with a free and clear house who will accept his $82,000 note for most of the purchase price. They may have to make numerous offers searching for a motivated seller who understands the benefits of such a trade. With persistence they can find such an owner. Next Sam would borrow from Insecurity Bank using the house as security for the loan. He has now generated cash out of his note.

There is always a path to cash. The path may not be direct. It may involve more than one move, but the path is there.

In these examples, we did not consider sales costs and commissions. Also, tax implications were not considered (and there are many). In Steve Speculator's case, he exchanged personal property, a note, for real property, a house. Any gain to the house seller (Sam Seller) is taxable as if Sam received cash. Gain/profit in the note is taxable to the note holder (Steve Speculator) as if he received cash. The house seller may be able to report the note at "fair market value" (translation for tax purposes: a discounted amount less than the current note balance). Consult your tax advisor.

#4. *Hypothecate or borrow against the note*

Suppose that two years ago Sam Seller carried back a $10,000 note secured by a 2nd deed of trust on Park Ave. on a sale to Bob Buyer. Sam now needs some cash. He contacts Ben Banker, the loan officer at Insecurity Bank, and asks for a loan of $5,000. The banker inquires about collateral for the loan. Sam offers to assign them the $10,000 note he is receiving payments on from Bob Buyer as collateral for this loan. The Banker is not impressed. Why? What is Ben Banker's problem with Sam's request?

The two parties in this proposed loan transaction are the lender, Insecurity Bank (1st party), and the borrower, Sam Seller (2nd party). Bob Buyer is a third party outside this current loan transaction. His note is called a third party note. Institutional lenders today are wary of making loans secured only by a trust deed note from a third party like Bob Buyer. Insecurity Bank has no financial information on Bob Buyer and has no right to get any information from him. Bob can take the position that it is none of their business. He need not cooperate in any way.

The reason lenders are wary is that lenders know nothing about the payor or the security for the note. They have no right to access the property. Individuals and privately held corporations are often approached to lend money on, and accept a third party note, as collateral. Some specialize in this type activity. Some individuals and privately held corporations are willing to buy existing third party notes. However, many will not originate a new loan secured by that third party note.

Before borrowing against a note, consider the costs. In addition to the interest rate charged, which is usually more than the face rate on the note, other points or costs charged by a lender may make borrowing expensive.

For example: Interest rates on loans funded by private investors and arranged by loan brokers in California frequently run 3% to 5% above the current rate for loans on owner-occupied single family homes funded by institutions to qualified buyers. Loan brokers may charge from 2 points to 10 or more points (1 point = 1% of the loan) for arranging a private investor-funded loan plus other normal charges. Usually these notes are payable interest only monthly and are all due and payable in 3 to 5 years. Review Chapter 5 for the problems inherent in loans with short term balloons.

TAX IMPACT: Borrowing on a note may be a taxable event.

Suppose Sam Seller held a $10,000 carryback note from Bob Buyer and was able to borrow $4,000 by pledging the note as collateral. For tax purposes, the $4,000 would be treated as if Sam had received a $4,000 principal payment from Bob. The payment may trigger a taxable event for Sam in proportion to the amount of gain he had in the note. **The tax treatment of money borrowed against a note is the same as receipt of the same amount of principal paid to the note holder.** This would happen ONLY if the sale in which the note originated was for more (even $1 more) than $150,000. When the sale is for $150,000 or less, no gain on the carryback is recognized if Bob pledges the note as collateral. For details, see Internal Revenue Code Section 453A(d). Such is not the case when borrowing against real estate, where money borrowed is not taxed on receipt. What you do later with the property determines whether a tax is paid on money borrowed.

> **To deduct interest on borrowed money, you must be able to show what the borrowed money was spent for, whether it was for business or personal expenses. Check with your accountant for details.**

TAX TRAP: As we showed on page 61 when your loan is greater than your cost basis, that difference may be taxable upon sale. In California during the high appreciation of the mid-to-late '80s some property owners refinanced their properties and pulled out cash. The market started to soften and prices began falling in '90, '91 and '92 leaving some owners with property that was encumbered with 100% or more debt. Property owners are said to be "Upside Down" when their loan exceeds the value of the property. If they gave it away to someone who assumed their loan or if they lost it in foreclosure, they would be liable for taxes on their gain. Gain here is the difference between their current loan balance(s) and their adjusted cost basis in the property. Adjusted cost basis on a rental property is the original purchase price, plus any capital improvements, less depreciation taken. If property owners and investors are to avoid serious tax problems and liability exposure, they must do a better job of planning their borrowing and pay-back strategy.

With the variety of ways to sell notes, such as selling so many payments (a "partial"), or part or all of a balloon payment, or the last few payments, or a portion of each payment, etc., **the idea of borrowing against a note, particularly with its adverse tax implications and personal liability for the borrower, may not be as favorable as selling all or a portion of the note to raise cash.**

For example: A note seller wants to sell a $15,000 note secured by a single family residence.

Nancy Notebuyer offers $10,000. The note seller winces and says, "I hate to take that large a discount when I only need $3,200." Nancy makes him a different offer. She offers to buy the next 28 payments of $165/mo. for $3,600 (less $400 costs) to net $3,200 to the note seller. Nancy will take a full assignment of both the note and deed of trust until she has received her 28 payments. Her purchase agreement covers what will happen in the event of a default or an early payoff. After receiving her 28 payments, she will assign the note and deed of trust back to the note seller, without recourse. The balance will then be $13,006. The seller receives the cash he needs and avoids the large discount ($5,000) required to sell the entire note. A prudent note seller should review the tax consequences with competent tax counsel prior to selling or borrowing on a note.

Owner Will Carry © 1998 by Bill Broadbent, SEC, CCIM, & George Rosenberg

In **ALL** real estate transactions when a real estate agent is involved on behalf of a client, an agent's role must be to benefit and protect the client. With that thought in mind, the obvious question a client must ask his/her agent is:

WHO DO YOU REPRESENT?

CHAPTER 7

AGENCY ISSUES INVOLVING TRUST DEEDS AND MORTGAGES

REAL ESTATE AGENTS: When seller carryback financing is involved in a transaction, the principals (seller and buyer) must understand whom the real estate agent(s) represent. Whom the agent represents can significantly influence the terms of a seller carryback note to one party's advantage.

Sometimes buyers are more aware of the possible advantages of seller carryback financing than the real estate agents involved (See Bob Bruss' column on page 14). Before looking for real estate to purchase, a buyer should ask himself, "DO I NEED REPRESENTATION in acquiring a suitable property?" If the answer is "Yes," then the buyer should consider employing his/her own agent. Employing a Buyer's Agent has numerous advantages. These are explained in the brochure, *Who Does Your Real Estate Agent Represent?* (**EX #21**). For your information we have reproduced this brochure on pages 190-193 in the back of this book.

To assist consumers and agents in establishing clear agency relationships, the authors developed (in 1982) the first agency disclosure statement (**EX #22, pgs 194-5** in back of book). This preceded mandatory agency disclosure requirements by any state.

Now over 44 states require agency disclosure by real estate agents telling the consumer whom the agent represents in a real estate transaction. Many consumer groups feel that these disclosures are inadequate. Hopefully they will be revised and improved for everyone's benefit.

> **When working with a real estate licensee, determine who the licensee will represent in the transaction at the very start of your relationship.**

For many buyers, perhaps up to half of all American families who can't meet the stringent Institutional requirements to obtain a real estate loan, seller carryback financing may be the difference between buying and not buying a home. *Seller financing is also very important to real estate investors.* If a buyer needs representation, then the buyer should carefully qualify the agent as to his/her experience in negotiating seller carryback financing before employing that agent to represent him. As all terms are negotiable in a real estate transaction, the agent who is experienced in negotiating seller carryback financing for the buyer's benefit is a <u>RARE</u> and VERY VALUABLE PERSON.

In their combined seventy six years of real estate practice, the authors have observed many examples of deals that could and should have been made, but were not, due to the "CASH ONLY" mentality of many real estate agents.

A seller, when interviewing agents to list his/her property for sale, should inquire as to their experience in dealing with seller carryback financing and/or alternative marketing methods, even though the seller prefers an all cash transaction. The agent who understands seller financing will be less likely to pass up a deal that can be made (with a little ingenuity) than the agent who doesn't comprehend or "bad mouths" anything but cash. As we have explained in this book, a thorough understanding of seller carryback financing can become a path to cash.

Some agents don't know that they don't know about seller financing and don't want to learn about anything other than cash. See the Bob Bruss column on page 14. An agent with a closed mind can be a serious roadblock to a transaction.

A MIND IS LIKE A PARACHUTE.
IT FUNCTIONS ONLY WHEN IT IS OPEN.

More on agent representation:

For most real estate agents, representation takes the form of full service brokerage where the agent's fee is contingent on a title transfer. However, agent does not necessarily equal commission! A few experienced agents are available to consumers on an hourly fee basis for transaction consulting; see pages 203 and 204. They perform limited real estate advisory services for one party (only) in the transaction and are paid an hourly fee for their services, regardless of whether a closing takes place.

In the event you have tried marketing your property at a fair price with attractive seller carryback financing (#2 below) and the market has not responded, then you need to consider the following marketing strategies:

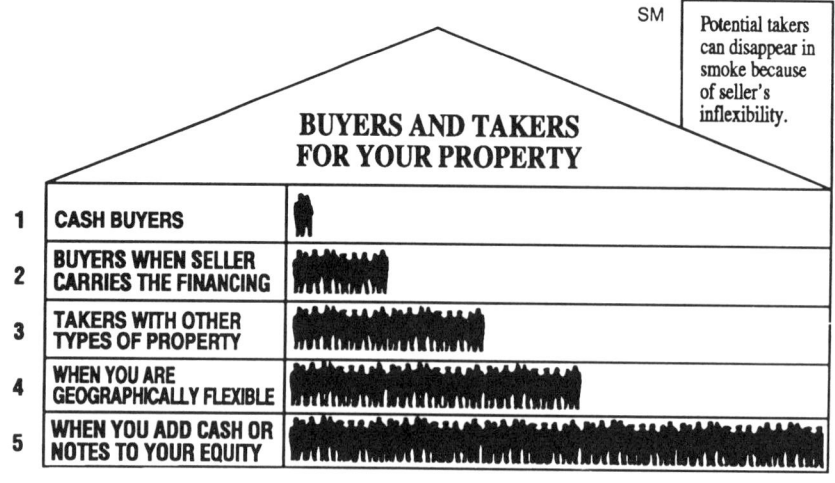

© 1986 by Who's Who in Creative Real Estate, Inc.

Look for:

(#3) Buyers/Takers with property equities in your immediate area.

(#4) Buyers/Takers with property equities outside your area, even outside your state!

If neither of the above two ideas is successful, consider #5 above, adding cash or existing notes (secured by other property) to your equity. This makes your equity MORE ACCEPTABLE TO MORE PEOPLE.

> **There are always more Buyers/Takers in the marketplace with notes and/or equity than CASH BUYERS!**

Look for an agent with extensive training and experience in creative marketing and exchanging to assist you. The agent you select should be grounded not only in technical skills, but should understand client representation. Ask your potential agent "Who will you represent?"

MORE ON REPRESENTATION: WHO REPRESENTS WHOM?

In California real estate licensees are permitted to arrange private money loans, and buy and sell existing trust deed notes. Some states such as Arizona and Florida have separate licenses for mortgage brokers. In some states this type of activity is not regulated. Investors who fund loans or buy discounted deeds of trust or mortgage notes should determine the license status and level of experience of the people with whom they deal. The principles of agency and client representation apply to transactions involving lending and the buying and selling of notes secured by mortgages and deeds of trust.

Many states are unregulated as to the buying and selling of discounted mortgages. Even in those states which require licensing the regulators have not yet formalized agency disclosure requirements. **Note brokers are not immune from agency issues.** It is the note seller's or in some cases the private investor's perception of your relationship that is important. In a 1976 case the California Supreme Court confirmed the broad proposition that "whenever the acts or omissions of a broker causes injury in a real estate transaction, then there is a compelling reason" to find that the broker was an agent of the injured person.

Note brokers should learn about agency issues and understand how fiduciary responsibilities work. Early in his/her encounter with consumers (the sooner the better), the note broker should discuss whom he is representing and document whom s/he represents. A note broker should also explain to the consumer what this means so that the consumer has <u>informed consent</u>. In one of the most significant agency cases in California history (which involved a $2,500 loan) the little old lady plaintiff admitted in court that she had signed the disclosure forms, but testified "that no one explained to me what it meant" and the court decided in her favor. The court pierced the lender's corporate veil, went after the principals individually, and levied significant damages both actual and punitive.

<u>INSTITUTIONAL LENDERS:</u>
Banks, Savings and Loans, Mortgage Bankers, Insurance Companies and the agents of each, represent themselves, not the borrower.

<u>INDEPENDENT MORTGAGE BROKER:</u>
Such brokers may have access to many lenders and are in a position to help locate a better loan for the borrower. Borrowers should discuss whom the loan broker/ agent represents early in their relationship to avoid any misunderstanding.

CAUTION: Beware of ANYONE who wants a substantial up-front fee to help you obtain a loan. Most legitimate loan agents and brokers are paid when the loan is funded.

An exception to this general rule may be a loan for commercial property or a special use property where an experienced agent charges the borrower a packaging fee. This fee is to set up a professional presentation that will assist the borrower in finding a loan. Ask the agent to show you a few samples of loan packages s/he prepared on loans that were funded where the borrower paid a packaging fee. Before paying a packaging fee, ask the mortgage broker for references from several other borrowers whom s/he has represented and who have paid him or her a packaging fee. Then <u>contact</u> those people to get their reaction and ask what results were achieved by the loan broker.

Another exception to up-front fees would be the cost of an appriasal.

<u>PRIVATE MONEY LOAN BROKERS:</u>
These are individuals who are usually licensed by the state to arrange loans secured by real property. Using money from individual investors rather than institutions, they assist nontraditional borrowers and/or place loans on nontraditional properties. Nontraditional refers to a person or a property that does not conform to institutional lending requirements. Examples can be found in Chapter 1.

How do you find a private money loan broker? Look in the yellow pages of the phone directory or in newspaper classified ads under the heading, "Real Estate Loans." CAUTION: This listing category also includes institutional lenders and mortgage bankers.

Private money loan brokers are viewed by most borrowers as the agent of the borrower. When a borrower **employs** an agent **with a written Employment Agreement** to find them a lender, that agent represents the borrower.

PRIVATE (INDIVIDUAL) MONEY LENDERS:

When a private money lender is <u>not</u> represented, the private lender or note investor would be wise to employ a real estate Consultant who understands loans to review the economics of the transaction from the lender's perspective. Private lenders should understand that such a Consultant may be employed for his/her expertise on an hourly rate basis. For an example of what can go wrong when a private lender is not represented, see **EX 23, pg 108**, "A TRUST DEED DISASTER." This disaster could easily have been avoided if the lender/investor had employed someone knowledgeable to represent them.

Be sure the paperwork is competently prepared. Review our checklist in Chapter #12. Using the list will minimize risk and maximize your potential for a safe and secure transaction. There are many facets to a loan or note purchase transaction. Employing an expert to guide you and interpret the technical aspects may be your best investment.

NOTE BROKERS

Ned Notebroker is licensed by his state to broker notes. He functions much like a real estate broker who sells real property. For example:

Sam Seller holds a note that he carried back when Arthur Agent listed and sold his house a year ago. Sam needs cash for a new business venture. He employs Ned Notebroker to be his agent under an exclusive employment agreement to market Sam's note. In the employment agreement Sam agrees to pay Ned a commission when the note sale closes. It is usually a percentage of the selling price of the note or a flat fee.

Ned has a fiduciary responsibility (a relationship of high trust and confidence) to Sam to get him the highest reasonable price for his note and to look out for Sam's interests throughout the transaction. Because of their agency relationship Ned will disclose to Sam anything that comes to his attention that might affect Sam's decisions relative to sale of Sam's note. Because he is Sam's agent he must place Sam's interests ahead of his own.

Some states have no licensing requirements for people who buy, sell and/or broker existing notes. Those that do usually issue licenses from either the Department of Real Estate, Department of Corporations, or Banking Department.

EXHIBIT 23

A Trust Deed DISASTER!

by William R. Broadbent

"EVERY PENNY GONE...RETIREMENT DREAM TURNS NIGHTMARE" the newspaper headline declared and the following story unfolded:

Mr. and Mrs. S moved into San Luis Obispo County, California. They settled in a rented house for what they hoped would be a "dignified retirement." The elderly couple looked around for ways to invest their life savings of $80,000. Six months after their arrival, they answered a newspaper advertisement offering a third deed of trust on a farm. Mr. S visited the property and met with the owner, Mr. J. Mr. S phoned the Better Business Bureau and the local Chamber of Commerce to check on Mr. J's apparently unblemished background.

S then agreed to lend J $80,000 for one year in return for $1,660 monthly interest. S placed the money in escrow with a local title company, ostensibly with instructions that it be given to J in return for a note and third trust deed on the farm.

To his surprise, S got a *fourth* deed of trust, not a third. Two prior loans on the property were already in foreclosure when he loaned the money. A foreclosure sale was conducted, the farm was sold, and, according to Mr. S, only the holders of the first two trust deeds got any money. Mr. and Mrs. S LOST EVERY PENNY.

How Could This Disaster Have Been Prevented?

Mr. and Mrs. S should have employed someone who understood trust deed investing to analyze this situation from their perspective. Obvious risks were:
1. Putting all their cash into one deal, leaving no reserve.
2. Being in a junior position (3rd or 4th) with 2 senior loans ahead of them.
3. Using vacant land as the security.
4. Having insufficient protective equity.
5. Asking the wrong people about Mr. J.

This is a case where a knowledgeable consultant could have prevented the disaster. A real estate agent (one with expertise in paper) or a mortgage broker would be paid for his or her time, knowledge and experience. In the above case, the consultant could have pointed out the problems and advised Mr. S against the investment.

Most People Think Agent = Commission

An investor may employ an agent/consultant on an hourly basis to represent him, just as he would an accountant or attorney. The consulting agent does not give legal or tax advice but knows what questions to ask and how to work with the client's attorney. When a potential investor brings me (as an agent/consultant) a trust deed he is considering, I review it with him to uncover any pitfalls, strengthen his position and help him to complete the transaction. I usually charge an hourly rate to the person who employs me. Or, on a few occasions, my investor clients have employed me to invest for them. Sometimes I've been paid a consulting fee by the investor to analyze a trust deed or mortgage investment. Here are some of the problems a mortgage broker/real estate agent consultant can point out:

* The potential liability if foreclosure becomes necessary.
* Insufficient security for a loan.
* Flawed or faulty appraisal or title report.
* Unusual terms in the document (when found either drop the deal or consult a real estate attorney).
* Usury.
* Terms in senior loans that could cause problems.
* Undesirable borrower/trustor/mortgagor.

Using a consultant could prevent costly mistakes, help solve unanticipated problems and provide an objective analysis. To find such a person try to find a mortgage broker or a real estate agent with personal experience in mortgage/trust deed investing. Real estate agents holding designations such as "S.E.C.", "C.C.I.M." or "C.R.E." should be among the better qualified agents to assist you.

©Copyright 1990 by William R. Broadbent

William R. Broadbent, S.E.C. - C.C.I.M., specializes in real estate investments, exchanges and consulting, all under Single Agency. He is President of Arnett and Broadbent, Inc. and has over 30 years of brokerage experience. For 15 years, Bill has been an active trust deed and mortgage investor, primarily for his own account. He is a nationally-recognized author and lecturer and teaches a 1 day seminar on consulting which is available on audio tapes with workbook as a home study course. For further information contact him at Arnett and Broadbent, Inc., 1380 Broad Street, San Luis Obispo, CA 93401 (805) 543-9100.

THE PAPER SOURCE, September, 1990

INVESTORS IN DISCOUNTED NOTES SECURED BY REAL ESTATE:

Note sellers can be clever, greedy, or worse, inept. There are some cases of outright fraud where phony notes have been sold to unsuspecting investors who are attracted by the potential "high yields." There are numerous other risks. If you are considering this type investment and don't understand the intricacies of notes secured by real estate, then employ someone with experience who does. This could be a real estate attorney, mortgage or note broker or real estate consultant. Employ someone who has experience he or she can verify in this specialized type of investment. They can be employed on an hourly basis to review any note offerings and determine any advantages or disadvantages to you.

In recent years the note business has attracted many amateurs with limited knowledge of notes, real estate, law, tax and investing. Unless you employ someone to represent <u>you</u>, the person offering to sell you a note represents him/herself or the note seller, <u>NOT YOU</u>. INVESTIGATE BEFORE YOU INVEST! It can save you headaches, heartaches, minimize your risk and protect your capital.

Suppose your real estate agent brings you a buyer who has enough cash for only a 10% down payment. Should you take the deal? What are the risks? Is there a safer way to structure the transaction? Understanding how these concepts work can save you headaches, ulcers and money. In this chapter we explore the risk of a low down payment, seller carryback transaction.

CHAPTER 8

WHAT'S WRONG WITH AN 80-10-10 SALE?

Perhaps nothing, maybe everything! First, let's define a typical 80-10-10 transaction by using an example:

Sam Seller sells his Park Ave. house to Bob Buyer for $100,000. Bob gets a new loan from Insecurity Bank for $80,000 (80% of the purchase price). Bob pays $10,000 cash down (10% of the purchase price) and Sam Seller carries back a note for $10,000 (10% of the purchase price) secured by a second deed of trust or second mortgage. The typical 80-10-10 transaction looks like this:

$80,000	=	80%	new loan with cash going to seller (loan payments $950/month)
$10,000	=	10%	cash down payment to seller from buyer
<u>**$10,000**</u>	=	<u>10%</u>	note secured by a 2nd trust deed or 2nd mortgage (carried by Seller)
$100,000	=	100%	equals the purchase price of the property

Sam's carryback 2nd note is payable interest only monthly (11% per year) with the entire principal balance due and payable 5 years from closing.

If Bob Buyer makes all payments on the first and second loans and pays the principal balance (balloon) due on the 2nd in 5 years, then Sam has no problem.

But, should Bob be unable to make his monthly payments or the balloon payment, then Sam must foreclose on his second trust deed or mortgage to try to salvage something or lose the $10,000 equity in his carryback note.

RISK ANALYSIS...

When Sam Seller carries back a note, there is always some risk. These risks include but are not limited to the following: death of the buyer, divorce, loss of job, serious illness or injury, etc., any of which could cause Bob Buyer to stop making his payments to Sam. If patience, perseverance and cooperation don't work, then Sam must resort to foreclosure to protect himself.

What problems could Sam face in the foreclosure process?

In California the foreclosure process usually requires about four months to complete. See the discussion beginning on page 149 for details. In many states the process takes longer. During this time Sam must make the payments of $950 per month x

Owner Will Carry © 1998 by Bill Broadbent, SEC, CCIM, & George Rosenberg

110

4 months to keep that first loan current and to prevent that lender from foreclosing. If no one else bids more for the property at the foreclosure sale, then Sam bids in the amount of his second trust deed note, ends up with the property, and is obligated to continue making payments on the first loan. Additional capital, risk and costs of sale are involved in a foreclosure. He may have to spend money for repairs, then either rent the property or keep it vacant while trying to sell it.

Q. *Why not rent it pending a sale?*

A. It is difficult to find a good tenant if they know the property is going to be sold out from under them.

A resentful tenant may hinder and sometimes kills a sale. A sloppy tenant can cause a lot of damage in a short time. Many residential real estate agents favor selling vacant houses because they don't have to make appointments with the seller to show the home.

Let's say Sam takes three months after the foreclosure sale to resell the house. Suppose with <u>luck</u> he receives the same price he obtained from Bob Buyer, and this time receives ALL CASH. The transaction summary would look like this:

Proceeds from sale of Park Ave. property		$100,000
(3 months after Sam acquired it at foreclosure sale)		
Less: 1st loan balance assumed by buyer		<u>$80,000</u>
Cash to Sam Seller		$20,000
Less: Sales costs (brokerage fee, title, escrow)	($8,000)	
Less: Payments on 1st loan during foreclosure period		
Four months @ $950/mo. **PITI**		
(**P**rincipal, **I**nterest, **T**axes, **I**nsurance)	($3,800)	
Less: Foreclosure fees & costs	($1,600)	
Less: Repair costs & cleanup for sale (estimate)	($2,000)	
Less: Payments on 1st loan during resale period		
Three months @ $950/mo. PITI	<u>($2,850)</u>	
Total cost during foreclosure and resale		- $18,250
Net proceeds after sale		$ 1,750

<u>Recap</u>

Cash to Sam Seller	$20,000
Total cost during foreclosure period	- $18,250
Net proceeds after sale	$ 1,750
Original amount of 2nd TD note carried by Sam	$10,000
Less: Net proceeds after sale of Park Ave.	- $ 1,750
Loss of equity in note	$ 8,250

This example recaps only the cash spent by Sam to protect himself. It does NOT consider the time he spent or the frustration involved in the foreclosure process. This **optimistic example** also assumes a cash sale for Sam, a stable price on the house, and ignored potential problems, such as a longer holding period to resell, higher fixup costs, a foreclosure delayed by a bankruptcy action, or the Soldier's and Sailor's Civil Relief Act, (50 U.S.C. Appen: §501 et seq.).

Some states allow a redemption period even after the foreclosure sale. A redemption period permits a foreclosed owner to reacquire the property during that period. Any glitch could further erode Sam's equity in the 2nd T/D note. A softening in market value could easily increase his loss. Can you see why many institutions who lend on real estate don't like to make loans for more than 80% of the value of the property? The 20% **protective equity** is their cushion against loss. Sometimes even that 20% equity is not enough to protect them from loss.

> **A seller who accepts an 80-10-10 deal sells his property, but incurs significant risk and probable loss in the event a foreclosure is necessary on the carryback note. In the above example the seller would have needed a cash reserve in excess of $8,000 to protect himself in the event of a default or foreclosure. Sellers who carry back a note, note brokers, and people who invest in trust deed and mortgage notes should understand the risks and have adequate cash reserves to protect themselves if foreclosure becomes necessary on a note in second (or any junior) position.**

Real estate agents representing sellers should explain to their seller/client what may go wrong with a seller carryback note **BEFORE** the seller agrees to accept such an offer. Such disclosure includes a credit report on the buyer, as well as the cash outlay and reserves necessary to process a foreclosure and resale.

(EX #24, pg 113) Use this Carryback Foreclosure Cost Sheet to estimate what could happen to you in the event of a foreclosure on a note you are about to carry back or purchase as an investment.

Sellers who carry back on an 80-10-10 transaction, and later try to sell their 2nd trust deed or mortgage note, often have difficulty in finding a buyer. **There are almost no buyers for these notes.** If they attract an offer they are shocked at the discount quoted for their note.

Considering the risks, a 50% to 70% discount may not be unreasonable. After analyzing the risk/reward ratio in this example, can you see why a note investor feels a substantial discount is necessary to offset the risks involved in buying a 2nd that originated in an 80-10-10 transaction?

A seller who accepts a low down payment (10% or less), and carries back a junior note is taking a very substantial risk. Most note investors won't buy these notes at any price. The risk of loss far outweighs the POTENTIAL YIELD. Here's why.

Suppose you buy the $10,000 second note from that 80-10-10 transaction at a 50% discount. The numbers would be:

EXHIBIT 24

CARRYBACK FORECLOSURE COST SHEET
Costs and Net Proceeds on Foreclosure and Resale

This estimate of costs required to foreclose and resell property under trust deed is prepared for the following:

☐ Purchase agreement
☐ Exchange agreement
☐ Counteroffer
☐ Escrow
☐ Option
☐ Trust deed & note

Dated _____ , 19 _____
at_____ , California.
Entered into by _____
Regarding property referred to as: _____
_____
Document number, if recorded: _____

This sheet is prepared and presented to sellers who carry back junior trust deeds and notes on the sale of property, as well as other junior lenders.

This disclosure assists the seller/lender to anticipate any funding needed to foreclose should buyer/borrower default in payments, and projects the net proceeds of any foreclosure and resale undertaken.

The figures estimated in this sheet may vary and thus cannot be guaranteed because of daily changes in lender demands, trustee's fees, repair costs and ownership expenses.

This form does not include costs incurred for interest on carryback, bankruptcy or hold-over problems with the buyer/borrower or any rents received prior to resale.

1. Estimated resale value of real estate . . . . $_____

2. Balances on senior trust deeds at resale:
   2.1 Underlying first . . . . $_____
   2.2 Underlying second . . . . $_____

3. Cash advances from default through resale:
   3.1 Taxes . . . . $_____
   3.2 Insurance . . . . $_____
   3.3 Payments on underlying trust deeds (Number of months_____) . . . . $_____

4. Foreclosure costs and fees:
   4.1 Publishing notice . . . . $_____
   4.2 Recording notice . . . . $_____
   4.3 Posting notice . . . . $_____
   4.4 Postage . . . . $_____
   4.5 Trustee's guarantee policy . . . . $_____
   4.6 Trustee's fees . . . . $_____
   4.7 Attorney's fees . . . . $_____
   4.8 Advertising, etc. . . . . $_____

5. Resale costs:
   5.1 Repairs and fixer-up costs . . . . $_____
   5.2 Title insurance premiums . . . . $_____
   5.3 Escrow fees and charges . . . . $_____
   5.4 Broker fees and charges . . . . $_____

6. Estimated loans, advances, costs and charges to foreclose and resell (2, 3, 4 and 5) . . . . (-) $_____

7. **Estimated net proceeds available to pay off carryback trust deed** . . . . $_____

Seller's Broker: _____
Agent: _____
Address: _____
_____ Phone: (__)_____
Date:_____ , 19 _____
Agent's Signature: _____
Broker's Approval:_____ __/__/ __

I have read and received a copy of this estimate.
Date:_____ , 19 _____
Seller's Name:_____
Address: _____
_____ Phone: (__)_____
Seller's Signature: _____
Seller's Signature: _____

N	**I**	**PV**	**PMT**	**FV**
60 mo.	solve for I	$5000	$91.67/mo.	$10000

I = 30.6% yield per year! The <u>potential yield</u> looks very attractive. But, if the deal ends up in foreclosure and you receive only $1,750 back in cash when you invested $5,000 (PV), then you have lost over $3,000. **Actual yield can be measured only in hindsight, after a note has been paid off and the final payment has cleared the bank.**

TWO ALTERNATIVE WAYS TO DISPOSE OF A 2ND MORTGAGE THAT ORIGINATED IN AN 80-10-10 TRANSACTION

Here are two possibilities, either of which involves takers for the note who usually live in the same community as the property securing the 2nd mortgage.

1. Locate investors who purchase and manage single family homes as long term investments. If the property would be a good rental and the first loan is a reasonable (under 8%) fixed interest rate loan, a single family home investor may buy the note hoping for a default where he/she could foreclose and add another rental to his portfolio. The discount will probably be substantial.

2. If the holder of the 2nd will consider acquiring other real estate, this note could be offered at face value as part of a down payment on the acquisition of a property in the same community. In any market there are usually a few sellers who are **sufficiently motivated** to dispose of their property that they will accept a note secured by other property (even a 2nd out of an 80-10-10 deal) at face value in order to get rid of their real estate.

A note from Bill Broadbent

PROOF OF THE PUDDING: I recall a transaction many years ago where my partner acquired his current residence using an unsecured note bearing no interest. He had received the note as part of a real estate transaction. It was seasoned 18 months, had a good payment record, and the payor had very good credit. He offered it at face value for part of the down payment on a vacant house listed by another real estate firm who represented a **motivated seller.**

My partner disposed of a no-interest note and found a larger home for his family. The seller sold a vacant house they were unwilling to rent. The sellers also got out from further mortgage payments on the vacant house. **BB**

What happens when the seller accepts a low down payment and carries back a First Mortgage?

Suppose the sale price was $100,000 and that Sam Seller accepts a 10% down payment from the Buyer, Dan Deadbeat. The terms of the carryback note are payments of $724.16/mo. including 9% interest , all due and payable in 10 years.

Normal sales costs (Commission, title, escrow etc.) total $8,000, which leaves Sam with $2,000 cash and his $90,000 note. Sam was in a hurry to sell and didn't bother to check Dan's credit (which was very bad) or other references.

Fifteen months after closing Dan defaults. By the time the foreclosure was completed 6 months had passed. After the property was cleaned up and listed for sale with Arthur Agent, another 4 months had passed. Ten months have passed with no payments on the $90,000 note.

Assuming the property sold for the same price, but with a higher down payment, the transaction summary would look like this.

Selling price		$100,000
Seller carry back note		$ 85,000
Down payment		$ 15,000
LESS: Sales costs		
Commission, Title , escrow, closing)	$ 8,000	
Delinquent taxes and insurance	$ 2,400	
Foreclosure costs	$ 1,600	
Repair and cleanup for resale	$ 2,000	
Total out of pocket expenses	$14,000	
Ten months of lost interest @ $675/mo.	$ 6,750	
Total cost to Sam		- $20,750
Down payment		$15,000
Sam's loss on this transaction		**$ 5,750**

These are fairly conservative estimates and in many cases the actual costs would exceed these amounts. In this example Sam Seller had to spend at least $1,600 to get the property back and received no payments on his note for 10 months. He then spent another $14,000 to resell the property.

REMEMBER, FORECLOSURES DON'T ALWAYS GO SMOOTHLY!
Some things that can stall the process and cost Sam Seller more money can include but are not limited to the following.

PROPERTY DAMAGE

When a buyer is losing a property, at best, they lose interest in maintaining it and in a worst case scenario, they will intentionally damage the property. This can add thousands of dollars to Sam's cost of fixing up the property for resale. The less equity a buyer has in a property the less incentive he/she has to keep it up or try to save it if he/she encounters financial difficulty.

BANKRUPTCY

Bankruptcies currently are at or near an historical high. Today filing for bankruptcy is an easy way to halt (stay) a foreclosure. Now Sam Seller may have to employ a

Bankruptcy attorney as it is a very specialized field of law. This attorney will file a petition to the Federal Bankruptcy court for a "relief of stay", asking the court to lift its stay and allow the foreclosure to proceed. Atttorney fees alone could cost Sam Seller a couple of thousand dollars in extra costs to get his property back from Dan.

In order to recover bankruptcy costs try putting this language in the promissory note when it is drawn: "In the event that Makers are hereafter involved as debtors in any bankruptcy proceeding under Title 11 of the United States Code, Makers agree that any costs or expenses incurred by Payees, including attorney's fees and court costs, in pursuing or otherwise enforcing Payees' rights hereunder, shall be repaid by Makers together with interest accruing at the same rate as herein provided for repayment of the principal balance. Such repayment and reimbursement of costs and expenses shall be fully due upon demand, or together with the next monthly installment due hereunder, whichever first occurs."

EVICTION

Sam finally receives the property back at the foreclosure sale because there are few (if any) bidders for highly encumbered properties. Dan Deadbeat still occupies the property and refuses to vacate. Sam goes back to his real estate attorney and has him file an unlawful detainer action to have the Sheriff forcibly remove Dan from the property. If necessary, this procedure could add another $800 to $1,500 in costs and from a month to a year in time to Sam's cost of repossession.

A difficult foreclosure could cost Sam 3 or 4 times the fees estimated in our original example. It could also extend the time during which Sam receives no income (interest) on his carryback note.

SUMMARY

This example further proves our point that there is no substitute for protective equity. Thin down payment sales are riskier for the Seller who originated the sale and for any future buyer of the note carried back by the seller. **The LOWER the down payment below 10%, the HIGHER the probability that the property sold for an inflated price above its actual fair market value.** It is not surprising that an experienced note buyer will expect a larger discount and higher yield on a note with a thin equity position to compensate for this extra risk.

It should also come as no surprise that the few buyers of non-performing paper (in default) not only expect but are entitled to larger discounts for the risk and expense they take on when they agree to purchase a note that is in default.

If you lose your capital, then all the <u>*POTENTIAL YIELD*</u> *GOES UP IN SMOKE.*

Those readers involved in buying, brokering, selling, or investing in notes should study this chapter very carefully!

As no seller wants to lose the equity in his carryback note, we have identified several alternatives that can strengthen his position and minimize his risk exposure. Let's look at them now.

CHAPTER 9

HOW TO REDUCE THE SELLER'S RISK WHEN CARRYING BACK A NOTE

Suppose Sam Seller receives an offer to purchase Park Ave. from Bob Buyer on 80-10-10 terms. Before responding to the offer, Sam or his agent should ask Bob three questions:

1. How do you plan to pay the balloon on the 2nd loan when it is due?
2. Do you own <u>other property</u>, and, if so, how much equity do you have in that property?
3. Are you receiving payments on a note secured by real property that you sold?

Each of these important questions leads to a way to <u>reduce the seller's risk</u> when carrying back a note. Agents working with a new buyer should ask questions two and three as part of their qualifying procedure prior to showing property.

I. PLANNING FOR THE BALLOON PAYMENT.

(This assumes the 2nd T/D note is NOT amortized and calls for a balloon payment in a few years.)

> **NOTE: Short term balloon payments, 1 to 3 years, can be very risky for both parties unless the buyer has a relatively sure source of funds to pay off the balloon WITHOUT RELYING ON A REFINANCE.**

Q#1. How do you plan to pay the balloon on the 2nd loan when it is due?

If the answer is "<u>By refinancing the property,</u>" it assumes that <u>the property will appreciate</u> in value enough that a refinance will be possible when the balloon payment comes due. Seldom does such appreciation occur on short term balloons of less than 3 years. A smart buyer should try to negotiate a due date of at least 5 to 7 years. We covered the reasons in Chapter 5. A smarter buyer would try to avoid any balloon. HERE'S WHY!

Let's review the sale that took place five years ago under the following terms:

Sam Seller's selling price	$100,000
Down payment from Bob Buyer:	$ 10,000
New 1st loan from Insecurity Bank:	$ 80,000
Carryback 2nd to Sam Seller:	$ 10,000

THE HIGH COST OF REFINANCING

Typical terms on a carryback 2nd deed of trust (Remember that note terms are always negotiable.):

AMOUNT	INTEREST RATE	PAYMENT	BALLOON	DUE DATE
$10,000	11% Interest Only	$ 91.66	$10,000	3 to 5 years

The $10,000 second loan is now due. Bob Buyer could easily pay $2,000 to $3,000 to refinance with a new first loan. Bob's original $80,000 first loan taken out five years ago would have a current balance due of $77,260. Bob's house would have to appraise for $112,500 to justify a new $90,000 loan at an 80% LTV. Loans whose amounts total more than 80% of the property's value, while available to a few highly qualified buyers on the original purchase, are NOT usually available to owners who are trying to refinance and pull out cash. Ninety percent loans on a refinance are available only to above-average borrowers with excellent credit and may require Private Mortgage Insurance (PMI).

Let's assume that interest rates have not changed and are still at 10%. Then the distribution of cash from the new first loan of $90,000 would be as follows:

$77,260	pays off the original first loan
$10,000	pays off the 2nd trust deed to Sam Seller
$ 1,240	Appraisal fee, Loan Policy of Title Insurance, etc.
$ 1,500	Finance charges (loan fee to Insecurity Bank)
$90,000	Total new loan for 30 years, @ 10% interest = $ 790/month

The cost of refinancing in the above case offsets the buyer's equity buildup to date.

Original first loan $80,000.00, 30 years @ 10% interest = $ 702/month
Increase in monthly payment on new first loan $ 88/month
Increased cost for 30 years: $88/mo. x 360 mos. = $31,680

If interest rates have increased, then this payment will be higher. Private Mortgage Insurance (PMI), if required, would cost about $500 up front for the first year. The monthly payment would increase another $30 to $45 per month from the 2nd year on if PMI was required by the new lender.

Refinancing can be expensive. Rather than set up a balloon payment, both buyer and seller would be better off amortizing the carryback 2nd TD note. This will avoid the uncertainty of a balloon payment and save the buyer a large amount of money in the long run.

Could the Buyers have negotiated a different pay-back arrangement? Perhaps one of the following:

ALTERN.	AMOUNT	INT. RATE	TERM	PAYMENT	BALLOON
(1)	$10,000	11%	5 Years	$217.42	0
(2)	$10,000	11%	7 Years	$171.22	0
(3)	$10,000	11%	10 Years	$137.75	0

Had the Buyers negotiated one of the three alternatives above, they would have received these benefits:

1. Avoided a balloon payment
2. Avoided the necessity and cost ($2,740 in the previous example) of refinancing the first loan
3. Eliminated $12,740 of debt ($90,000 new loan minus $77,260 old loan balance)
4. Maintained the $702 payment during the remaining term of their original $80,000 first mortgage
5. Had their home paid off five years sooner, as the refinancing (new loan of $90,000) would start a new 30 year debt structure
6. Saved up to $31,680 in extra payments over the life of the first loan

Had the buyers negotiated a 10 year pay-out on their 2nd at $137.75, they would have established a budget pattern during that time. At the end of 10 years (when the 2nd paid off), they would have two prudent financial options available to them relative to the $137.75 a month.

1. If they have the financial awareness and ability to earn more than 10% on their money (10% is the interest rate on their first loan), then they should put that $137.75 each month into such an investment. Suppose they could earn 12% on that money. If they put $137.75 monthly into something that earned 12% per annum, at the end of 20 years when their home loan paid off, they would have $136,270 more for their retirement. This accumulation is before payment of income taxes (such as contributing it to an IRA, Keogh account, 401K or other tax sheltered pension or profit sharing plan). Review graph on page 35.

2. Suppose they <u>don't</u> know how to earn 10% or more on their money. They could apply the $137.75 per month as an additional principal payment on their first T/D or mortgage loan. This would pay off the first loan sooner and save the payor 10% interest. When the 2nd loan paid off at the end of 10 years, their first loan would have a balance of $72,762, amortized over 20 years (240 months) at $702/month. Increasing their monthly payment by $137.75 to $839.75 would pay their loan off in 155 months, a little less than 13 years. They would save 85 months (240 less 155) of payments times $702 per month or $59,670.

> **The financial options, one and two above, represent two sound money management principles which can also be applied by a seller who carries back a small note secured by a property he/she sold. Otherwise the small income stream (payments received on the note) will usually be spent or lost forever.**

II. THE USE OF OTHER PROPERTY AS SECURITY

Q #2. Do you own other property, and, if so, how much equity do you have in that property?

Suppose Bob Buyer owns a smaller home on Main Street.

Bob's Main St. home value	$75,000
1st Loan	$35,000
Bob's equity	$40,000

Sam could ask Bob Buyer to create (write) a deed of trust for $10,000. Bob, or his escrow officer or attorney (depending on your state), would put a blank form in the typewriter and would type the security instrument, mortgage or deed of trust, in favor of Sam. The deed of trust or mortgage on the Main St. house is <u>additional security</u> to secure the $10,000 note Sam Seller carries back on the Park Ave. property. There would be **one note for $10,000 secured by two separate deeds of trust,** one on Park Ave., the other on Main Street. If a default occurred, Sam could foreclose on both.

EX #25, pg 121 - DEED OF TRUST AS ADDITIONAL SECURITY (TO SECURE EXISTING NOTE)

The Main St. deed of trust could remain in effect until the Park Ave. note is paid in full.

Or, by mutual agreement the Main St. deed of trust could be reconveyed (released as security) at the end of two or three years, provided the payments had been made on time on the note secured by Park Ave. REMEMBER, all terms are negotiable in a real estate transaction.

What if the note were secured only by the Main Street property?

Would Sam Seller be better off accepting a $10,000 note secured only by Bob Buyer's Main St. property or by carrying a 2nd trust deed note on the Park Ave. property he is selling?

Here is a comparison of the two situations:

	Bob's Main St. House		**Sam's Park Ave. House**	
Market value		$75,000		$100,000
Less 1st loan	$35,000		$ 80,000	
Less 2nd loan	$10,000		$ 10,000	
Total loans		$45,000		$ 90,000
Protective equity		$30,000 (30%)		$ 10,000 (10%)

Total loan to value ratios
(45,000÷75,000) = 60% LTV   (90,000 ÷ 100,000) = 90% LTV

EXHIBIT 25
T/D AS ADDITIONAL SECURITY
(TO SECURE EXISTING NOTE)

WHEN RECORDED MAIL TO:

Sam and Sally Seller
123 Elm Street
Anytown, CA 99999

SPACE ABOVE THIS LINE FOR RECORDER'S USE

DEED OF TRUST WITH ASSIGNMENT OF RENTS
(This Deed of Trust contains an acceleration clause)

This DEED OF TRUST, made March 1, 1991 , between

Bob Buyer and Betty Buyer, husband and wife   herein called TRUSTOR,

whose address is   999 Main Street   Anytown   CA
                   (Number and Street)   (City)   (State)

FIRST AMERICAN TITLE INSURANCE COMPANY, a California corporation, herein called TRUSTEE, and

Sam Seller and Sally Seller, husband and wife as joint tenants
, herein called BENEFICIARY,

WITNESSETH: That Trustor grants to Trustee in Trust, with Power of Sale, that property in the   city of
Anytown,   County of   SLO   , State of California, described as:

Lot 471 of Tract 51101, in the city of Anytown, County of SLO,
State of California as per map recorded in Book 65, page 29 of   MAIN STREET
Maps, in the office of the County Recorder of said County.   PROPERTY

This deed of trust secures payment of a note described on Exhibit A attached.

If the trustor shall sell, convey or alienate said property, or any part thereof, or any interest therein, or shall be divested of his title or any interest therein in any manner or way, whether voluntarily or involuntarily, without the written consent of the beneficiary being first had and obtained, beneficiary shall have the right, at its option, except as prohibited by law, to declare any indebtedness or obligations secured hereby, irrespective of the maturity date specified in any note evidencing the same, immediately due and payable.

Together with the rents, issues and profits thereof, subject, however, to the right, power and authority hereinafter given to and conferred upon Beneficiary to collect and apply such rents, issues and profits.

For the Purpose of Securing (1) payment of the sum of $ 10,000.00 with interest thereon according to the terms of a promissory note or notes of even date herewith made by Trustor, payable to order of Beneficiary, and extensions or renewals thereof, and (2) the performance of each agreement of Trustor incorporated by reference or contained herein (3) Payment of additional sums and interest thereon which may hereafter be loaned to Trustor, or his successors or assigns, when evidenced by a promissory note or notes reciting that they are secured by this Deed of Trust.

To protect the security of this Deed of Trust, and with respect to the property above described, Trustor expressly makes each and all of the agreements, and adopts and agrees to perform and be bound by each and all of the terms and provisions set forth in subdivision A, and it is mutually agreed that each and all of the terms and provisions set forth in subdivision B of the fictitious deed of trust recorded in Orange County August 17, 1964, and in all other counties August 18, 1964, in the book and at the page of Official Records in the office of the county recorder of the county where said property is located, noted below opposite the name of such county, namely:

COUNTY	BOOK	PAGE	COUNTY	BOOK	PAGE	COUNTY	BOOK	PAGE	COUNTY	BOOK	PAGE
Alameda	1288	556	Kings	858	713	Placer	1028	379	Sierra	38	187
Alpine	3	130-31	Lake	437	110	Plumas	166	1307	Siskiyou	506	762
Amador	133	438	Lassen	192	367	Riverside	3778	347	Solano	1287	621
Butte	1330	513	Los Angeles	T-3878	874	Sacramento	5039	124	Sonoma	2067	427
Calaveras	185	338	Madera	911	136	San Benito	300	405	Stanislaus	1970	56
Colusa	323	391	Marin	1849	122	San Bernardino	6213	768	Sutter	655	585
Contra Costa	4684	1	Mariposa	90	453	San Francisco	A-804	596	Tehama	457	183
Del Norte	101	549	Mendocino	667	99	San Joaquin	2855	283	Trinity	108	595
El Dorado	704	635	Merced	1660	753	San Luis Obispo	1311	137	Tulare	2530	108
Fresno	5052	623	Modoc	191	93	San Mateo	4778	175	Tuolumne	177	160
Glenn	469	76	Mono	69	302	Santa Barbara	2065	881	Ventura	2607	237
Humboldt	801	83	Monterey	357	239	Santa Clara	6626	664	Yolo	769	16
Imperial	1189	701	Napa	704	742	Santa Cruz	1638	607	Yuba	398	693
Inyo	165	672	Nevada	363	94	Shasta	800	633			
Kern	3756	690	Orange	7182	18	San Diego	SERIES 5	Book 1964, Page 149774			

shall inure to and bind the parties hereto, with respect to the property above described. Said agreements, terms and provisions contained in said subdivisions A and B, (identical in all counties, and printed on the reverse side hereof) are by the within reference thereto, incorporated herein and made a part of this Deed of Trust for all purposes as fully as if set forth at length herein, and Beneficiary may charge for a statement regarding the obligation secured hereby, provided the charge therefor does not exceed the maximum allowed by law.

The undersigned Trustor, requests that a copy of any notice of default and any notice of sale hereunder be mailed to him at his address hereinbefore set forth.

STATE OF CALIFORNIA   }
COUNTY OF _____ }ss.
                       }

Signature of Trustor

On _____ before me, _____

Bob Buyer

_____,

Betty Buyer

personally appeared _____

EXHIBIT A (Usually on a separate page attached to T.D.)

(This refers to the T/D on Park Ave.)

This deed of trust secures payment of a promissory note dated March 1, 1991, executed by Bob Buyer and Betty Buyer in favor of Sam Seller and Sally Seller in the amount of $10,000.00.

This note is additionally secured by a deed of trust recorded March 5, 1991 as Document No. 91-44455 in the official records of SLO County, California.

From the above comparison isn't it <u>obvious</u> that Sam would be much safer accepting a $10,000 2nd trust deed note secured by Bob's Main St. property than by carrying back a $10,000 2nd trust deed note secured only by his own Park Ave. property?

Sam Seller has **THREE times as much protective equity** in dollar terms and **FOUR times** as much **protective equity** in percentage terms on the Main St. house protecting his note. He would have a much smaller first loan to make payments on in the event he has to foreclose on the Main St. property.

If Bob intends to sell the Main St. property, then Sam could negotiate for a shorter due date, as the 2nd will be paid off when the Main St. property sells.

> **IMPORTANT: NO CASH changes hands relative to the $10,000 note secured by Bob's Main St. property. Bob and Betty Buyer sign a promissory note for $10,000 secured by a trust deed on their Main St. property in favor of Sam and Sally Seller. There are institutional lenders who will treat a created note secured only by Bob's Main St. property as a cash equivalent down payment and give Bob a new loan for the balance to purchase Sam Seller's Park Ave. property.**

The deed of trust on Main Street is recorded and a loan policy of title insurance, insuring the seniority position of the deed of trust, should be issued in favor of the Sellers. Before agreeing to such a transaction, you should review our checklist in Chapter 12, page 139 which covers additional risks.

Income tax impact: A transaction structured this way currently has <u>no disadvantages</u> either to the Buyers who create the note or the Sellers who receive it. The tax status is no different than if the Sellers carried back on their own property. From a safety and security standpoint Sam and Sally Seller are <u>much more secure</u>. They have more **protective equity** on Main Street than on Park Ave.

Using alternate security (Main St. property only), as discussed above, or cross security (both Main St. and Park Ave.) in the example before that, Sam Seller can turn a risky 80-10-10 transaction into a much safer deal. Should Sam subsequently need additional cash, he could sell his $10,000 note secured by Main St. He would find many more buyers and receive more money from the note sale than if he had carried back the $10,000 second secured only by his own property on Park Ave. The reason is that the Main St. note has more **protective equity** and represents a lower risk to a note buyer like Nancy Notebuyer or an investor like Norman Noteholder.

NOTE: Seller carryback notes secured by the property sold (in California & some other states) carry no personal liability. The property is the sole security for the debt.

If the note is secured only by <u>other</u> property, then the payor will be personally liable in the event of a default or foreclosure.

III. THE USE OF EXISTING NOTES.

Q#3. *Are you receiving payments on a note secured by real property that you sold?*

Suppose that in December 1990 Bob Buyer sold a lot he owned on Oceanview Terrace to Irving Investor for $160,000. Irving had paid $140,000 cash down. Bob carried back the difference with a note for $20,000 secured by a deed of trust on the lot. Terms: Interest only at 11% ($183.33/mo.), all due and payable in December 1995. Bob can use that note in one of several ways.

1. Bob could offer to assign the $20,000 note to Sam Seller as the entire down payment on Sam's Park Ave. house.

Selling price of Park Ave. house	$100,000
Assignment of Bob's trust deed note on the Oceanview Terrace lot as down payment. (Lot is now owned by Irving Investor)	$ 20,000
Bob gets a new loan on Park Ave. from Insecurity Bank in the amount of	$ 80,000

Loan proceeds are paid to Sam and Sally Seller at closing.

TAX IMPACT: If Bob paid less than $160,000 for Oceanview Terrace, he has some gain in his $20,000 note. Assigning the note to Sam as a down payment will cause the remaining gain to be taxed. Sam could claim on his income tax return that the $20,000 note has a fair market value less than its face value. Let's assume a $15,000 value. For Sam's income tax purposes, receiving this note is equivalent to Sam receiving $15,000 cash. When the entire note pays off at $20,000, Sam will pay tax on an additional gain of $5,000.

IMPORTANT: When existing notes are used to acquire real property, they are frequently transferred at their present balance, as they facilitate the sale of property. When a seller is <u>motivated</u> to sell a property he or she is more likely to accept an existing note at face value than to try and discount it. This is a *different mind set* (the focus is on disposing of real estate) than if the seller had cash and was out to buy a note at a discount for an investment. When an existing trust deed or mortgage note is sold for cash, the note is usually discounted. The reason is that cash now is certain. Cash to be received in the future is not! Payors on notes can default. The economy can change and property values can decline. Discounts vary depending on a variety of factors. Remember our thought in Chapter 6, **THERE IS NO SUCH THING AS A "STANDARD DISCOUNT."**

2. Bob could use this note as collateral security for a new note to Sam.

What else could Bob Buyer do with his $20,000 note on Oceanview Terrace? He could use that note as collateral and assign the note and deed of trust as collateral security to Sam Seller. Such a collateral assignment would secure the $10,000 note Bob asked Sam to carry back on the 80-10-10 sale of the Park Ave. property.

	Irving Investor's Oceanview Terrace Lot		Sam's Park Ave. House
Selling Price	$160,000		$100,000
Cash down payment	$140,000		$ 10,000
New first loan			$ 80,000
Seller Carryback:		assigned to Sam	
1st TD (to Bob)	$ 20,000	to secure 2nd TD of	$ 10,000

In the proposed situation Sam would have a $20,000 note securing his $10,000 note **(50% protective equity)** and a $160,000 lot securing the $20,000 note **(actually 94% protective equity overall; this $10,000 note is ultimately secured by a $160,000 lot)**.

The diagram on the next page illustrates this example.

Sam's security would be far better under either #1 or #2. If (as in #1) Bob assigns the $20,000 note to Sam for the down payment, he may benefit by getting a slightly better interest rate on the $80,000 institutional first loan on the purchase of Sam's house. Institutional lenders feel more secure with an 80% loan-to-value (LTV) ratio than with a 90% LTV ratio. On 90% loan-to-value situations a lender frequently requires the buyer to pay for private mortgage insurance (PMI). The extra mortgage insurance would cost about $500 the first year and in the following years increase the buyer's payment, in this case by about $30 to $45 per month. A lender may allow the payor to drop PMI when the loan-to-value (LTV) reaches 80% or less. This decision must be supported by a new appraisal (at payor's expense) and a good payment record by the borrower.

TAX IMPACT OF COLLATERAL ASSIGNMENT OF A SECURED NOTE
VERY IMPORTANT!

If Bob had a gain in his $20,000 note, using it as collateral for a $10,000 note would trigger some gain recognition. It would be the same as Bob receiving a $10,000 principal payment. (See Internal Revenue Code Section 453A(d)). This would happen ONLY if the sale in which the note originated was for more (even $1 more) than $150,000. When the sale is for $150,000 or less, no gain on the carryback is recognized if Bob pledges the note as collateral. The $150,000 rule DOES NOT apply for pledges of installment notes arising from sales of personal use property (such as the principal residence) or property used in the business of farming.

Such techniques as using another note for collateral are not new. They just are not frequently used. Here is another simple technique that could help close many sales, which frequently fail to close.

$10,000 NOTE

———————
———————

Note from Bob Buyer
to Sam Seller.

$20,000 NOTE

———————
———————
———————
———————

The $10,000 note from Bob Buyer to Sam Seller is secured by a $20,000 note from Irving Investor to Bob Buyer.

Bob assigns this $20,000 note to Sam Seller as collateral for Bob's $10,000 note to Sam Seller.

$160,000 PROPERTY

Bob Buyer's $20,000 note from Irving Investor is secured by a $160,000 property, a lot on Oceanview Terrace, now owned by Irving Investor.

July 1990: Bob Buyer sells lot to Irving Investor for $160,000 and carries back a $20,000 note at $183/month. Due date on that note is July 1995.

SEQUENCE OF EVENTS

1. July 1990: Bob Buyer sells his $160,000 lot to Irving Investor.
   Bob carries back a note for $20,000. Irving Investor now owns Bob's Oceanview Terrace Lot. Irving's note is all due July 1995.

2. December 1992: Bob Buyer assigns Irving's note to Sam Seller.

3. December 1992: At the same time as Bob assigns Irving's note as collateral to Sam Seller, Bob writes a $10,000 note payable to Sam Seller. The $10,000 note is used as part of the down payment for Sam Seller's Park Avenue property.

BOB'S $10,000 NOTE IS COLLATERALIZED BY IRVING'S $20,000 NOTE, WHICH IN TURN IS SECURED BY A $160,000 LOT ON OCEANVIEW TERRACE OWNED BY IRVING.

HOW TO DO AWAY WITH CONTINGENT SALES *(Attention: Agents and Sellers)*

PROBLEM: You have a house listed for sale. A buyer's broker has a buyer who will buy it - IF the buyer can sell his present home. The buyer makes an offer to purchase contingent upon (subject to) selling his house. If your seller/client accepts this offer, he may remove his property from active market exposure. Should the buyer not complete the purchase, you and your client may have lost some sale opportunities. Is there another approach that completes a sale now? YES!

SOLUTION: Inquire about the equity in the buyer's house. If there is enough equity (in terms of loan to value) to **safely create a note** secured by Bob Buyer's house, then you can complete the sale of your listing. The note created by Bob and Betty Buyer for perhaps a year or less is made payable to Sam and Sally Seller, whose house Bob Buyer wants to buy. When Bob's house sells, the note is paid off.

EXAMPLE:
Bob Buyer owns a house on Bowser Lane that he wants to sell. His wife Betty spots a For Sale sign on Sam and Sally Seller's house on Park Ave. Bob and Betty <u>really</u> <u>like</u> the Park Ave. house and want to buy it, but are short of cash for the down payment until their Bowser Lane house sells. Let's look at the numbers.

Value of Bowser Lane:	$90,000
Loan(s)	-0-
Equity	$90,000

Bob would create a lst trust deed note for $20,000 on the Bowser Lane house payable to Sam and Sally Seller. The note could be due in a year or so and bear interest at any rate the parties agree to. Interest (if any) to accumulate and not be payable until the note is due or Bowser Lane sells, whichever event occurs first. Sam agrees to accept the created note instead of a cash down payment.

Terms of sale on Sam's Park Ave. house:

Price	$100,000	
Down payment note (due l yr.)	20,000	secured by Bowser Lane house
Balance due Sam	$ 80,000	

If Sam needs a sizable amount of cash, then Bob must get a new first loan on Park Ave. As long as the note created for the down payment is secured only by the Bowser Lane house, some institutional lenders will treat it as a cash equivalent down payment ($20,000 = 20% in this example) and give Bob a new loan on Park Ave. of $80,000 (80%) to complete the purchase from Sam Seller. If Sam needs cash only for commissions and transactions costs, then he could sell or borrow against the $20,000 down payment note, and still carry back a note for $80,000 on the Park Ave. house. Suppose Bob cannot sell Bowser Lane in a year. In that event Sam can extend Bob's note, or, Bob will have to get a new loan from either Insecurity Bank or a private investor to pay the $20,000.

With the large protective equity in Bowser Lane the Sellers are very well secured and can anticipate that the note will be paid. In this case, everybody wins! Here's how:

Seller completes a sale, receives cash plus a well secured note, and can go on with his life.

Buyers get the house they really want. Agents get a cash commission now.

Terms on the note the buyer creates can be tailored to fit his circumstances. As you learned in Chapter 2, ALL TERMS ARE NEGOTIABLE. Isn't this better than tying up the seller on a contingent purchase agreement on Park Ave.? If the created note has a due date of a year or less, the buyer will be realistic about his selling price and terms to complete a sale of his Bowser Lane property.

Real estate agents can accomplish more for their sellers or buyers by utilizing these techniques.

DON'T FORGET
WHEN CARRYING BACK PAPER OR
WHEN INVESTING IN TRUST DEEDS & MORTGAGES,
THERE IS JUST NO SUBSTITUTE
FOR PROTECTIVE EQUITY!

MAKING SELLER FINANCING WORK FOR YOU
a special message for Buyers

As a buyer you must realize that most sellers don't understand how to take back a mortgage without being taken and haven't read the book OWNER WILL CARRY which explains how. This also applies to most real estate agents. Someone has to have this knowledge and information.

John Schaub, a successful single family house investor for 28 years, said, "Understanding owner financing allowed me to buy without borrowing from banks. I learned that when sellers really wanted out of a property, they would loan money (carry back a note) on terms a bank would never approve. Lower-than-market interest rates geared not to the loan amount, but to the cash flow from the property, were often acceptable. Sellers wanted me to buy because I would take a problem off their hands. They were less concerned about my financial statement or credit <u>than about how I was able to solve their problem.</u>"

The first thing you need is a <u>motivated seller</u> who is capable of providing the type of financing you need. You must be sensitive to the seller's needs and objectives or there will be <u>no deal</u> for you. If the subject property is a house, then a good opportunity may be to find one that is vacant whose owner has already purchased another home. This eliminates a common objective to seller financing, " I need cash so I can buy another home."

Another good candidate is the "Don't Wanter". This is usually a frustrated owner who is fed up with tenants and toilets (or other ownership responsibilities) and just wants to divest himself of those responsibilities.

Many sellers need some cash. If they don't see it coming from your down payment then you must be able to structure the carryback note(s) so that a seller can receive a reasonable amount of cash. Many ideas in this book can help you generate cash from notes.

One of the best is suggesting that the owner split the carryback paper into two notes secured by the property. If s/he has enough confidence in his property and you as a buyer, s/he can keep the junior note and with the help of a note broker, sell off the senior note to generate the cash needed.

When a real estate agent has the property listed, such an agent can be a positive or negative influence, depending on his or her knowledge of seller financing. As the listing agent represents the seller, you as a buyer are usually better off employing an agent to represent you. Before employing a Buyer's agent you should qualify that agent as to his knowledge and experience with seller financing and his willingness to pursue For Sale By Owner (FSBO) opportunities. Ask the agent to tell you about how he has benefited other buyers he has represented. CAUTION: Many so-called "Buyer's Agents" in this country claim to understand seller financing. Most do not. Many are not good negotiators for their buyer clients. Those who are willing to improve their performance capability could benefit greatly from reading this book. You should recommend it to them. This idea <u>is more self serving to you than to the authors.</u>

**You can use seller financing to make a good deal great,
but not to make a bad deal good**

To overcome a seller's or buyer's fear of the unknown each must know what items need to be in a note. We covered this in Chapter 3.

Balloon payments should either be avoided like the plague they can be, or structured so you can live with them. In Chapter 5 we also showed a technique that avoids the balloon but gets the seller his money back sooner.

In Chapter 10 we explain the critical difference between a "NO MONEY DOWN" and "NOTHING DOWN" deal. One can be good for both parties (win-win) while the other may be OK for the buyer but is almost a sure loser for the seller (and most sellers reject them), unless, of course, the seller has read how to use substitute security/collateral techniques described in Chapter 11 in this book. Active developers, rehabbers and investors moving in and out of title to properties will find that the ability to substitute security will facilitate the acquisition and disposition of property and minimize the buyer's use of cash.

Seller Financing and the Buyer's Broker
a message to Agents representing Buyers

The primary function of an employed buyer's agent is to represent the client and help Bob Buyer locate the best property and negotiate the best price AND TERMS for Bob.

When the Buyer's Agent locates a suitable property and sees enough equity in a seller's property to allow for a seller carryback note, the buyer's agent should diligently pursue seller financing. All terms of seller financing are negotable and the financing structure will depend upon how motivated the seller is to sell. Motivated sellers on occasion have agreed to carry back at very low or even NO INTEREST at all. Interest only terms, due in 10 or 15 years, or fully amortized over 25 or 30 years are possible.

To avoid a balloon payment, a buyer's agent might suggest a stepped payment note where the monthly payment increases each year. Stepped payments give the seller more dollars to spend and keep pace with inflation. Such payments also protect the buyer against a future responsibility to meet a balloon payment obligation.

The note and mortgage need not be secured by the property being sold. Bob Buyer may offer to create a note at a below-market interest rate secured by another property he owns. Sam may accept that note because it accomplishes his primary objective, which is to sell his property. As we have illustrated in previous examples, the note may be better secured than if Sam carried back on his own property.

By omitting a due-on-sale provision on the created note, Bob may make his property even more salable, as it offers seller financing someone else can assume.

Understanding how to create, maneuver, and negotiate carryback financing is one of the greatest talents a buyer's agent can possess. Along with negotiating price for the buyer client, seller financing can provide more terms benefits to the client than anything else. Unfortunately, most real estate agents, including those who profess to be "Buyer's Agents", lack the appropriate knowledge, skills and experience on this subject. Over a period of years we accepted calls from consumers (nationwide) who were looking for a Buyer's Agent to represent them. They ALL wanted two things, (1) an agent who understood seller financing and (2) someone who would be an advocate and negotiate for their interest. **They were tired of the inept, order-taking mentality that dominates the real estate industry. Many licensees who claim to represent buyers fit this description.**

Realizing that the industry in general isn't ready to help them, they purchased this book to learn the intricacies of seller financing.

We finished Chapter 9 by showing you a transaction where Bob Buyer acquired Sam Seller's property using a "No Money Down" technique. Sam was protected because Bob created a $20,000 down payment note to Sam, secured by the Bowser Lane property to acquire the Park Ave. property. Bob could lose his Bowser Lane property if he did not make his payments.

There IS a difference between a "Nothing Down" and a "No Money Down" transaction. When properly done, a "No Money Down" transaction can benefit both buyer and seller. Such a win-win situation for both buyer and seller is different from a "Nothing Down" deal, possibly a win for the buyer, or a loss for the seller.

CHAPTER 10

A "NO MONEY DOWN" TRANSACTION VS. A "NOTHING DOWN" DEAL

What's the difference?

A "NOTHING DOWN" DEAL:

A "nothing down" deal describes a transaction where the buyer risks no cash, no equity in real or personal property, and has no liability on any debt. NOTHING DOWN = NO RISK TO BUYER.

Example:

Steve Speculator reads a newspaper ad. An owner wants to sell and will carry back part of the financing. Steve makes the following offer:

Purchase Price	$100,000
Steve takes title "subject to" an existing loan of record	$ 65,000
Steve offers the seller a note secured by a 2nd deed of trust for	$ 35,000

and makes the property the "sole security"
for the 2nd T/D note carried back by the seller.

From the Seller's perspective this is even weaker than the 80-10-10 transaction we discussed earlier.

Here the seller has **NO PROTECTIVE EQUITY!** Steve Speculator risks nothing.

A variation of the above transaction is where the Buyer takes out a new $70,000 first loan from Insecurity Bank to pay off the existing loan, gives the seller some cash, then has the seller carry back a $30,000 second deed of trust for the difference. While the Buyer may be liable to the Bank on the first loan, the seller holding the second has **NO PROTECTIVE EQUITY** and a substantial risk.

A buyer has nothing at risk in states like California, whose laws limit the borrower's liability to the property securing any seller carryback loan. Such laws are called anti-deficiency statutes. Anti-deficiency means that if the Buyer can't pay and the

Seller forecloses, the Buyer will lose <u>only</u> the property. His other assets may not be attached. Anti-deficiency legislation only applies to a carryback note secured by the property being sold.

In California when a seller takes back a purchase money note (the note is a part of the purchase price) and deed of trust secured by the property sold to the buyer, the seller can recover only the property back if the note is not paid. He cannot sue the buyer (borrower) for payment. If the property purchased is residential property, 1 to 4 units, one of which is occupied by the buyer, and the purchase price is financed by an institution, the institution is limited to recovery of the property by foreclosure and cannot sue for payment if a deficiency results due to foreclosure (in California).

A "NO MONEY DOWN" TRANSACTION:

In the "no money down" transaction below versus the "nothing down" deal above, a buyer can lose the property and the seller is protected in the event of foreclosure. This type of transaction could benefit Bob Buyer and is far more secure for Sam and Sally Seller than either of the "nothing down" transactions outlined above.

For another variation on a valid "no money down" transaction, let's look at Bob Buyer's Main Street property again. This time Sam Seller's first loan is $50,000 and assumable.

	Bob Buyer's Main Street House	Sam Seller's Park Ave. House
Home Value	$75,000	$100,000
1st Loan (existing)	$35,000	$ 50,000
Equity	$40,000	$ 50,000

Bob Buyer offers to write a $20,000 note payable to Sam Seller as a down payment on Sam's Park Ave. house. NO CASH IS INVOLVED! This note is to be secured by a 2nd trust deed on Bob's Main Street house. You can see in the above example that the $40,000 equity in Main St. will secure the $20,000 note Bob is creating. After creating (writing) the $20,000 2nd, there still will be $20,000 in **protective equity**.

ATTENTION BUYERS & INVESTORS:
THE ABOVE EXAMPLE ILLUSTRATES ONE OF THE MOST USEFUL AND UNDERUSED WAYS TO ACQUIRE REAL ESTATE.

Bob can qualify for a new loan of $70,000 on Park Ave. with Insecurity Bank and suggests that Sam carry back a note for $10,000 (behind the new $70,000 1st), secured by a 2nd trust deed on the Park Ave. house. He asks Sam to pay all closing costs.

The transaction profile :

Down payment 2nd trust deed note created by Bob on his Main St. House	$ 20,000
New loan on Park Ave. by Bob Buyer pays off Sam's $50,000 loan	$ 70,000
2nd trust deed note carried by Sam Seller on Park Ave. House	$ 10,000
Park Ave. house value (total purchase price)	$100,000

Did Bob put any cash down on this transaction? NO. Does Bob have anything to lose? YES. If he fails to make his payments, he could default and lose both properties, Main St. and Park Ave.

Sam sold his Park Ave. house and received no money down from Bob. Does Sam get any cash? **YES!** The old loan on Park Ave. was $50,000. Bob took out a new loan at Insecurity Bank for $70,000, which paid off the old loan and put $20,000 cash in Sam's pocket. He uses some of the cash to pay transaction costs and a cash commission to his real estate agent. Real estate agents are frequently negative about "nothing down" deals because they don't see a way to get paid a cash commission. They must learn, or you may have to show them how to convert seller carryback notes to cash. In some cases they may be able to take a note for their commission. Sam sells the property for "no money down," yet ends up with cash and two properly secured notes. Should he need additional cash in the future, Sam could sell all or a portion of either carryback note

Property profiles after closing: Bob now owns both properties with the following debt structure.

Main Street House Value $75,000

1st loan	$35,000	
2nd loan (to Sam Seller)	$20,000	
Total loans		$55,000
Protective Equity		**$20,000 (27%)**

Park Avenue House Value $100,000

1st loan (to Insecurity Bank)	$70,000	
2nd loan (to Sam Seller)	$10,000	
Total loans		$80,000
Protective Equity		**$20,000 (20%)**

The two notes Sam is carrying each have 20% or more in **protective equity** behind the last dollar of debt. From the above example you can see that THERE IS A BIG DIFFERENCE between a "NO MONEY DOWN" TRANSACTION and a "NOTHING DOWN" DEAL!

Could this transaction have been made without Insecurity Bank?
Suppose Insecurity Bank had rejected Bob's request for a $70,000 loan. How else could the transaction have been structured and closed?

Owner Will Carry © 1998 by Bill Broadbent, SEC, CCIM, & George Rosenberg

One way would be for Bob to take over Sam's existing $50,000 assumable first loan. Sam would still carry back two notes. One would be written with a short term to sell at a low discount. The other would be Sam's note to keep, written for a longer term with lower payments. Sam could sell the short term note if he needed cash. If Sam's needs do not require much cash, he could sell some of the payments (a partial to Nancy Notebuyer).

You can see that with a little imagination Sam can make the transaction work without any help from Insecurity Bank. Again remember, NO MONEY CHANGED HANDS BETWEEN BOB AND SAM.

Recap of proposed transaction:

1st loan assumed by Bob Buyer	$ 50,000
2nd loan carryback by Sam Seller	$ 30,000
Down payment note secured by Main Street	$ 20,000
Total Purchase Price	$100,000

Let's assume that Bob Buyer plans to sell or exchange the Main Street property within a year. He does not want to pay off the balance on the $20,000 note (secured by the Main St. property) he owes to Sam Seller. Sam Seller is comfortable with Bob being the payor, but is reluctant to accept a substitute payor he doesn't know who will acquire the Main St. property from Bob. Here is a solution that benefits both parties:

CHAPTER 11

THE SUBSTITUTION OF SECURITY ALTERNATIVE

Before Sam and Bob close on Park Ave. they enter into a Substitution of Security Agreement. This agreement permits Bob to substitute other security for his note to Sam. The agreement sets out specific parameters under which Sam will accept property other than Main Street to secure the remaining balance on Bob's $20,000 down payment note. Bob will secure this note with another property he owns. The deed of trust on Main Street will be reconveyed (released) and a new deed of trust drawn that references the old note and pledges a different property as security. A loan policy of title insurance to insure the seniority position of the trust deed or mortgage Sam will own is issued to Sam Seller on the substituted property. If the terms of the note do not change when real property security is substituted, there is no tax impact on the substitution of the security. If the terms of the note are substantially modified at the time the security is substituted, Sam may have tax consequences.

Having nothing more than a simple statement in the deed of trust that Sam agrees to accept substituted security may be too vague, and as a result, unenforceable. The sample Agreement to Substitute Security shown here, while not guaranteed, illustrates some specific parameters. Please check with competent legal help in your state. Sam is not being asked to agree in advance to a blank check of unknowns.

EX #26, pg 135: AGREEMENT TO SUBSTITUTE SECURITY

Whenever an Agreement to Substitute Security is developed by a property seller for a specific transaction, its terms should be tailored to benefit and protect that seller/payee/beneficiary/mortgagee/holder of the security. These terms will be more conservative for a person of modest means, who does not have extensive financial knowledge and strength. He/she may need a lower loan to value ratio, more protective equity and a smaller first loan. A wealthy person with considerable assets, liquidity, and who understands the principles in this book, may be comfortable with a higher loan to value ratio or larger first loan because he/she can consider larger deals and is capable of handling the accompanying financial risks.

The security substituted may be either real property or it could be personal property collateral, i.e., an existing third party note (third party is a party not involved with the buyer's or seller's transaction).

EX #27, pg 136: AGREEMENT TO SUBSTITUTE COLLATERAL

EXHIBIT 26

AGREEMENT TO SUBSTITUTE SECURITY

on Lot_____ in Block_____ ,City _____.

County _____ State _____

BUYER/Trustor;_____

SELLER/Beneficiary;_____

Deed of Trust dated_____ Recorded_____

Instrument#_____ Book _____ Page _____

Beneficiary agrees to substitute other security in place of the security described in the above deed of trust securing payment of the note to Beneficiary if the following formula is met:

A. Substitute real property used to secure the Beneficiary's note must meet the following criteria:

1. If the security is unimproved land, the note must be in first lien position and represent a loan to value ratio of 50% or less.

2. If the security is improved property, the note must be in either first or second lien position with a loan to value ratio not to exceed 75% of the current fair market value of the property securing said lien. Any senior lien may not have an unpaid balance over $ _____ .

3. When the note is in second lien position, then that first lien must be due and payable at least two years beyond any due date on the second note .

4. If there are any questions concerning the value of a property offered as security for the note , then the Beneficiary may request an appraisal and the cost of that appraisal will be shared between the Beneficiary and Trustor. Beneficiary chooses the appraiser.

5. Should Trustor need to sell or exchange the substituted property then Trustor has the right to substitute another property under the terms outlined in this agreement.

6. Trustor, at Trustor's expense, will provide title insurance on all security used to secure the note to Beneficiary. Trustor will pay other costs relative to the substitution.

Date_____   Date_____

_____   _____
              Signature   Signature

NOTE: If the Trustor/Mortgagor holds one or more notes they would prefer to substitute in place of the property referenced above then use the **Agreement to Substitute Collateral** on page 136
                    If they have both real estate and notes and are willing to use either, then both of these agreements could be used in the same transaction.

EXHIBIT 27
AGREEMENT TO SUBSTITUTE COLLATERAL

on lot _____ in Block _____, City _____, County _____, State _____
BUYER/Trustor: _____
SELLER/Beneficiary: _____

Beneficiary agrees to substitute other collateral in place of the security described in the deed of trust securing payment of the note to Beneficiary is the following formula is met:

COLLATERAL SUBSTITUTION FORMULA

If Trustor requests to substitute other collateral for the security described in the deed of trust held by Beneficiary, then the collateral will be established under the terms and conditions set forth herein.

Trustor agrees to secure the note being carried by Beneficiary with one or more trust deed notes having a minimum current aggregate balance of 110 percent of the balance due on the Beneficiary's note. As the principal balance is reduced on the Beneficiary's note, the aggregate balance in the substitute trust deed note(s) may be reduced as long as the 110 percent ratio is maintained.

All notes in the group securing Beneficiary's notes must meet the following criteria:

1. If secured by unimproved land, the note must be in first lien position with a loan to value ratio of not more than 50 percent.

2. If secured by improved property, it must be either a first or second lien provided the total loan to value ratio does not exceed 70 percent of the current fair market value of the property securing said lien and the prior lien (if any) does not have an unpaid balance over $250,000.

3. When the secured note is in second lien position, then that second lien must be due and payable no later than two years before any due date on the senior lien ahead of it.

4. If there is any question concerning the value of the property securing a note that has been offered as collateral, then the Beneficiary may request an appraisal and the cost of that appraisal will be shared between the Beneficiary and Trustor.

5. All notes used as collateral must bear interest of at least 9 percent per annum with payments of (at least) interest only semiannually.

6. If a note used as collateral is being paid off, then Trustor shall have the right to substitute another trust deed note of equal or greater quality and current balance.

7. If a note used as collateral is in default in payment for forty five days then the Trustor within 15 days thereafter must substitute another note of equal or greater quality. If Trustor fails to substitute another note of equal or greater value within 15 days, then Beneficiary may elect to declare all unpaid principal and accrued interest on the secured note executed by Trustor immediately due and payable, regardless of the due date specified in the secured note.

Some sellers and agents mentally FREEZE at the suggestion of securing a note with property other than the one being sold. The idea need not be an obstacle and MAY BE A BETTER OPPORTUNITY. Sellers may find that the substituted property provides more equity protection than the property they are selling! We earlier saw an example of this in Chapter 9 when Bob Buyer secured a note to Sam Seller with Bob's Main St. property, rather than the Park Ave. property he was buying from Sam.

Another use of substituted security (real property) or substituted collateral (personal property)

SUBSTITUTED SECURITY/COLLATERAL USED TO SECURE THE SELLER'S CARRYBACK NOTE MAY HAVE MORE PROTECTIVE EQUITY THAN THE SELLER'S OWN PROPERTY.

An owner of vacant land is approached by a developer. The developer wants to buy the land with 25% cash down and have the seller carry back a note for 75% of the purchase price. The developer also asks the seller to subordinate (become junior in seniority to) the carryback note to a new construction loan of $250,000.

Developer's Proposal
Value of seller's land	$100,000
Developer's cash down payment	$ 25,000 **(protective equity)**
Seller's carryback note (subordinated)	$ 75,000 to a $250,000 new loan

Is subordination of the carryback note a risky deal for the seller? If the developer defaults on his loan payments, he may leave the seller with additional debt ($250,000 new construction loan) secured by the property, more debt than the undeveloped, unfinished property is worth when the seller's $75,000 second is added. During foreclosure the seller would have to keep the payments current on the first loan and then find a competent builder to finish the project.

Suppose the developer owned an income property worth $300,000 on which he owed a $100,000 first loan. In most cases wouldn't it be safer for the seller to carry back $75,000 secured by a proven income property?

Let's compare the two situations:

SUBSTITUTED SECURITY APPROACH
Value of developer's income property		$300,000
Less: Existing first loan	$100,000	
Less: Second note to land seller	$ 75,000 (created)	
Total debt	$175,000	
Protective equity		**$125,000 (42%)**

TYPICAL SUBORDINATION APPROACH

Potential value of developer's new project		$350,000
Less: New first loan	$250,000	
Less: Second note to land seller (subordinated carryback)	$ 75,000	
Total debt		$325,000
Protective equity		**$ 25,000 (7%)**

There is $100,000 more **protective equity** ($125,000 vs. $25,000) on the proven income property than there would be if the seller carried back on his own property. Also, the first loan is smaller and easier to handle in the event of default and/or foreclosure. The first loan is a $100,000 long term loan, rather than a $250,000 short term construction loan.

Suppose the developer had offered the equity in an income property, whose value is $1.2 million with an existing first loan of $400,000, to secure the $75,000 carryback note. At first glance the larger first loan appears to make it a higher risk situation. BUT, when we add the $75,000 2nd to the $400,000 first loan ($475,000 ÷ $1,200,000), we find a Loan to Value (LTV) of 39.6%. This leaves a 60% protective equity vs. a 42% protective equity on the smaller property. In either case we have eliminated the normal "what ifs" concerning the new, unproved development project by placing the debt on an existing income property with a track record.

IMPORTANT: The use of substitute or alternate security (real property) or collateral (personal property) may be far safer for many sellers/payees/ beneficiaries/mortgagees than subordinating to a new construction loan with its inherent and significant risks!

You should refer to the checklist in Chapter 12 before accepting an alternate property as security.

CHAPTER 12

TO PREVENT SURPRISES, HERE IS A CHECKLIST TO USE BEFORE YOU AGREE TO CARRY BACK A NOTE OR BEFORE YOU BUY AN EXISTING NOTE

Our fifteen point checklist:

1. Get a credit report on Bob and Betty Buyer.
Sellers should get the buyers' social security numbers and the buyers' written permission to run a credit check. This will assure the sellers that Bob and Betty Buyer are people with a history of paying their bills on time.

CREDIT REPORT AUTHORIZATION

Date: _____
To any credit reporting agency:

To enable Mr. and Mrs. Sam Seller to make a final decision concerning the sale of their Park Ave. property to us on terms, we are providing our social security numbers and authorize you to issue the Sellers a credit report on us.

_____

Bob Buyer   Social Security Number

_____

Betty Buyer   Social Security Number

_____

Current Home Address: Street   City   State   Zip   Phone

_____

Previous home address within the last five years

_____

Currently employed by   Work Phone

_____

Signature authorization   Signature Authorization

2. Try to get a current financial statement on the buyers.

This becomes important in states where the buyer has personal liability when signing a carryback note secured by real estate. **EX #28, pg 141:** Statement of Assets & Liabilities.

3. If there is any doubt about the value of a substitute property, then get an independent fee appraisal from a professional fee appraiser, one <u>you select</u>, who is licensed and not in the business of marketing real estate.

This should be available for a few hundred dollars on a small property like Bob's. On an apartment or office building the cost could easily be several thousand dollars or more.

4. Prior to closing, get a Beneficiary's Statement or loan status report for any senior loan to be sure it is current.

In California a beneficiary must respond within 21 days or be subject to a fine and damages under CC § 2943(e)(4). Ask Bob for a copy of the first T/D loan documents. You should know all terms and conditions of the loan with priority over your note. This is the obligation you will make payments on if you have to foreclose on a 2nd T/D or mortgage you hold. Rule of thumb: If the first loan has a due date (balloon payment), that due date should be <u>at least</u> eighteen months to two years beyond the due date on any junior note you carry or buy.

Does the law in your state allow a junior lien holder the right to obtain the details (terms) of the senior lien from that lender? If so please send Bill Broadbent a copy of the code section or case law on this. Mail to:

> **Bill Broadbent**
> **Arnett & Broadbent, Inc.**
> **1380 Broad St.**
> **San Luis Obispo, CA 93401-3910**
> **Fax (805)543-0438**
> **e-mail: bill@arnettbroadbent.com**

Watch out for negative amortization. If a Senior lien has an adjustable interest rate or payment amount, the loan may allow negative amortization (when the interest payment is greater than the total payment, interest not covered by the total payment is added to the loan balance). Negative amortization can quickly erode the **protective equity** of a junior lien holder. Even without negative amortization, increases in the interest rate on an Adjustable Rate Mortgage (ARM) will increase the monthly payment, which could eventually force the payor into default. Such an ARM note increases the risk to anyone holding a junior note behind a first mortgage with an adjustable interest rate.

5. Look for a due-on-sale provision in the first loan documents.

If the loan has such a clause and you are forced to foreclose, the first loan holder can call his loan due and payable in full. The reason is that after foreclosure the former owner/borrower has alienated (gone out of) title. To prevent this from happening, try to get the first loan holder to sign a Non-Acceleration Letter. That is your best protection. We know of several institutional lenders who have signed such a letter. It protects you in acquiring the property through foreclosure if you keep their loan current. If you resell, then they still have the right to accelerate their loan

EXHIBIT 28
STATEMENT OF ASSETS & LIABILITIES
(To be used along with your credit report)

NAME: _____

(please print)

ADDRESS: _____

_____

PHONE #: _____

WHAT I/WE OWN   AND   WHAT I/WE OWE

ASSETS (I/we own)		IN DOLLARS	LIABILITIES (I/we owe)		AMOUNT
	BANK OFFICE NAME & NO.	(OMIT CENTS)	NOTES PAYABLE TO BANKS	BANK OFFICE NAME & NO.	(OMIT CENTS)
CASH					
STOCKS AND BONDS	Publicly Traded _____		OTHER NOTES & ACCOUNTS PAYABLE	Mobilehome Loans	
	Privately Held _____			Real Estate Loans	
				Loans on Life Ins. Policies	
NOTES RECEIVABLE (COLLECT-IBLE)	Relatives & Friends		TAXES PAYABLE	Current Yr's Income Taxes Unpaid	
	Trust Deeds & Mortgages			Prior Yr's Income Taxes Unpaid	
	Other			Property Taxes Unpaid	
REAL ESTATE	Improved		CREDIT CARD BALANCES	1)	
	Unimproved			2)	
FURNITURE				3)	
			OTHER LIABILITIES		
LIFE INSURANCE	Cash Surrender Value				
OTHER PERSONAL PROPERTY	Vehicles: 1)			Total Liabilities	
	2)		NET WORTH CALCU-LATION	TOTAL ASSETS	
	Other:			Less: TOTAL LIABILITIES	
	TOTAL ASSETS			NET WORTH	

Owner Will Carry © 1998 by Bill Broadbent, SEC, CCIM, & George Rosenberg

unless they approve the new buyer. This is a win-win arrangement for you and the senior lender.

IMPORTANT: Conservative investors who fund 2nd trust deed or mortgage loans or who buy discounted seller carryback notes also may find that having the senior lender sign a Non-Acceleration letter makes sense.

EX #29, pg 143: SAMPLE NON-ACCELERATION LETTER
(for seller carryback)

EX #30, pg 144: SAMPLE NON-ACCELERATION LETTER
(when buying a note)

6. Get a Preliminary Title Report or a Commitment To Insure from an established, reputable title insurance company on any property that will be used to secure the newly created note. This will protect you against a flawed title, liens or other encumbrances that could cause future problems. If the Title Report looks okay, Bob Buyer should provide a loan policy of title insurance to insure the priority position of the deed of trust he creates on Main St. in favor of Sam and Sally Seller.

In California when Sam Seller sells his property to Bob Buyer and carries back a note secured by a deed of trust, Bob usually receives a policy of title insurance. This policy insures Bob's title to the property and **also insures Sam Seller** the priority of the trust deed note that Sam carries back. It is referred to as a <u>joint protection</u> policy. In the event that Sam sells his note at a later date to Nancy Notebuyer or Norman Noteholder, Nancy or Norman can get an assignee's endorsement (104.1) to the original title policy. This endorsement will insure that the priority of the deed of trust remains the same and that the assignment is valid. Buying this endorsement is less costly than getting a new title policy.

NOTE: The title insurance system <u>does not</u> work this way in all states. States other than California may require a separate loan policy or endorsement to insure the seniority position of the original deed of trust or mortgage for the Beneficiary/ Mortgagee. Without a separate loan policy or endorsement, the note holder's position may not be insured. It is usually safer and cheaper to insure the seniority position of the deed of trust when it is originated than to pay for a new title insurance policy later on when the note is being sold.

7. If your state laws provide for it, record a Request for Notice of Default.
When recorded, this Request for Notice **(EX#31, pg 145)** requires a senior lien holder to notify junior lien holders in the event the senior lien holder starts a foreclosure action.

States that don't have a "Request for Notice of Default" law should consider adopting one. Such a notice benefits and protects consumers.

WARNING: A few senior lien holders have let the trustor (payor) get behind six to ten months or more before they file a foreclosure action. The seller who

EXHIBIT 29

NON ACCELERATION LETTER TO SENIOR LIEN HOLDER
(TO BE USED WHEN CARRYING BACK A JUNIOR NOTE)

Insecurity Bank   Date_____
789 Cash Lane
Anytown, USA
Re: Loan #
To who it may concern:

You are the holder of a first Deed of Trust recorded on _____
as Document/Instrument No. _____ in Volume/Book _____
Page _____,of Official Records of _____ County, State
of_____,on property located at_____.
I intend to carryback a note secured by a junior Deed of Trust on the same property.

Although I am carrying this note in the expectation that it will be paid in a timely manner, it is possible that in the future it might be necessary for me to begin Trustee's Sale proceedings to protect my interest. The purpose of this letter is to confirm that if such proceedings ever become necessary, you will not exercise the Due-On-Sale Clause in your first Deed of Trust if I acquire the property at either the Trustee's Sale or by a Deed in lieu of foreclosure. However, you do reserve the right to accelerate your note if some other party acquires the property at the Trustee's Sale, or by Deed from the present Trustor, or by Deed from me after I acquire the property at the Trustee's Sale.

I may want to sell my note at some future time. In that event this agreement shall inure to the successors and assigns of the undersigned.

I would appreciate it if you would sign the enclosed copy of this letter and return it to me for my records. A stamped envelope is enclosed for your convenience.

                  Very truly yours,

                  _____
                                        Beneficiary

Confirmed:

Lender: _____

By: _____

Title: _____

EXHIBIT 30

NON ACCELERATION LETTER
(WHEN BUYING A NOTE)

Date _____

_____
_____
_____

RE: Loan # _____
     Property Address: _____

To Whom it May Concern:

You are the holder of a first Mortgage recorded on _____, as Document/ Instrument No. _____ in Volume _____ Page _____, of Official Records of _____ County, State of _____.

I intend to purchase a promissory note secured by a junior mortgage on the above property. Although I expect that your mortgage is being paid in a timely manner, if for any reason payments to you become delinquent I would like to know so that I can make the payments and keep your mortgage from going into default. I would make the payment to you within ten days after receiving your notice, and would then begin foreclosure of my junior mortgage.

If I acquire the property either at a foreclosure sale or by a deed in lieu of foreclosure, I would ask that you not exercise any right to call your loan immediately due and payable because of the change of title. It would not be a problem, however, if you were to exercise a due-on-sale (acceleration) provision if some other party acquires the property at the foreclosure sale, or upon transfer of the property from me to another party. I will give you advance notice in writing of any proposed transfer of the property by me.

I would appreciate it if you would sign the agreement below and return this letter to me for my records. A stamped envelope is enclosed for your convenience.

Very truly yours,

_____
Potential Mortgagee

If there is a senior lien that can accelerate without notice, use this:
The undersigned lender agrees that it will give written notice to _____ at _____ if the first mortgage is in default for more than _____ days, and will give _____ an opportunity to cure the default before any foreclosure proceedings are started on the first mortgage. If _____ acquires the property at a foreclosure sale, or by a deed in lieu of foreclosure, because of a default in the junior mortgage, the undersigned lender will not accelerate the due date of the first mortgage because of the transfer of title to _____.

Lender

By: _____
       Name and Title

EXHIBIT 31

REQUEST FOR NOTICE OF DEFAULT

Order No.
Escrow No.
Loan No.

WHEN RECORDED MAIL TO:

Sam and Sally Seller
123 Elm Street
Anytown, CA 99999

SPACE ABOVE THIS LINE FOR RECORDER'S USE ONLY

Request For Notice Under Section 2924b Civil Code

In accordance with Section 2924b, Civil Code, request is hereby made that a copy of any Notice of Default and a copy of any Notice of Sale under the Deed of Trust recorded as instrument No. ___432100___

on ___February 20___, 19_88_, in Book ___8460___, Page ___2002___, Official Records of ___SLO___ County, California, and describing land therein as

Lot 3 of Tract No. 890, Whispering Pines Subdivision in the County of SLO, State of California, as per map recorded in Book 12, Pages 4 and 5 of Maps, in the office of the County Recorder of said County.

executed by ___Bob Buyer and Betty Buyer, husband and wife___, as Trustor,

in which ___Sam Seller and Sally Seller, husband and wife as joint tenants___ is named as

Beneficiary, and ___First American Title Insurance Company___, as Trustee,

be mailed to ___Sam and Sally Seller___,

at ___123 Elm Street___,

Number and Street

___Anytown, CA 99999___

City and State

NOTICE: A COPY OF ANY NOTICE OF DEFAULT AND OF ANY NOTICE OF SALE WILL BE SENT ONLY TO THE ADDRESS CONTAINED IN THIS RECORDED REQUEST. IF YOUR ADDRESS CHANGES, A NEW REQUEST MUST BE RECORDED.

STATE OF CALIFORNIA }

COUNTY OF _____ } ss.

On _____,

before me, the undersigned, a Notary Public in and for said State, personally appeared _____

_____

personally known to me (or proved to me on the basis of satisfactory evidence) to be the person(s) whose name(s) is/are subscribed to the within instrument and acknowledged to me that he/she/they executed the same.

WITNESS my hand and official seal.

Signature _____

Sam Seller
_____

Sally Seller
_____

(This area for official notarial seal)

carried back a junior note will have to make up the back payments on senior loans in a foreclosure action.

In California, whenever a junior loan is to be secured by one to four units, the junior lender can require that a **Request for Notice of Delinquency (EX #32, pp 147-8)** of payment on the senior loan be recorded. If the trustor becomes four months delinquent on their payments, the senior lien holder must notify the junior lien holder. The Junior Lien Beneficiary requesting this notice must pay a $40 fee to the Senior Beneficiary.

8. Notice To Senior Lender.

In states which have no provision for such default notices, a good idea for you as a junior lien holder is to notify the senior lien holder in writing that you hold a junior lien and you would like to be notified in the event he does not receive his payment within thirty days of its due date. The senior note holder will usually respond, as he wants to know that his loan will be paid by you if his borrower does not pay.

9. Be sure that the Trustor/Mortgagor carries fire insurance at least equal to the replacement cost of the improvements and that you are named as a mortgagee/loss payee.

If the improvements burn down, you will be protected.

SPECIAL RISKS:
If the property is located in an area that is subject to earthquakes or flooding, then Sam Seller could require Bob to carry appropriate insurance to cover these special risks. The specifics on this should be set forth in the deed of trust or mortgage.

INSURANCE GAP: Where a building's use does not conform to the land's zoning requirements.

Suppose Sam Seller is selling a small commercial building that is on land now zoned for residential use. The building's use as a retail store does not conform to the land's residential zoning. Such a use is called a legal, non-conforming use. Its use does not conform to the land's required use. If Sam is carrying back a note secured by this property, the non-conforming element could affect him.

If more than 50% of the building is destroyed by fire, some local ordinances may prohibit the owner from rebuilding the building to be used for retail commercial purposes. This could have a negative effect on the value of the property.

Many insurance policies will pay only to rebuild what was destroyed. If the building is not being rebuilt, the owner will have to pay for demolition of that portion (up to 50%) of the building that remains before starting a new building which conforms to the land's zoning. A special endorsement is available, usually at a reasonable cost, to cover the demolition expense. Sam Seller, as part of his sales agreement with Bob Buyer, could require Bob to carry such an endorsement on his fire insurance policy. Sam will then be named as a loss payee on the policy.

EXHIBIT 32 - Page 1 of 2

Order No:
Escrow No.
Loan No.

WHEN RECORDED MAIL TO:

SPACE ABOVE THIS LINE FOR RECORDER'S USE

REQUEST FOR NOTICE OF DELINQUENCIES UNDER
SECTION 2924e CIVIL CODE

In accordance with Section 2924e California Civil Code, request is hereby made that a written notice of any or all delinquencies of four months or more, in payments of principal or interest on any obligation secured under the Deed of Trust recorded as Instrument Number _____ in Book _____ and Page _____, on _____, 19_____, Official Records of _____ County, California, loan number _____ and describing land therein as:
(if available to requesting party)

be sent to _____
(requester beneficiary)

at _____ , _____
(address)   (city)

_____
(state)   (zip)

1. The ownership or security interest of the requester, is the beneficial interest under that certain deed of trust recorded as Instrument

Number # _____ in Book _____ and Page _____ on _____, 19_____, of the Official

Records of _____ County, CA. Wherein _____ is the trustor or mortgagor.

2. _____ is the date on which the interest of the requester will terminate as evidenced by the maturity date of the note of the trustor/mortgagor in favor of the requester.

3. _____ is the name of the current owner of the security property described above.

4. The street address of the security property as described above is: _____

_____

(continued on reverse side)

1161 (1/94)
Page 1 of 2

EXHIBIT 32 - Page 2 of 2

CONSENT BY OWNER/TRUSTOR

I, _____ , AUTHORIZE
                                    (TRUSTOR)

_____
                              (SENIOR LIENHOLDER)

TO DISCLOSE IN WRITING TO _____
                                    (REQUESTING BENEFICIARY/MORTGAGEE)

NOTICE OF ANY AND ALL DELINQUENCIES OF FOUR MONTHS OR MORE, IN PAYMENT OF PRINCIPAL OR INTEREST

ON ANY OBLIGATION SECURED BY THAT SENIOR LIEN MORE PARTICULARLY DESCRIBED AS INSTRUMENT

NUMBER _____ IN BOOK _____ AND PAGE _____ , RECORDED

ON _____ , 19_____ , IN OFFICIAL RECORDS OF _____ COUNTY, CALIFORNIA.

_____   _____

_____   _____
         (TRUSTOR/OWNER)   (REQUESTER BENEFICIARY/MORTGAGEE)

DATED_____ ,19_____

This Document Must Be Notarized To Be Recorded.

Older buildings which burn down may require higher standards when rebuilt, in part due to changes in building, fire and safety codes. Another special endorsement is available at reasonable cost that a seller could require a buyer to carry on the fire insurance policy. The endorsement protects against these added costs due to upgrade changes in building codes.

Some casualty insurance policies cover both of the above mentioned risks within the same endorsement. Talk to a property casualty insurance specialist (CPCU designation) for details.

The buyer of an existing note would have no leverage with the property owner on this issue unless the note is to be extended or modified. Such terms should be included in negotiations for modification or extension.

10. Check once a year with the county tax collector to make sure the Trustor/ Mortgagor has paid his property taxes.
Institutional lenders frequently employ a tax service to do this. First American Title Insurance Company will provide this service to an individual investor for a one-time fee.

Nonpayment of either fire insurance and/or property taxes constitutes a default on most loans and may give you the right to foreclose. Foreclosure procedures are important.

11. Understand the foreclosure laws in your state.
California Foreclosure Procedures follow:

TYPICAL PRIVATE SALE FORECLOSURE PROCEDURE AS IT WOULD OCCUR IN CALIFORNIA TODAY

A. Lender notifies trustee of default.

B. Trustee requires:
  1. Original promissory note.
  2. Original or certified copy of the trust deed.
  3. Declaration of default.
     Describes exact nature of what the lender considers the default to be.
  4. Foreclosure report (sometimes referred to as "Trustee's Sale Guarantee" or"TSG").
     Shows condition of title but insures ONLY the Trustee and Beneficiary.
  5. Statement from lender concerning no knowledge of borrower declaring bankruptcy.
  6. Non-military affidavit. (Federal Law, applies nationwide)
     Soldier's and Sailor's Civil Relief Act prevents credit proceedings on individuals called into active duty after loan obligations were originated.
  7. Cash deposit from lender to cover costs of foreclosure.

C. Trustee records "Notice of Default." **(EX #33, pg 151)**
1. Within 10 business days trustee must mail a copy of "Notice of Default" to anyone who has recorded a Request for Notice.
2. Within one month trustee must mail a copy of "Notice of Default" to anyone who has a recorded interest in the property.
3. As of 7/1/85 Senior lenders must notify junior lenders, who make a written "Request for Notice of Delinquency" and pay a $40 fee, within four months and 15 days from the time a payment is not made (2924e CA Civil Code). Must have borrower's consent or notify borrower in 10 point bold type in loan document.

D. Three months must be allowed to pass during which borrower has the right to "reinstate" the loan. "Reinstatement" means to make up all past due payments plus pay any penalties, costs, and charges.

E. After a minimum of three months have passed, the trustee may start advertising "Notice of Sale."
1. Trustee must mail by registered or certified mail a copy of the Notice of Sale to any interested parties a minimum of 21 days prior to the date of the sale.
2. Trustee must record the Notice of Sale a minimum of 14 days prior to the date of the sale.
3. Trustee must publish the Notice of Sale in a newspaper of general circulation in the city, county, or judicial district in which the property is located, at least once each week for three successive weeks.
4. Trustee must post the Notice of Sale in a public place at least 20 days prior to the date of the sale.
5. Trustee must post the Notice of Sale in some conspicuous place on the property (if possible, on the front door) at least 20 days prior to the date of the sale.
6. Substitution of trustee after the Notice of Sale records requires a new Notice of Sale process.

F. Once advertising "Notice of Sale" starts, an additional period is provided for reinstatement. The Trustor may reinstate (make up delinquent payments and costs) up to 5 days prior to the Trustee's Sale. Now only the last 5 business days immediately preceding the sale date are provided for "redemption." Redemption means to pay off the entire loan obligation, plus all advances and costs to be able to keep the property.

G. Postponements
1. Lender can postpone a maximum of 3 times. After 3 postponements the lender or Trustee will have to re-post, republish and mail a new Notice of Sale.
2. Trustee can postpone if he considers it necessary for the protection of the interests of either the borrower or the lender.
3. The borrower's one day, automatic, right of postponement if the reason stated for the postponement is to secure funds to redeem the property has been repealed CC § 2924g.

H. The foreclosure sale
1. Must take place in a public place in the county in which the property is located.

EXHIBIT 33

SPACE ABOVE THIS LINE FOR RECORDER'S USE

NOTICE OF DEFAULT

IMPORTANT NOTICE

IF YOUR PROPERTY IS IN FORECLOSURE BECAUSE YOU ARE BEHIND IN YOUR PAYMENTS, IT MAY BE SOLD WITHOUT ANY COURT ACTION, and you may have the legal right to bring your account in good standing by paying all of your past due payments plus permitted costs and expenses within the time permitted by law for reinstatement of your account, which is normally five business days prior to the date set for the sale of your property. No sale date may be set until three months from the date this notice of default may be recorded (which date of recordation appears on this notice).

This amount is ___$30,825.00___ as of ___August 1, 1992___, and will increase
(Date)
until your account becomes current. While your property is in foreclosure, you still must pay other obligations (such as insurance and taxes) required by your note and deed of trust or mortgage. If you fail to make future payments on the loan, pay taxes on the property, provide insurance on the property, or pay other obligations as required in the note and deed of trust or mortgage, the beneficiary or mortgagee may insist that you do so in order to reinstate your account in good standing. In addition, the beneficiary or mortgagee may require as a condition to reinstatement that you provide reliable written evidence that you paid all senior liens, property taxes, and hazard insurance premiums.

Upon your written request, the beneficiary or mortgagee will give you a written itemization of the entire amount you must pay. You may not have to pay the entire unpaid portion of your account, even though full payment was demanded, but you must pay all amounts in default at the time payment is made. However, you and your beneficiary or mortgagee may mutually agree in writing prior to the time the notice of sale is posted (which may not be earlier than the end of the three-month period stated above) to, among other things, (1) provide additional time in which to cure the default by transfer of the property or otherwise; or (2) establish a schedule of payments in order to cure your default; or both (1) and (2).

Following the expiration of the time period referred to in the first paragraph of this notice, unless the obligation being foreclosed upon or a separate written agreement between you and your creditor permits a longer period, you have only the legal right to stop the sale of your property by paying the entire amount demanded by your creditor.

To find out the amount you must pay, or to arrange for payment to stop the foreclosure, or if your property is in foreclosure for any other reason, contact:

Sam and Sally Seller
(Name of Beneficiary or Mortgagee)

123 Elm Street
(Mailing Address)

Anytown, CA 99999

(012) 345-6789
(Telephone)

If you have any questions, you should contact a lawyer or the governmental agency which may have insured your loan.

Notwithstanding the fact that your property is in foreclosure, you may offer your property for sale, provided the sale is concluded prior to the conclusion of the foreclosure.

Remember, YOU MAY LOSE LEGAL RIGHTS IF YOU DO NOT TAKE PROMPT ACTION.

2. Trustee must accept cash or its equivalent.
   a. Cashier's check from a recognized financial institution.
   b. The Trustee or Lender in foreclosure can bid the amount of their loan as the equivalent of cash, or can add additional cash to compete with other qualified bidders.

> **There are good reasons (legal and tax) for a note holder bidding less than the loan balance due (an "underbid"). Review this idea with legal and tax counsel.**

3. At conclusion of bidding, trustee may or may not immediately deliver trustee's deed to high cash bidder, transferring title to and possession of the property to the high cash bidder. Follow-up and get the Trustee's deed recorded as soon as possible.

Bidders, including lenders in foreclosure, should satisfy themselves as to the condition of the property, condition of title, and the right of parties in possession immediately prior to the sale.

In California a trustee's sale (foreclosure) is final; there is no redemption period. This is true in other states as well. Some states allow a redemption period (usually a few months) during which the foreclosed owner may re-aquire the property by paying off the loan in full. Check the foreclosure statutes that apply in your state.

12. Seller Carryback Disclosure Statement: Several years ago, due to problems that sellers and buyers had incurred with seller carryback financing, the California legislature decided that both parties would be better informed if a Seller Carryback Financing Disclosure statement was filled out by the real estate agent who handled the transaction and was signed by both buyer and seller. Here is a sample.

EX #34, pg 153: Seller Carryback Disclosure Statement used in California.

13. If the entity signing the note is a partnership or a corporation, seek legal advice. Additional safeguards may be needed.

14. When buying a note, get an Offset Statement, Statement of Balance Due or Estoppel Letter, all mean about the same. This should be signed by the current payor/trustor/mortgagor confirming that the balance due and other terms of the note concur with what the note seller has told you and confirmed in writing on a Beneficiary Statement. Getting a written statement prevents future problems.

15. Personal guarantees (when a note is being sold, with recourse):
Note buyers may ask note sellers to personally guarantee the note being purchased. This means that if the payor (Bob Buyer) does not pay and the note buyer (Norman Noteholder) forecloses and does not receive payment in full, then the note seller (Sam Seller) will make up the difference.

EXHIBIT 34

SELLER CARRYBACK DISCLOSURE STATEMENT

DATE:_____,19____, at _____, CA
and an attachment to the following contract:

☐ Purchase agreement

☐ Counteroffer

☐ Exchange agreement

☐ Option to purchase (with or without lease)

Dated_____, 19_____
Entered into by_____

> This statement is required by California Civil Code Section 2956 when the seller carries back a note executed by the buyer as part of the sales price for property containing four or less family units.
>
> This statement is prepared and presented by the broker or agent, to the party who offers or counteroffers to buy, sell, exchange or option as part of the offer or counteroffer received by the broker or agent.
>
> A copy of the statement shall also be delivered to the party accepting the offer or counteroffer. The statement is signed by the broker or agent who prepares it. Both buyer and seller sign it acknowledging they have read and received a copy.

DISCLOSURES:

1. General information concerning note to be executed by Buyer to Seller:

1.1 Note to be executed by Buyer in the original amount of $_____, payable in constant monthly _____ installments of $_____ to include _____ percent per annum interest, ☐ until paid ☐ all due and payable with a **final/balloon payment** on _____, 19____ in the approximate amount of $_____.

1.2 The note will be secured by a trust deed on the property._____

1.3 If this note contains a **FINAL/BALLOON PAYMENT**, the debt is not fully amortized. When this remaining balance is due and payable, there can be no assurance that refinancing, modification or extension of the balloon payment will be available to the Buyer.

1.4 Unless stated and explained in an attached addendum, the note contains a fixed rate of interest with no variable or adjustable interest rates which would increase payments or result in a negative amortization of the debt: _____

1.5 Unless stated, the original amount of the note will be adjusted by endorsement at close of escrow to reflect differences in the then remaining balance of any underlying trust deed obligation(s) being assumed or obtained.

1.6 If an All-Inclusive Note and Trust Deed are carried back by Seller, they will contain provisions passing through to the Buyer any prepayment penalties, late charges, due-on sale or further encumbrance acceleration and future advances.

2. Special provisions & disclosures concerning the carryback note & trust deed:

2.1 If an all-inclusive note and trust deed are carried back by the Seller, they will contain provisions that the Seller will place the note on contract collection with any institutional lender, escrow officer or real estate broker, other than the Seller, and that the collection agent is instructed to first disburse funds on payments due senior encumbrances.

2.2 A joint protection CLTA policy of title insurance will be delivered to Buyer and Seller insuring their interests in title on the close of escrow.

2.3 The trust deeds and grant deeds or land sale contracts to be executed will be recorded with the county recorded at close of escrow.

2.4 The Seller will be named, through escrow, as a loss payee under the hazard and fire insurance assigned to or obtained by the Buyer.

2.5 No tax reporting service shall be obtained for the Seller and Seller will assure himself that real estate taxes have been paid while he holds the note. _____

2.6 Requests for Notice of Default and Notice of Delinquency under California Civil Code Sections 2924b and 2924e will be recorded and served on behalf of Seller on encumbrancer senior to the carryback.

2.7 Seller is aware that in the event of a default under the carryback note and trust deed, his sole source of recovery is limited to the net proceeds from foreclosure or his subsequent resale; and he is not entitled to rental value or deficiency money judgment under the note. [CCP §580b]

2.8 Unless entered, Buyer shall receive no net proceeds or cash back upon the close of escrow. Amount to be received $_____; source of funds _____; reason for receipt _____
_____

2.9 The note shall include the following provision: "This note is subject to Section 2966 of the Civil Code, which provides that the holder of this note shall give written notice to the trustor, or his successor in interest, of prescribed information at least 90 and not more than 150 days before any balloon payment is due."

3. Encumbrances senior & prior to Seller's carryback trust deed & note:

3.1 Conditions of encumbrances, with priority over the Seller's carryback note and trust deed which will remain or be placed of record at time of closing are as follows:

	First Trust Deed	Second Trust Deed
Original balance:	$_____	$_____
Current balance:	$_____	$_____
Interest rate:	_____% ☐ VIR	_____% ☐ VIR
	Type:_____	Type:_____
Monthly payments:	$_____	$_____
Due date:	_____, 19__	_____, 19__
Balloon payment:	$_____	$_____
Current defaults:	$_____	$_____

3.2 If any of the senior encumbrances contain a due date, it may be difficult or impossible to refinance, modify or extend the balloon payment in the conventional mortgage marketplace.

4. Buyer credit information (supplied by Buyer):

Buyer to hand Seller a completed credit application on acceptance. Seller may terminate the agreement within _____ days of acceptance by delivering to Buyer, Buyer's broker or escrow written Notice of Cancellation based on disapproval of Buyer's credit.

5. Broker disclosures:

5.1 Credit data is supplied by Buyer. Broker knows of no falsity or omission concerning the Buyer's credit information.

5.2 This statement and its contents being statutorily required disclosures do not limit the broker's duties to disclose other facts material to the Buyer or Seller.

5.3 The Buyer and Seller are not to sign this statement until they have read and understood all of the information in it. All parts of the form must be completed before signature.

5.5 ☐ See attached addendum for additional disclosures which are made a part hereof.

5.6 This statement was prepared by:_____.

6. Other provisions:_____
_____
_____
_____
_____
_____
_____
_____
_____
_____
_____

Buyer's Broker: _____
Address:_____
_____ Phone (_____) _____
By: _____
I have read and received a copy of this statement.
Date: _____ 19 _____
Buyer: _____
Buyer: _____
Broker's approval: _____ ___/___/___

Seller's Broker: _____
Address:_____
_____ Phone (_____) _____
By: _____
I have read and received a copy of this statement.
Date: _____ 19 _____
Seller: _____
Seller: _____
Broker's approval: _____ ___/___/___

FORM 300   09-96   ©1996 **first tuesday**, P.O. BOX 20069, RIVERSIDE, CA 92516 (909) 781-7300

Owner Will Carry © 1998 by Bill Broadbent, SEC, CCIM, & George Rosenberg

Personal guarantees are only as good as the person signing the guarantee. Check his/her credit. Get a financial statement on the note seller/guarantor, but keep in mind that PEOPLE, not financial statements, pay notes. Personal financial circumstances change, sometimes rapidly. For example, a note seller guaranteed a $12,000 note he sold. During the next 18 months he lost $129,000. He probably could not have made good on the guarantee he signed when he sold the note. Remember: Guarantees require judicial action (going to court), which is expensive, time consuming and frustrating.

Properly secured and structured seller carryback notes with adequate protective equity and/or additional security (real property) or collateral (personal property) are simpler and safer than a personal guarantee. That is why we have emphasized and explained these additional security and/or collateral concepts in this book.

By following our 15 point checklist a seller will minimize the risk when carrying a note, especially when accepting notes secured by other property. The seller will also have better quality paper, which will bring a better price, if he/she later needs to sell all or a portion of the note to raise cash.

IMPORTANT: **WE DO NOT LIVE IN A RISK FREE WORLD!** Some risks relative to notes cannot be anticipated or eliminated. Examples would include, but are not limited to, earthquakes, hurricanes, tornadoes, floods, riots, any one of which may cause extensive property damage and not be adequately covered by insurance. Changes in government regulations can also seriously affect a property's value. The owner of a note secured by an affected property may not be able to do anything about such government regulations. An example would be down-zoning. Bankruptcy of a Trustor/Mortgagor will always be a risk. Some defect in construction could surface years later and cause problems that no one could reasonably anticipate. Another risk will be the year-2000 (Y2K) problem, also known as the "Millenium Bug."

Having noted these words of caution, we think that a view of the real world of notes from our perspective is important.

In spite of the risks mentioned above, our experience with seller carryback notes over several decades is that the vast majority of notes pay off without significant problems. Most payors are honest and honor their debt obligations.

By following our prudent guidelines above, more property can be sold safely with seller carryback financing. Both buyer and seller will benefit.

A NEW RISK: FORFEITURE

The government may sieze private property by filing either a:

Civil suit, filed against the property itself and not limited to the criminal's interest in the property; or a

Criminal suit filed against the individual, for example:
Suppose Sam Seller sold his property to Dan Deadbeat and carried back a note. Dan was arrested in a drug bust and law enforcement pursued a civil forfeiture action. What must Sam do? He must respond promptly to protect his interest. The Department of Justice has established policies and procedures which may benefit the lender if utilized properly and in a timely manner. Upon receipt of a Civil Forfeiture complaint, Sam should immediately contact appropriate legal counsel and file a claim to protect his interest. The time periods are short and bonding of costs may be required.

CONSULT WITH AN EXPERIENCED REAL ESTATE ATTORNEY.

Our first use of multiple notes was in Chapter 4 when Sam Seller carried back two or three smaller notes instead of one large note to sell his property. Here are more examples where using multiple notes can solve problems:

CHAPTER 13

USE MULTIPLE NOTES FOR MORE FLEXIBILITY

Problem:

Suppose Sam and Sally Seller have separated, are planning a divorce, and have put their jointly-owned home up for sale. They receive a purchase offer from Bob and Betty Buyer offering them a cash down payment and asking the Sellers to carry back a note secured by a 2nd deed of trust in the amount of $20,000, payable $200 or more per month including interest at 10%, all due and payable 5 years from closing. Sam and Sally Seller's relationship has deteriorated. They do not want to be involved with each other after the divorce. Having joint interests in the same note creates involvement.

Solution:

One spouse could carry back a $10,000 note secured by a 2nd deed of trust and the other could carry back a $10,000 note secured by a 3rd deed of trust. However, this arrangement creates unequal priority for one of them. If this approach is used, then the person who is financially strongest should carry the note in 3rd position while the other person carries the note in 2nd position. The title should also be searched to confirm the priority of any newly created deed(s) of trust.

A more equitable solution would be for the Buyers to execute two notes for $10,000 each, one to Sam and one to Sally, with identical terms, secured by a single deed of trust. Place the original notes with a neutral note collection service, preferably a bank or escrow company that will hold the original documents until the notes are paid off. Have a provision in each note that "default on one note constitutes a default on both." With individual notes Sam and Sally need have no further mutual involvement. Each can receive a check either directly from the Buyer or from a collection service. Either of them may sell, borrow or exchange their $10,000 note without consulting the other. In terms of priority and **protective equity**, each note is equal to the other. Each note says that a payment default on one note is a default on both. This provision can be used in any multiple note situation.

Isn't this superior to each divorced spouse having an undivided 1/2 interest in one $20,000 note?

EX #35, pg 157: DEED OF TRUST THAT SECURES TWO NOTES OF EVEN DATE.

The separate note solution can also be effective when multiple owners are selling a property.

EXHIBIT 35

DEED OF TRUST SECURING TWO NOTES OF EVEN DATE

WHEN RECORDED MAIL TO:

Sam Seller
123 Elm Street
Anytown, CA 99999

SPACE ABOVE THIS LINE FOR RECORDER'S USE

DEED OF TRUST WITH ASSIGNMENT OF RENTS
(This Deed of Trust contains an acceleration clause)

This DEED OF TRUST, made   October 1, 1992   , between

Bob Buyer and Betty Buyer, husband and wife   herein called TRUSTOR,

whose address is   999 Main Street   Anytown   CA
                   (Number and Street)   (City)   (State)

FIRST AMERICAN TITLE INSURANCE COMPANY, a California corporation, herein called TRUSTEE, and

Sam Seller, a married man as his separate property, and Sally Seller, his wife, as her separate property
, herein called BENEFICIARY,

WITNESSETH: That Trustor grants to Trustee in Trust, with Power of Sale, that property in the   City of
Anytown,   County of   San Luis Obispo,   State of California, described as:

Lot 3 of Tract No. 890, Whispering Pines Subdivision in the County of San Luis Obispo, State of California as per map recorded in Book 12, Pages 4 and 5 of Maps, in the office of the County Recorder, San Luis Obispo County, California.

If the trustor shall sell, convey or alienate said property, or any part thereof, or any interest therein, or shall be divested of his title or any interest therein in any manner or way, whether voluntarily or involuntarily, without the written consent of the beneficiary being first had and obtained, beneficiary shall have the right, at its option, except as prohibited by law, to declare any indebtedness or obligations secured hereby, irrespective of the maturity date specified in any note evidencing the same, immediately due and payable.

Together with the rents, issues and profits thereof, subject, however, to the right, power and authority hereinafter given to and conferred upon Beneficiary to collect and apply such rents, issues and profits.

For the Purpose of Securing (1) payment of the sum of $ 20,000 (two notes)* with interest thereon according to the terms of a promissory note or notes of even date herewith made by Trustor, payable to order of Beneficiary, and extensions or renewals thereof, and (2) the performance of each agreement of Trustor incorporated by reference or contained herein (3) Payment of additional sums and interest thereon which may hereafter be loaned to Trustor, or his successors or assigns, when evidenced by a promissory note or notes reciting that they are secured by this Deed of Trust.

To protect the security of this Deed of Trust, and with respect to the property above described, Trustor expressly makes each and all of the agreements, and adopts and agrees to perform and be bound by each and all of the terms and provisions set forth in subdivision A, and it is mutually agreed that each and all of the terms and provisions set forth in subdivision B of the fictitious deed of trust recorded in Orange County August 17, 1964, and in all other counties August 18, 1964, in the book and at the page of Official Records in the office of the county recorder of the county where said property is located, noted below opposite the name of such county, namely:

COUNTY	BOOK	PAGE	COUNTY	BOOK	PAGE	COUNTY	BOOK	PAGE	COUNTY	BOOK	PAGE
Alameda	1288	556	Kings	858	713	Placer	1028	379	Sierra	38	187
Alpine	3	130-31	Lake	437	110	Plumas	166	1307	Siskiyou	506	762
Amador	133	438	Lassen	192	367	Riverside	3778	347	Solano	1287	621
Butte	1330	513	Los Angeles	T-3878	874	Sacramento	5039	124	Sonoma	2067	427
Calaveras	185	338	Madera	911	136	San Benito	300	405	Stanislaus	1970	56
Colusa	323	391	Marin	1849	122	San Bernardino	6213	768	Sutter	655	585
Contra Costa	4684	1	Mariposa	90	453	San Francisco	A-804	596	Tehama	457	183
Del Norte	101	549	Mendocino	667	99	San Joaquin	2855	283	Trinity	108	595
El Dorado	704	635	Merced	1660	753	San Luis Obispo	1311	137	Tulare	2530	108
Fresno	5052	623	Modoc	191	93	San Mateo	4778	175	Tuolumne	177	160
Glenn	469	76	Mono	69	302	Santa Barbara	2065	881	Ventura	2607	237
Humboldt	801	83	Monterey	357	239	Santa Clara	6626	664	Yolo	769	16
Imperial	1189	701	Napa	704	742	Santa Cruz	1638	607	Yuba	398	693
Inyo	165	672	Nevada	363	94	Shasta	800	633			
Kern	3756	690	Orange	7182	18	San Diego	SERIES 5	Book 1964, Page 149774			

shall inure to and bind the parties hereto, with respect to the property above described. Said agreements, terms and provisions contained in said subdivisions A and B, (identical in all counties, and printed on the reverse side hereof) are by the within reference thereto, incorporated herein and made a part of this Deed of Trust for all purposes as fully as if set forth at length herein, and Beneficiary may charge for a statement regarding the obligation secured hereby, provided the charge therefor does not exceed the maximum allowed by law.

The undersigned Trustor, requests that a copy of any notice of default and any notice of sale hereunder be mailed to him at his address hereinbefore set forth.

*   This deed of trust secures payment of a $10,000 note to Sam Seller and a $10,000 note to Sally Seller.

Signature of Trustor

STATE OF CALIFORNIA   }ss.
COUNTY OF _____}

On _____ before me,

_____'

personally appeared_____

_____,

personally known to me (or proved to me on the basis of satisfactory evidence) to be the person(s) whose name(s) is/are subscribed to the within instrument and acknowledged to me that he/she/they executed the same in his/her/their authorized capacity(ies), and that by his/her/their signature(s) on the instrument the person(s) or the entity upon behalf of which the person(s) acted, executed the instrument.

WITNESS my hand and official seal.

Signature _____

Bob Buyer

Betty Buyer

More flexibility for the heirs:

When settling an estate, real property may be distributed and several heirs could be in ownership of a single property. If the property is salable for cash, no problem. Sell it and divide the cash.

If seller carryback financing is required to complete a sale at a good price (very important on land sales, which are usually difficult to finance through institutions), then several people may end up holding undivided interests in a single note and deed of trust. If one heir wants to sell his or her position and the other heir(s) are not willing to buy it, that heir would find his/her position difficult to sell. Wouldn't everyone be better off with his/her own note in an amount based on their percentage interest in the property? All notes could be secured by a single deed of trust and have equal priority. A default in payment on one note is a default on all. The notes should be placed in a collection service that would hold the original documents until the notes were paid off. The collection service would receive one payment check from the buyer/trustor and would disburse individual checks to each note holder/beneficiary. The collection service would provide continuous accounting and handle year end reporting chores to the IRS of interest received when applicable.

Each note holder would have more autonomy and flexibility. If one heir needed to borrow, sell or exchange his/her note, the heir could do so without permission of the other beneficiaries.

Dissolving a partnership:

Leon owned some property his friend Ted said was suitable for development. Ted had some experience and a better financial statement, so they decided to form a joint venture for the development. Leon contributed his property to the partnership and they acquired an adjoining property as well. Subsequently the market softened. Leon panicked. He employed a real estate Consultant who reviewed the situation and advised Leon that it would be very risky for him to continue. Leon lacked cash to protect himself if something went wrong. Ted was convinced the project would succeed but didn't have the cash to buy out Leon's interest. Ted owned several other properties.

A price of $120,000 for Leon's interest in the development property was agreed on with Ted. The Consultant suggested that Ted create three separate notes to Leon - $20,000, $40,000 and $60,000 - each one secured by a 2nd deed of trust on a separate property. No further encumbrance was placed on the development parcel. Interest was to accrue on the new notes for one year. Title searches were conducted.

At the end of that year payments were to begin on each note. The due dates were staggered. One note was due in two years, one due in three years, and one due in 4 years. All notes had due-on-sale provisions. Request For Notice of Delinquency forms were filed on each property for Leon's protection. The staggered payment structure of these notes gave Ted some breathing room to finish the new project. Ted also had time to market one or more of the other properties. Most important, Leon was out from under the worry, headache and risk of the joint venture and received three secured notes in return for his joint venture equity.

Some authors of informational books (like this) save the later chapters for miscellaneous thoughts on the subject. Not here. When we write of other uses for trust deeds and notes, we want the reader to know that we have saved some of the best for last. A Performance note and a Performance deed of trust are two of the more powerful tools in the creative tool kit. Either one, correctly used, can make the difference between an average deal and a great deal.

CHAPTER 14

OTHER USES OF TRUST DEEDS AND MORTGAGES

REDUCING YOUR RISK AS A GUARANTOR:

Situation #1:
Suppose a close friend or relative (Brown Jr.) wants to buy a house. Insecurity Bank considers his loan application marginal. If he had a Guarantor, his loan application would be approved. Brown Jr. approaches Brown Sr. to be the Guarantor. Brown Sr. wants to keep things on a business-like basis. What if Brown Jr. defaults and doesn't make his payments? Brown Sr. has the liability on the loan, but no ownership interest and no way to protect himself if Brown Jr. defaults.

Solution:
Brown Sr. asks Brown Jr. to execute a deed of trust (no note is involved) to be recorded behind (after) the loan to Insecurity Bank in favor of Brown Sr. This deed of trust will secure Brown Jr.'s performance (making the loan payments to Insecurity Bank) in this transaction. This T/D is called a Performance trust deed. Should Brown Jr. default on the first loan where Brown Sr. was Guarantor, then Sr. could make up the delinquent payments and foreclose on the Performance deed of trust. Brown Sr. would end up with the property if Brown Jr. did not cure the default. If Brown Sr. has to foreclose on Brown Jr., Insecurity Bank should be happy with the situation and not accelerate on Brown Sr.

EX #36, pg 160: AGREEMENT FOR PERFORMANCE DEED OF TRUST (Protects Guarantor)

Where unrelated parties are involved, the borrower may pay a fee to the Guarantor to compensate him for taking the risk. Our sample agreement provides for such a fee payment, where appropriate.

Situation #2:
Suppose you are buying a business of some type, which may or may not include any real estate, perhaps a small store in a resort area. The Seller is willing to carry some of the financing. Suppose the business is either unproved or seasonal in nature. You are worried about being able to make the same payment each month.

EXHIBIT 36

AGREEMENT FOR PERFORMANCE DEED OF TRUST

Brown Jr. and Brown Sr. are cosigners of a promissory note to Insecurity Bank in the principal amount of $_____, payable in monthly installments of $_____ until _____, when all principal and interest is due and payable in full. The note is secured by a deed of trust to _____as Trustee,

recorded_____ in Volume _____ at Page _____ of the

Official Records of _____ County, _____.

Brown Sr. has cosigned the note as an accommodation to Brown Jr., **(alternative: In consideration of the payment of $_____, Brown Sr. has cosigned the note)** to enable Brown Jr. to obtain a loan from Insecurity Bank. Brown Jr. agrees to make each note payment before the payment becomes delinquent. Brown Jr. further agrees to indemnify Brown Sr., and hold him harmless from all loss and expense arising from any default by Brown Jr. to comply in a timely manner with all obligations set forth in the note and deed of trust, including but not limited to payment of monthly note installments, real property taxes, and insurance premiums. If Brown Jr. fails to comply with any of the terms and conditions of the note and deed of trust, Brown Sr. is hereby given the right to cure the default without notice, and Brown Jr. shall reimburse to him upon demand the full amount expended by Brown Sr. to cure the default, plus interest at 10 percent per annum or the maximum rate permitted by law, whichever is less.

This agreement shall be secured by a second deed of trust encumbering the real property described in the deed of trust securing payment of the note to Insecurity Bank. The deed of trust shall recite that it secures full performance of all obligations set forth in this agreement, which may be referred to in the deed of trust as a "written guaranty agreement" dated _____."

Brown Jr. agrees that he will not sell the real property without requiring either (a) payment in full of the note to Insecurity Bank, or (b) buyer's assumption of the note to Insecurity Bank with a full release (novation) of Brown Sr. from all liability for payment of the note.

If any action or proceeding is filed to enforce or interpret any provision of this agreement, the prevailing party shall be entitled to recover reasonable attorney's fees from the other party.

Dated:_____

_____
Brown Sr.

_____
Brown Jr.

Solution:

Structure the carryback financing in such a way that the payment is relative to the volume of business. This calls for a Performance Note which is secured by a standard deed of trust. For example, a summer resort owner could pay high payments from June through September and lower than average payments from October through May. Payments on the Performance Note could be a percentage of the gross sales volume of the business. When buying property that includes a business, the buyer may not be comfortable with the seller's representations as to the sales volume of the business. The sales volume affects the buyer's ability to make loan payments. One way for the buyer to be more certain he/she can make the payments is to set up a seller carryback note whose pay-back rate is determined by sales volume of the business. Such a Performance Note is secured by a deed of trust (or mortgage). An **illustration** of such a note follows.

EX #37, pgs 162-164: PERFORMANCE NOTE AND DEED OF TRUST (3 Pages)

IMPORTANT: Before using the Performance Deed of Trust or Performance Note, be sure to have the documents reviewed by the proposed Trustee, so that you know the Trustee is willing to foreclose in the event of default. A Trustee is not obligated to foreclose. If the Trustee declines to foreclose, you, as the Beneficiary, can either substitute another Trustee or pursue a judicial foreclosure.

DEED OF TRUST & INSTALLMENT NOTE

DO NOT DESTROY THIS NOTE: When paid, this note and the Deed of Trust must be surrendered to the First American Title Insurance Company with request for reconveyance.

INSTALLMENT NOTE

(INTEREST INCLUDED)

(This note contains an acceleration clause)

$ 85,000   Anytown , California, October 1, 1992

In installments and at the times hereinafter stated, for value received   Bob Buyer and Betty Buyer
promise__S__ to pay to

Sam Seller and Sally Seller, husband and wife as joint tenants

or order, at   123 Elm Street, Anytown, CA 99999
the principal sum of   eighty-five thousand and no/100   Dollars,
with interest from   October 1, 1992   on the amounts of principal remaining from time to time
unpaid, until said principal sum is paid, at the rate of   nine   per cent, per annum. Principal and interest due
in monthly installments of   seven hundred fifty and no/100*   Dollars,
($ 750.00), or more on the   first   day of each and every month, beginning on the   first   day
of   November , 19 92

> * The monthly installment is subject to being increased pursuant to the percentage of gross receipts formula attached to this note as Schedule A, and incorporated by reference.

and continuing until said principal sum and the interest thereon has been fully paid. AT ANY TIME, THE PRIVILEGE IS RESERVED TO PAY MORE THAN THE SUM DUE. Each payment shall be credited first, on the interest then due; and the remainder on the principal sum; and interest shall thereupon cease upon the amount so credited on the said principal sum. Should default be made in the payment of any of said installments when due, then the whole sum of principal and interest shall become immediately due and payable at the option of the holder of this note.

If the trustor shall sell, convey or alienate said property, or any part thereof, or any interest therein, or shall be divested of his title or any interest therein in any manner or way, whether voluntarily or involuntarily, without the written consent of the beneficiary being first had and obtained, beneficiary shall have the right, at its option, except as prohibited by law, to declare any indebtedness or obligations secured hereby, irrespective of the maturity date specified in any note evidencing the same, immediately due and payable.

Should suit be commenced to collect this note or any portion thereof, such sum as the Court may deem reasonable shall be added hereto as attorney's fees. Principal and interest payable in lawful money of the United States of America. This note is secured by a certain DEED OF TRUST to the FIRST AMERICAN TITLE INSURANCE COMPANY, a California corporation, as TRUSTEE.

_____   _____
                                        Bob Buyer

_____   _____
                                        Betty Buyer

CALCULATION OF MONTHLY INSTALLMENTS

This schedule is an attachment to an Installment Note dated October 1, 1992 in the original principal amount of $85,000, signed by Bob Buyer and Betty Buyer, hereafter collectively referred to as "Buyer," in favor of Sam Seller and Sally Seller, husband and wife as joint tenants, hereafter collectively referred to as "Seller."

The minimum monthly installment payment to be made by Buyer to Seller is $750, which shall be due on the first day of each calendar month until all unpaid principal and accrued interest have been paid in full.

Buyer is the owner of a restaurant business known as the "Anytown Coffee Shop," located at 999 Elm Street, Anytown, California. In addition to the minimum monthly installment payment of $750, Buyer agrees to pay to Seller, on the first day of each calendar month, the amount (if any) by which six percent (6%) of Buyer's "gross income" from the Anytown Coffee Shop exceeds the minimum monthly installment payment. The percentage payment shall be based upon gross income received during the preceding month, and shall be sent together with a statement of gross income for the period covered by the percentage payment.

The term "gross income" shall mean gross sales, receipts, charges and revenues of every kind, nature, character and description, including service and sales for cash, or on a charge basis; and the gross amount received by Buyer from any and all other sources of income from business conducted by the Anytown Coffee Shop. There shall be deducted from "gross income" only the following:

   (a) Charges actually paid by Buyer in connection with credit sales (e.g., American Express, Visa, Mastercard, or such other companies);

   (b) The amounts actually paid by Buyer to operators of coin-operated machines for actual sales from said machines, if any, located at the Anytown Coffee Shop; and

   (c) The amount of sales tax payable by reason of such sales or services, payable under any tax law, according to laws then in effect, or which are adopted in the future by a duly constituted governmental taxing authority. The amount deducted must actually be paid to a governmental authority before Buyer shall be entitled to a deduction from "gross income," and then only if the amount was actually included as a part of the "gross income" of Buyer.

Upon demand, Buyer shall furnish to Seller a copy of Buyer's sales tax returns, and Seller shall have a right to inspect the accounting books and records of the Anytown Coffee Shop, for the purpose of verifying the gross income reported by Buyer to Seller.

WHEN RECORDED MAIL TO:

_____

SPACE ABOVE THIS LINE FOR RECORDER'S USE

DEED OF TRUST WITH ASSIGNMENT OF RENTS
(This Deed of Trust contains an acceleration clause)

This DEED OF TRUST, made   October 1, 1992   , between
Bob Buyer and Betty Buyer, husband and wife as joint tenants   herein called TRUSTOR,

whose address is   **999 Main Street**   **Anytown**   **CA 99999**
(Number and Street)   (City)   (State)

FIRST AMERICAN TITLE INSURANCE COMPANY, a California corporation, herein called TRUSTEE, and

Sam Seller and Sally Seller, husband and wife as joint tenants   , herein called BENEFICIARY,

WITNESSETH: That Trustor grants to Trustee in Trust, with Power of Sale, that property in the
County of   Elbert   State of California, described as:

Lot 2, Block 6 of Tract Map 104, filed of record on March 28, 1958 in Book 6 of Maps at Page 142, in the office of the Recorder for Elbert County, California.

See Exhibit A

If the trustor shall sell, convey or alienate said property, or any part thereof, or any interest therein, or shall be divested of his title or any interest therein in any manner or way, whether voluntarily or involuntarily, without the written consent of the beneficiary being first had and obtained, beneficiary shall have the right, at its option, except as prohibited by law, to declare any indebtedness or obligations secured hereby, irrespective of the maturity date specified in any note evidencing the same, immediately due and payable.

Together with the rents, issues and profits thereof, subject, however, to the right, power and authority hereinafter given to and conferred upon Beneficiary to collect and apply such rents, issues and profits.

For the Purpose of Securing (1) payment of the sum of $ **85,000** with interest thereon according to the terms of a promissory note or notes of even date herewith made by Trustor, payable to order of Beneficiary, and extensions or renewals thereof, and (2) the performance of each agreement of Trustor incorporated by reference or contained herein (3) Payment of additional sums and interest thereon which may hereafter be loaned to Trustor, or his successors or assigns, when evidenced by a promissory note or notes reciting that they are secured by this Deed of Trust.

To protect the security of this Deed of Trust, and with respect to the property above described, Trustor expressly makes each and all of the agreements, and adopts and agrees to perform and be bound by each and all of the terms and provisions set forth in subdivision A, and it is mutually agreed that each and all of the terms and provisions set forth in subdivision B of the fictitious deed of trust recorded in Orange County August 17, 1964, and in all other counties August 18, 1964, in the book and at the page of Official Records in the office of the county recorder of the county where said property is located, noted below opposite the name of such county, namely:

COUNTY	BOOK	PAGE	COUNTY	BOOK	PAGE	COUNTY	BOOK	PAGE	COUNTY	BOOK	PAGE
Alameda	1288	556	Kings	858	713	Placer	1028	379	Sierra	38	187
Alpine	3	130-31	Lake	437	110	Plumas	166	1307	Siskiyou	506	762
Amador	133	438	Lassen	192	367	Riverside	3778	347	Solano	1287	621
Butte	1330	513	Los Angeles	T-3878	874	Sacramento	5039	124	Sonoma	2067	427
Calaveras	185	338	Madera	911	136	San Benito	300	405	Stanislaus	1970	56
Colusa	323	391	Marin	1849	122	San Bernardino	6213	768	Sutter	655	585
Contra Costa	4684	1	Mariposa	90	453	San Francisco	A-804	596	Tehama	457	183
Del Norte	101	549	Mendocino	667	99	San Joaquin	2855	283	Trinity	108	595
El Dorado	704	635	Merced	1660	753	San Luis Obispo	1311	137	Tulare	2530	108
Fresno	5052	623	Modoc	191	93	San Mateo	4778	175	Tuolumne	177	160
Glenn	469	76	Mono	69	302	Santa Barbara	2065	881	Ventura	2607	237
Humboldt	801	83	Monterey	357	239	Santa Clara	6626	664	Yolo	769	16
Imperial	1189	701	Napa	704	742	Santa Cruz	1638	607	Yuba	398	693
Inyo	165	672	Nevada	363	94	Shasta	800	633			
Kern	3756	690	Orange	7182	18	San Diego	SERIES 5	Book 1964, Page 149774			

shall inure to and bind the parties hereto, with respect to the property above described. Said agreements, terms and provisions contained in said subdivisions A and B, (identical in all counties, and printed on the reverse side hereof) are by the within reference thereto, incorporated herein and made a part of this Deed of Trust for all purposes as fully as if set forth at length herein, and Beneficiary may charge for a statement regarding the obligation secured hereby, provided the charge therefor does not exceed the maximum allowed by law.

The undersigned Trustor, requests that a copy of any notice of default and any notice of sale hereunder be mailed to him at his address hereinbefore set forth.

STATE OF CALIFORNIA }
COUNTY OF _____ }ss.

Signature of Trustor

On _____ before me,

_____ ,

personally appeared _____

_____ ,

Bob Buyer

Betty Buyer

EXHIBIT A (Usually on a separate page attached to T.D.)

This is an attachment to a deed of trust dated October 1, 1992, executed by Bob Buyer and Betty Buyer as Trustor, and Sam Seller and Sally Seller as beneficiary.

The monthly installment payment on the note referred to in this deed of trust is subject to being increased pursuant to a percentage of gross receipts formula attached to the original note as Exhibit A.

Mobile homes have become an affordable alternative to high priced residential housing. As mobile home rules differ from single family residential rules, we've included this new chapter in our book. If you are involved in buying, selling or carrying back a note secured by a mobile home, you should make this chapter "must reading."

CHAPTER 15

MOBILE HOME NOTES

Mobile home notes are different from notes secured by real property:

1. Mobile homes are personal property.

Wheels on or wheels off, a mobile home is still personal property.

To transfer such property you may elect to pay state sales tax on transfer. You receive a license plate and then pay an annual renewal fee to the state agency which keeps track of mobile homes. In California the agency is called the Department of Housing and Community Development (Dept. of HCD). For less than thirty dollars you can run a title search on any mobile home in the state through that agency. The computer search takes about a minute.

Some states permit mobile home owners on transfer of ownership to put their home on the county property tax roles. By transferring, an owner avoids any state sales tax and/or state annual licensing fees. The owner may then believe the mobile home has become real property. Not so. A mobile home becomes real property only when it is attached to a foundation and the proper documents are recorded in the local county recorder's office to make the home a part of the land on which it stands.

Regarding the type of security for such personal property: In many states a financing statement is used. To put the world on notice, this security (financing) document is signed, notarized, and may be recorded with the county recorder.

If you don't want to use a financing security statement, you may not need to. As the lender is the legal owner of the home and the buyer/borrower is the registered owner, for foreclosure purposes, a separate security document is not required. In California a legal owner may foreclose on the registered owner with proper public notice in 45 days without filing a financing/security statement.

2. Most mobile homes are in parks where the land space is rented.

When parks raise the rent, a mobile's value may fall. The reason is that most mobile home buyers have a certain monthly payment budget. With low space rent an owner can afford to make larger payments on his mobile home. So, where park owners are not greedy and maintain rents at or below inflation, mobiles in that park will hold their value and may even appreciate.

Depending on a park's rent policy, carryback mobile paper may be more or less risky. The paper is more risky when a park has a policy of high percentage raises (no rent control) or a history of surprises.

For example, management in a mobile home park recently told new home buyers not to worry about raises. The last raise had been two years ago and none were planned for this year. One month later rent raises of 20% across the board were mailed. Surprise! Prices on homes in that park dropped just about the same 20%. For mobile home buyers, sellers, and note buyers such a move immediately wipes out a substantial part of protective equity in a carryback note. Many mobile home owners are living on relatively fixed incomes. They cannot easily adjust to large increases in space rent.

3. Mobile park owners change policies.
Way back when, mobile home parks, like drive-in movie theaters, were built on land whose time of highest use had not arrived. For example, a local mobile home park's land value today is close to ten million dollars for a higher and better use. As a park its rental income caps to a value of perhaps a million dollars. The owner is 80. What will his heirs do? Want to bet they sell? Whether your mobile home note is secure could depend on what the new land owners do and what state and local laws require the owners to do. Laws may require that the park owners pay the mobile home owners for moving.

4. Mobiles are easily damaged by adverse weather.
Common knowledge is that when natural disasters hit, nature's first target is the nearest mobile home park. In the last California earthquake 59 mobiles in a 200 space park simply slid off their jacks and fell on the ground. In another park the mobile owners were not so lucky. When the quake hit, mobiles slid around on their jacks and broke gas lines in many homes. About 40 homes in a 150 space park completely burned. Burn time was less than 15 minutes.

A solution to the sliding problem is to anchor the jacks supporting the mobile to steel bars attached under the mobile. When done, the result is called "earthquake bracing." Cost can be anywhere from two to four thousand dollars, depending on the home and the contractor.

5. Mobiles can have insurance problems.
Suppose you buy a mobile to resell. While you are painting and fixing, the mobile is vacant. Most insurance companies will not insure a vacant mobile. A fire means you probably have lost your investment.

6. Mobile home prices are more volatile than single family home prices.
Mobile home prices in California rose as much as 50% in the three years from 1988 through 1990, only to fall the same 50% in the next three years.

The cause of such volatility may be government policies, business cycles, or interest rate moves. No matter the cause, adverse consequences are the same.

One result of tight money policies may be local factory layoffs. As many mobile home owners are blue collar workers, carryback note payments may slow or stop.

Two companies publish data which may help you place a value on a mobile home:

1. The Kelley Blue Book, Manufactured Housing Guide
   Phone: 800-BLUE-BOOK
   Web:www.kbb.com
   Cost, approx. $50 per year

2. National Automobile Dealers Association (NADA), Manufactured Housing Appraisal Guide
   Phone: 800-966-6232
   Web: www.nadaguides.com
   Cost, approx. $100 per year

These guides are just what their names imply. They are guides only. As we noted, a mobile home's value reflects its condition, location and park space rent, along with other variables, just as with a conventional home.

Seller considerations
Often buyers at the mobile price level have not saved money. Without at least something down (5% to 10%) and good credit most mobile home lenders like Greentree Financial will not lend. Also, most institutional lenders avoid homes more than 20 years old. So, where either the buyer or the mobile home does not qualify, sellers who must sell need to consider the carryback alternative.

Investor and Note Buyer considerations
Mobile home paper involves greater risk than real estate paper and so warrants a higher yield. Many years ago Baron Rothchild was asked what type of investments to buy. His answer, as applicable then as now, was, "Young man, do you want to eat well or sleep well?"

To both eat well and sleep well
Here is how to protect yourself when you either carry back or buy notes secured by a mobile home:

A mobile home buyer should have at least two of the following three attributes:
1. Good credit. Forget about excellent credit. It seldom exists.
   ALWAYS draw a credit report from a reliable agency. If you are a seller carrying back a loan, be sure to get the cost of the credit report (usually around $20 per person) in cash. Rejected buyers may stop payment on a check.

2. A 20% down payment.
   This too is generally not available.
   Try using step payments (described in Chapter 5 this book) to shorten the term of your note and help a buyer build equity faster. Balloon payments should be avoided as mobile homes are usually more difficult to refinance than real estate.
   Consider something besides cash to enhance the down payment.
   For example:

Take a car's ownership as collateral. If the buyer does not own a free and clear car, perhaps a friend or family member will offer such collateral for your buyer to use.

Would a relative write a note secured by real property (see Chapter 11) as additional or substitute collateral for the mobile home buyer? Ask. While you are asking, also designate who will pay the title fees and possible escrow costs. Include such costs in your calculations.

3. Good payment record from past landlords or lenders.

Leave a space for such names on your credit application form. These name blanks can be inserted just below the employer verification space. A sample form is shown on page 169.

When you find a buyer who meets at least two of the above three qualifications, you may have the best of both worlds - minimum risk and sufficient reward.

EXHIBIT 39

SHOEHORN MOBILE HOME SERVICES ("We'll fit you in")

Mobile Melvin, Proprietor (000) 942-2180

CREDIT REPORT AUTHORIZATION

To any credit reporting agency: Date:_____

To enable Shoehorn MH Services, (Seller) to make a final decision concerning the sale on terms of the property at _____ we are providing our Social Security numbers and authorize you to issue a credit report on us. Actual cost of each credit report is $_____ per person. I hand you $_____ cash for each person, a non-refundable cost, to cover the cost of each credit report.

Borrower: Co-borrower:

Name _____   Name _____
       (please print)   (please print)
Address _____   Address _____

_____   _____

Phone _____   Phone _____

Soc. Sec. # _____   Soc. Sec. # _____

I authorize you to contact:
a) Our present landlord for verification of monthly rental payments, and,
b) Our employers to verify employment.

Present landlord: Name: _____   Phone _____
                       (please print)
Monthly rent you are now paying: _____

Employer _____   Employer _____

Work Phone_____   Work Phone_____

Supervisor _____   Supervisor _____

Monthly Income_____   Monthly Income_____

Has an unlawful detainer been filed against either of you? _____

Has either of you ever declared bankruptcy? ____ If yes , when_____Status? ____

Authorizing signatures (sign below):

_____   _____
        Borrower   Co-borrower

EXHIBIT 40

(this form can be used when the proposed buyer is self-employed)

SHOEHORN MOBILE HOME SERVICES ("We'll fit you in")
Mobile Melvin, Proprietor (000) 942-2180

Business Verification References
(all information is confidential)

This information is furnished to _____, only for the

purpose of facilitating seller financing on _____ real property _____ personal property

located at: _____

Name of proposed property buyer _____

Buyer's home phone# _____   Buyer's business phone# _____

Name of business _____

Landlord's name _____

Landlord's phone #_____

Material/or service providers _____

Approximate Gross Sales per year _____

Approximate net profit per year _____

Business references: _____

Name:_____ Phone #_____

Name:_____ Phone #_____

Please return both this sheet and the Credit Report Authorization, along with the
appropriate credit reporting fee to:

Mobile Melvin,
SHOEHORN MOBILE HOME SERVICES
123 Park Ave.
Anytown, USA
Tel: (000) 942-2180
Fax: (000) 942-2181

CHAPTER 16

TIPS FOR SELLING YOUR BUSINESS AND TAKING BACK A SAFE AND SALABLE NOTE

Walter Poser, President, Poser Investments, Inc., Arcadia, CA

WHEN SELLING A BUSINESS

(Just like real estate) you will have more buyers when you the owner/seller will carry a portion of the financing for the buyer.

BUYER EXPERIENCED IN YOUR TYPE OF BUSINESS

If you are carrying back a note: You may not be lucky enough to sell your business to someone experienced in your business or industry, but it certainly is to your advantage to do so. The more experience the buyer has, the more likely s/he is to be successful making payments to you.

BUYER'S CREDIT (check it out to avoid Dan Deadbeat)

As a potential lender, you have every right to information that shows the buyer is able and willing to honor his credit obligations. Obtain financial statements from the buyer and obtain the buyer's authorization for you to get a credit report. The report should show that s/he has a history of paying debts in a timely manner. That **authorization should be for as long as you have a business relationship! (EX #41, pg 172)** If you decide to sell to a person with a poor credit record, insist on a larger down payment and consider that it may be more difficult, if not impossible, to sell your note.

Refer to Chapter 3, page 44, for what items need to be in a note. Here are some additional considerations applicable to business notes.

DOCUMENTS

When you sell your business, there are many documents besides a purchase agreement that need to be prepared. The other three main documents are the note, security agreement and the Uniform Commercial Code financing statement (UCC-1).

THE PURCHASE AGREEMENT

This document sets forth the terms of the sale, i.e., the down payment, carryback note, and other terms and details of the sale between the seller and the buyer. A standard fill-in type form might (if state law allows it) be completed by a Business Opportunity Broker, or better yet an attorney experienced in handling the sale of businesses.

EXHIBIT 41

CREDIT REPORT AUTHORIZATION
(___Loan ____ Owner carry back)

To any credit reporting agency: Date: _____

Borrower:

_____

_____

Attention: _____

To enable Sam Seller (lender/seller) to make a final decision concerning a carry back note on the business he may sell us, we are providing our social security numbers and authorize you to issue a credit report on us to him. *This authorization to you to issue a credit report to Mr. Seller is a continuing one for the life of the loan; that is until the following date: _____. If the due date of the loan is extended and you are provided with a copy of the written extension agreement, this authorization to issue a credit report shall continue until the expiration of the extension period.*

_____   _____

Print Name   First   Middle Initial   Last   Social Security Number

_____   _____

Print Name   First   Middle Initial   Last   Social Security Number

_____

Current home address   Street   City   State   Zip   Home Phone

_____

Previous home address within last five years

_____   _____

Currently employed by   Phone # at work

_____   _____

Signature authorization   Signature authorization

THE BUSINESS NOTE

A business note is a seller carryback note that results from the sale of a business. In some ways a business note is similar to a seller carryback real estate note, but in many ways it is different. A major difference between a business note and a real estate note is the note's security. A business note is normally secured by only the physical assets and goodwill of the business, whereas a real estate note is secured by real estate.

The value of business assets and goodwill fluctuate much more and much faster than the value of real estate. The actions of the owner of a business are the primary factor in determining the success or failure of a business. So, a business seller who is considering carrying back a note should be more selective in determining to whom he is going to sell his business than the seller of a piece of real estate.

In the event the buyer of real estate quits making payments, the carryback seller can foreclose, resell the property and recover most, if not all, of the balance of his note. This assumes that the original property sale and note were sensibly structured. The holder of a business note is usually not that fortunate. By the time the seller repossesses the business, its value may have deteriorated substantially. The buyer may have destroyed customer loyalty, terminated good employees, alienated suppliers, etc. The business may have very little, if any, value. Instead of reselling the business and recovering the amount of the note, the note holder may have to either close the business, sell it at a large loss, or invest a lot of time and effort in attempting to rebuild it.

In spite of the risks of holding a business note, selling a business and taking back a business note can be an excellent way to sell your business quickly and at a good price. It's difficult for a small business buyer to get bank financing and it's difficult to find a buyer willing, and able to pay all cash for your business. That's why more than 75% of small business sale transactions involve seller carryback financing.

If you're considering selling your business by taking back a note, here is some information that could be beneficial to you, especially if you ever need to sell your business note for cash some day. The way a business note is planned and written can have a lot to do with its safety and future sale value. The NOTE is your evidence that the buyer owes you money.

The SECURITY AGREEMENT: EX #42, pgs 174-177 lists the items that serve as security for the note, the duties of the buyer, and your rights in the event the buyer defaults on the loan.

The UCC-1, (Uniform Commercial Code financing statement, California version: EX #43, pg 178; and National version: EX #44, pg 179) when it is filed (recorded) with the Secretary of State and sometimes the county recorder, puts the public on notice that you have a lien on the assets that serve as security for the note. A recorded UCC-1 automatically expires after 5 years in most states. There is a provision which allows the secured party (seller) to unilaterally extend the UCC filing. The extension form must be recorded prior to the date the UCC-1 expires. The Note,

WOLCOTTS FORM 1095–SECURITY AGREEMENT (Personal Property)–With Promissory Installment Note–Interest Included–Rev.4-94 (Price class 1A) ©1994 WOLCOTTS FORMS, INC.

SECURITY AGREEMENT
(Personal Property)

THIS SECURITY AGREEMENT is made this ___31st___ day of ___July___ , ___1995___ ,

by and between __Bob Buyer & Betty Buyer__ of __Any City, California__ ,

County of ___Los Angeles___ , State of __Calif.__, (hereinafter "Debtor")

and __Sam Seller & Sally Seller__ of __Same City, California__ ,

County of ___Los Angeles___ , State of __Calif.__, (hereinafter "Secured Party").

Debtor hereby grants to the Secured Party a security interest in all that certain personal property (hereinafter "Security"), now owned or hereafter acquired (except consumer goods acquired more than ten (10) days after the Secured Party gives value, unless those goods are installed in or affixed to such property), and the proceeds and products thereof, described and situated as follows:

> All fixtures and equipment, tradename, goodwill, telephone number, stock in trade, leasehold interest owned by Seller and franchise from GREETING CARD, INC., including tangible assets of the business known as GREETING CARD, INC. (Site #179), located at 123 Central Avenue, Any City, California as set forth on inventory attached hereto and made a part hereof as Exhibit "A".

Owner Will Carry © 1998 by Bill Broadbent, SEC, CCIM, & George Rosenberg

as security for the payment to Secured Party of SEVENTY FIVE THOUSAND and no/100------------

--- ($75,000.00**) Dollars,

according to the terms and conditions of a certain Promissory Note, of even date herewith, in substantially the following form:

PROMISSORY INSTALLMENT NOTE - INTEREST INCLUDED

$ __75,000.00__   __Any City__ ___(CITY)___ , __California__ ___(STATE)___   __July 31__ ___(DATE)___ , __1995__

In installments as herein stated, for value received, the undersigned maker(s) promise(s) to pay to __Sam Seller &__

__Sally Seller, husband and wife as joints tenants_____ , or order

at __place designated by beneficiary_____

the sum of __SEVENTY FIVE THOUSAND AND NO/100---------------------------__ DOLLARS,

with interest from ___---August 2, 1995---------------------___ on the unpaid principal at the rate of

__NINE (9.0%)__ percent per annum; principal and interest payable in installments of ____ONE THOUSAND____

__THREE HUNDRED FIFTY TWO AND 25/100----------------------------------__ Dollars

or more on the__second__ day of each __and every_____ month, beginning_____

on the __2nd__ day of __September, 1995, and continuing until paid._____

_____

_____ and continuing until said principal and interest have been fully paid.

Each payment shall be credited first to interest then due, and the remainder applied to principal; and interest shall thereupon cease upon the principal so credited. Should default be made in payment of any installment when due, the whole sum of principal and accrued interest shall become immediately due, without notice, at the option of the holder of this note. Interest after maturity will accrue at the rate indicated above. Principal and interest are payable in lawful money of the United States. Each maker will be jointly and severally liable, and consents to the acceptance of security or substituted security for this note, and waives presentment, demand and protest and the right to assert any statute of limitations. A married person who signs this note agrees that recourse may be had against his/her separate property for any obligation contained herein. If any action be instituted on this note, the undersigned promise(s) to pay such sum as the Court may fix as attorney's fees. This Note is secured by a Security Agreement (Personal Property) of even date herewith.

Bob Buyer   *Betty Buyer*

Bob Buyer   Betty Buyer

Owner Will Carry © 1998 by Bill Broadbent, SEC, CCIM, & George Rosenberg

This Security Agreement also secures: (a) any and all extensions or renewals of said promissory note; (b) the repayment of all sums, including but not limited to legal expenses, that may be advanced or incurred by Secured Party for the maintenance , protection or preservation of the Security, or any part thereof; (c) any and all other sums that may hereafter be advanced by Secured Party to or for the benefit of Debtor; (d) any and all other expenditures that may hereafter be made by Secured Party pursuant to the provisions hereof; and (e) any and all other debts and obligations of Debtor to Secured Party that may hereafter be incurred.

Debtor shall execute such Financing Statements and other documents and do such other acts and things as Secured Party may from time to time require to establish and maintain a valid, perfected security interest in the Security; and Debtor shall permit Secured Party and Secured Party's representatives to inspect the Security and/or the records pertaining thereto from time to time at any reasonable time.

Debtor shall keep the Security in good condition and repair, and shall not use it for any unlawful purpose; and shall not remove, nor permit to be removed, any part of the Security from the above premises without the prior written consent of Secured Party, which shall not be unreasonably withheld; and shall provide, maintain and deliver to Secured Party physical damage and loss insurance policies covering the Security in amounts and with insurance companies satisfactory to Secured Party, naming Secured Party as loss payee, as Secured Party's interest may appear.

Debtor hereby declares and warrants to Secured Party that Debtor is the absolute and sole owner, and is in possession of all of the Security, and that the same is free and clear of all liens, encumbrances, adverse claims, and any other security interests. Debtor shall not sell or offer to sell or otherwise transfer the Security or any interest therein without the prior written consent of Secured Party; nor shall Debtor sell, assign or create or permit to exist any lien on or security interest in the Security in favor of anyone other than Secured Party, unless Secured Party consents thereto in writing. Debtor shall, upon Secured Party's request, remove any authorized lien or security interest on the Security, and defend any claim affecting the Security; and Debtor shall pay all charges against the Security, including but not limited to taxes, assessments, encumbrances and insurance, and upon Debtor's failure to do so, Secured Party may pay any such charge as it deems necessary and add the amount paid to the indebtedness of Debtor secured hereunder.

If Debtor fails to make payment of any part of the principal or interest as provided in said promissory note at the time and in the manner therein specified, or if any breach be made of any obligation, promise or warranty of Debtor herein contained, then the whole principal sum unpaid on said promissory note, with accrued interest thereon, shall immediately become due and payable, without notice, at the option of Secured Party, and Secured Party, at its option, may: (a) sell, lease or otherwise dispose of the Security at public or private sale; unless the Security is perishable and threatens to decline speedily in value or is a type customarily sold on a recognized market, Secured Party will give Debtor at least ten (10) days prior written notice of the time and place of any public sale or of the time after which any private sale or any other intended disposition may be made; (b) retain the Security in satisfaction of the obligations secured hereby, with notice of such retention sent to Debtor as required by law; (c) notify any parties obligated on any of the Security consisting of accounts, instruments, chattel paper, choses in action or the like to make payment to Secured Party and enforce collection of any of the Security herein; (d) require Debtor to assemble and deliver any of the Security to Secured Party at a reasonably convenient place designated by Secured Party; (e) apply all sums received or collected from or on account of the Security, including the proceeds of any sales thereof, to the payment of the costs and expenses incurred in preserving and enforcing the rights if Secured Party, including but not limited to reasonable attorneys' fees, and the indebtedness secured hereby in such order and manner as Secured Party in its sole discretion determines; Secured Party shall account to Debtor for any surplus remaining thereafter, and shall pay such surplus to the party entitled thereto, including any second secured party who has made a proper demand upon Secured Party and has furnished proof to Secured Party as requested in the manner provided by law; in like manner, Debtor agrees to pay to Secured Party without demand any deficiency after any Security has been disposed of and proceeds applied as aforesaid. Secured Party shall have all the rights and remedies of a secured party under the Uniform Commercial Code in any jurisdiction where enforcement is sought. Debtor agrees to pay all costs incurred by Secured Party in enforcing its rights under this Security Agreement, including but not limited to reasonable attorneys' fees. All rights, powers and remedies of Secured Party hereunder shall be cumulative and not alternative. No delay on the part of Secured Party in the exercise of any right or remedy shall constitute a waiver thereof, and no exercise by Secured Party of any right or remedy shall preclude the exercise of any other right or remedy or further exercise of the same remedy.

It is further agreed, subject to applicable law, that upon any sale of the Security according to law, or under the power herein given, that Secured Party may bid at said sale, or purchase the Security, or any part thereof at said sale.

Debtor warrants that if Debtor is a business entity, the execution, delivery and performance of the aforesaid promissory note and this Security Agreement are within its powers and have been duly authorized.

If more than one Debtor executes this Security Agreement, the obligations hereunder are joint and several. All words used herein in the singular shall be deemed to have been used in the plural when the context and construction so require. Any married person

who signs this Security Agreement expressly agrees that recourse may be had against his/her separate property for all his/her obligations to Secured Party.

This Security Agreement shall inure to the benefit of and bind Secured Party, its successors and assigns and each of the undersigned, their respective heirs, executors, administrators and successors in interest. Upon transfer by Secured Party of any part of the obligations secured hereby, Secured Party shall be fully discharged from all liability with respect to the Security transferred herewith.

Whenever possible each provision of this Security Agreement shall be interpreted in such manner as to be effective and valid under applicable law, but, if any provision of this Security Agreement shall be prohibited or invalid under applicable law, such provisions shall be ineffective only to the extent of such prohibition or invalidity, without invalidating the remainder of such provisions or the remaining provisions of this Security Agreement.

In the event Debtor, without the prior written consent of the Secured Party, sells, agrees to sell, transfers or conveys its interest in said real property or any interest therein, Secured Party may at its option declare all sums secured hereby immediately due and payable.

IN WITNESS WHEREOF, Secured Party and Debtor have executed this instrument.

Bob Buyer	*Sam Seller*
Bob Buyer, Debtor	Sam Seller, Secured Party
Betty Buyer	*Sally Seller*
Betty Buyer, Debtor	Sally Seller, Secured Party
Secured Party	Debtor

Page 4 of 4

EXHIBIT 43

This STATEMENT is presented for filing pursuant to the California Uniform Commercial Code

1. FILE NO. OF ORIG. FINANCING STATEMENT 0000100	1A. DATE OF FILING OF ORIG. FINANCING STATEMENT Aug 15, 1995	1B. DATE OF ORIG. FINANCING STATEMENT July 31, 1995	1C. PLACE OF FILING ORIG. FINANCING STATEMENT Sacramento, C

2. DEBTOR (LAST NAME FIRST) Buyer, Bob		2A. SOCIAL SECURITY NO., FEDERAL TAX NO. 000-11-0000

2B. MAILING ADDRESS 789 Park Street	2C. CITY, STATE Anytown, CA	2D. ZIP CODE 90000

3. ADDITIONAL DEBTOR (IF ANY) (LAST NAME FIRST) Buyer, Betty		3A. SOCIAL SECURITY OR FEDERAL TAX NO. 000-22-0000

3B. MAILING ADDRESS 789 Park Street	3C. CITY, STATE Anytown, CA	3D. ZIP CODE 90000

4. SECURED PARTY
NAME   Sam Seller & Sally Seller
MAILING ADDRESS   123 Elm Street
CITY   Anytown   STATE   CA   ZIP CODE   90001

4A. SOCIAL SECURITY NO., FEDERAL TAX NO. OR BANK TRANSIT AND A.B.A. NO.
111-00-1111

5. ASSIGNEE OF SECURED PARTY (IF ANY)
NAME
MAILING ADDRESS
CITY   STATE   ZIP CODE

5A. SOCIAL SECURITY NO., FEDERAL TAX NO. OR BANK TRANSIT AND A.B.A. NO.

6.

A ☐ CONTINUATION—The original Financing Statement between the foregoing Debtor and Secured Party bearing the file number and date shown above is continued. If collateral is crops or timber, check here ☐ and insert description of real property on which growing or to be grown in Item 7 below.

B ☐ RELEASE—From the collateral described in the Financing Statement bearing the file number shown above, the Secured Party releases the collateral described in Item 7 below.

C ☐ ASSIGNMENT—The Secured Party certifies that the Secured Party has assigned to the Assignee above named, all the Secured Party's rights under the Financing Statement bearing the file number shown above in the collateral described in Item 7 below.

D ☐ TERMINATION—The Secured Party certifies that the Secured Party no longer claims a security interest under the Financing Statement bearing the file number shown above.

E ☐ AMENDMENT—The Financing Statement bearing the file number shown above is amended as set forth in Item 7 below. (Signature of Debtor required on all amendments.)

F ☐ OTHER

7.

All fixtures and equipment, tradename, goodwill, telephone number, stock in trade, leasehold interest owned by Seller and franchise from GREETING CARD, INC., including tangible assets of the business known as GREETING CARD, INC., (Site #179), located at 123 Central Avenue, Any City, California as set forth on inventory attached hereto and made a part herof as Exhibit "A".

8.
(Date) _____ 19___

By: _____
SIGNATURE(S) OF DEBTOR(S)   (TITLE)

By: _____
SIGNATURE(S) OF SECURED PARTY(IES)   (TITLE)

CODE: 1 2 3 4 5 6 7 8 9

9. This Space for Use of Filing Officer (Date, Time, Filing Office)

10. Return Copy to
NAME
ADDRESS
CITY AND
STATE

EXHIBIT 44

THIS SPACE FOR USE OF FILING OFFICER

FINANCING STATEMENT— FOLLOW INSTRUCTIONS CAREFULLY

This Financing Statement is presented for filing pursuant to the Uniform Commercial Code and will remain effective, with certain exceptions, for 5 years from date of filing.

A. NAME & TEL. # OF CONTACT AT FILER (optional)	B. FILING OFFICE ACCT. # (optional)

C. RETURN COPY TO: (Name and Mailing Address)

D. OPTIONAL DESIGNATION [if applicable]: ☐ LESSOR/LESSEE ☐ CONSIGNOR/CONSIGNEE ☐ NON-UCC FILING

1. DEBTOR'S EXACT FULL LEGAL NAME - insert only one debtor name (1a or 1b)

1a. ENTITY'S NAME

OR

1b. INDIVIDUAL'S LAST NAME	FIRST NAME	MIDDLE NAME	SUFFIX

1c. MAILING ADDRESS	CITY	STATE	COUNTRY	POSTAL CODE

1d. S.S. OR TAX I.D.#	OPTIONAL ADD'NL INFO RE ENTITY DEBTOR	1e. TYPE OF ENTITY	1f. ENTITY'S STATE OR COUNTRY OF ORGANIZATION	1g. ENTITY'S ORGANIZATIONAL I.D.#, if any ☐ NONE

2. ADDITIONAL DEBTOR'S EXACT FULL LEGAL NAME - insert only one debtor name (2a or 2b)

2a. ENTITY'S NAME

OR

2b. INDIVIDUAL'S LAST NAME	FIRST NAME	MIDDLE NAME	SUFFIX

2c. MAILING ADDRESS	CITY	STATE	COUNTRY	POSTAL CODE

2d. S.S. OR TAX I.D.#	OPTIONAL ADD'NL INFO RE ENTITY DEBTOR	2e. TYPE OF ENTITY	2f. ENTITY'S STATE OR COUNTRY OF ORGANIZATION	2g. ENTITY'S ORGANIZATIONAL I.D.#, if any ☐ NONE

3. SECURED PARTY'S (ORIGINAL S/P or ITS TOTAL ASSIGNEE) EXACT FULL LEGAL NAME - insert only one secured party name (3a or 3b)

3a. ENTITY'S NAME

OR

3b. INDIVIDUAL'S LAST NAME	FIRST NAME	MIDDLE NAME	SUFFIX

3c. MAILING ADDRESS	CITY	STATE	COUNTRY	POSTAL CODE

4. This FINANCING STATEMENT covers the following types or items of property:

5. CHECK BOX [if applicable] ☐ This FINANCING STATEMENT is signed by the Secured Party instead of the Debtor to perfect a security interest (a) in collateral already subject to a security interest in another jurisdiction when it was brought into this state, or when the debtor's location was changed to this state, or (b) in accordance with other statutory provisions [additional data may be required]

7. If filed in Florida (check one) ☐ Documentary stamp tax paid ☐ Documentary stamp tax not applicable

6. REQUIRED SIGNATURE(S)

8. ☐ This FINANCING STATEMENT is to be filed [for record] (or recorded) in the REAL ESTATE RECORDS Attach Addendum [if applicable]

9. Check to REQUEST SEARCH CERTIFICATE(S) on Debtor(s) [ADDITIONAL FEE] (optional) ☐ All Debtors ☐ Debtor 1 ☐ Debtor 2

(1) FILING OFFICER COPY — NATIONAL FINANCING STATEMENT (FORM UCC1) (TRANS) (REV. 12/18/95)

WOLCOTTS FORM UCCNAT01 (price class 13C)

Security Agreement, UCC-1, as well as a number of other documents, should be prepared by a professional, such as an attorney or an escrow officer who is experienced in handling the sale of businesses. **Search carefully**, as few escrow officers or attorneys have experience in this highly specialized work.

DOWN PAYMENT

The down payment should be as large as possible, at least 30% of the selling price. A larger down payment means the purchaser has more equity at risk, has less debt, and lower payments. These items make the business note safer and more salable. Make sure the down payment is paid out of the purchaser's funds rather than out of funds borrowed from friends or relatives. Politely but firmly inquire about where the money for the down payment is coming from and make your selling decision accordingly.

Regardless of the amount of the down payment, it should be made through an escrow company, title company or attorney who is handling the transaction so it shows up on a settlement statement as a legitimate down payment. It is difficult to prove a down payment was actually made if it is made outside the escrow company, title company, or attorney. Also many states require a "bulk sale escrow" to put creditors of a business on notice of the sale.

You should avoid "nothing down" buyers. Making no down payment is a shrewd way to purchase a business but a bad way to sell one. Making delayed down payments over time ($10,000 today, $10,000 in six months, etc.) is just another version of the "nothing down" purchase. Consider carefully if you really want to sell your business to a buyer who is unwilling or unable to financially commit himself or herself to the business you are selling. The exception may be if the deferred down payment is coming from a well secured source, i.e., equity in real property which is for sale, a CD that is maturing in 6 months, or a payment from a structured settlement that is due in less than a year from a strong, well rated insurance company.

The best down payment is cash, but there are legitimate down payment alternatives. For example: The buyer may hold a seasoned note secured by real estate that s/he sold. The note may be an acceptable down payment if there is sufficient equity in the real estate and if the note has a good payment history. The Buyer might own free and clear real estate or have substantial equity in mortgaged real estate. Taking a note from the buyer secured by such real estate, or even taking title to the real estate, may be an acceptable down payment and result in a more secure carryback note for the balance of the purchase price.

In the event a non-cash down payment is offered, the business seller should determine the value of what s/he is being offered. Property securing an existing note can be appraised. So can a lot or rental house that the seller might accept as part of a down payment. Anything tangible with a measurable value that increases the down payment makes the seller's carryback note more secure. A seller's objective should be to get the buyer committed to a substantial down payment in the form of cash, notes or solid equity in real property.

INTEREST RATE

The interest rate on your business note should be approximately the same as interest rates being charged on mortgages, but don't turn down an otherwise acceptable opportunity to sell your business just because the interest rate is low. The interest rate is not as crucial on a business note. Business notes most often amortize over a much shorter period of time than real estate notes. Although a higher interest rate is better for the seller, you should consider that accepting a lower interest rate may make it easier for you to sell your business.

AMORTIZATION (TERM) OF NOTE

Most business notes are fully amortized over three to five years with some being amortized over as long as seven or eight years.

Here's a good rule of thumb: If the business does not generate enough cash flow (after expenses and a reasonable income for the buyer) to amortize the loan over a maximum of seven years, perhaps both the seller and the buyer should consider whether the business is overpriced.

As the buyer, you may want a longer term so your payment will be smaller. As the seller, the shorter the amortization the better. To shorten the term of the business note, you can ask the buyer to increase the down payment and/or increase the size of monthly payments. Avoid a balloon. It is seldom possible to get institutional financing to pay off a balloon. Stepped payments (Chapter 5) or a performance note (Chapter 14) might be alternatives to consider.

Both parties benefit by structuring the term so the payments can easily be made from income the business generates. Neither party benefits by having payments that are larger than the business can support. If the income from the business fluctuates seasonally, then the payments should be set higher during the higher income months and set lower during the low income months. Either a percentage of gross income or a fixed dollar amount may be used.

LATE PAYMENT CHARGE

Be sure you include a late payment penalty in the note. This gives the buyer an incentive to make payments on time. Typical late charges range from 5% to 10% of the amount of the payment. The buyer should not object to this provision if s/he intends to make the payments on time.

Payments postmarked after the grace period can still incur a late charge. If you are charging daily interest, payments postmarked before the due date should be charged interest, only to the date of the postmark .

Your note could also require the new owner to provide you with a current profit and loss statement on the business in the event you ever need to sell all or a portion of your note. Here is some language that could be included in your seller carryback note.

If the holder of this note ("Holder") decides to sell or assign all or any portion of the holder's interest in this note to another person ("Assignee"), the maker or other payor ("Payor") shall furnish to the proposed Assignee, within 10 days after receipt of the Holder's written request, such financial statements as are reasonably required to assure the proposed Assignee that note payments will be made in a timely manner in the future by Payor. If Payor fails or refuses to provide such financial statements within such ten day period, Holder, upon ten days prior written notice to Payor, may accelerate the due date of the note and call all unpaid principal and interest of the note immediately due and payable in full.

INSURANCE

The buyer of the business must, as part of the sale, maintain adequate liability and hazard insurance. You should have a copy of the policy showing you (the note holder) as a Loss Payee and showing that the insurance company has been instructed to notify you if the policy is canceled for any reason.

PERSONAL LIABILITY

It is to your advantage to have the buyer personally liable for repayment of the note. This means that in the event you have to take the business back and resell it for less than you are owed, you can get a deficiency judgment against the buyer. Some buyers will not agree to personal liability. Instead, they insist on buying the business (and executing a note) in the name of a small closely held corporation or Limited Liability Company (LLC), which may have no assets other than the business you are selling. When you are presented an offer in which the buyer is a small corporation or LLC, consider the possibility that in the event the buyer does not make payments, the only recourse you have may be to take back the business. Also consider that by the time you take the business back, the buyer may have allowed it to deteriorate substantially. See Chapter 14 regarding co-signors/guarantors.

WHAT TO EXPECT FROM THE SALE OF A BUSINESS NOTE.

- Business notes are riskier than notes secured by real property.
- There are fewer buyers for business notes than for notes secured by real estate.
- Business note buyers frequently require six months to one year seasoning. If the new owner of a business (Payor) has any complaints against the seller (note holder/payee) they usually surface within the first year after the sale.
- These factors indicate that the Buyer of a note secured solely by a business will expect a higher yield on his/her investment than buyers of notes secured by real estate.

So why should you as a note buyer take on the risks of buying a note secured only by a business? Your hope would lie in the potential reward. By following the suggestions in this chapter, you should be able to have a safe and secure note.

SUMMARY

Having read this book, you can become the lender and finance the sale of your property! Perhaps you will do a much better job than Ben Banker who frequently says, "NO!" You are now able to say, "YES!" and be confident that you are well-secured with minimal risk. Having such security may be the magic key to a fast sale. YOU CAN NOW TAKE BACK A NOTE OR MORTGAGE WITHOUT BEING TAKEN!

We started by looking at some considerations you as a seller must think through when receiving a note, or, more appropriately, when carrying back part or all of the financing. Discussed were sins committed and, worse, problems resulting from omissions.

Having reached this point, the reader should now understand the elements of a note to complete a well-structured transaction. We showed you the importance of **protective equity.** Some alternative ways to take back one note or several notes were also covered as well as a thorough discussion on wraparound financing.

Using several examples, starting with a balloon payment note, we saw the most advantageous way for a seller to structure such notes. We presented alternatives to balloon payment notes and showed how to avoid balloon payments entirely. Knowing all this, you as a seller or buyer can negotiate for the alternative you prefer.

Once the note is in place, you as a note holder have some choices: Keep, sell, exchange, or borrow against the note. This chapter explored your options, along with the pros and cons of each, as a proud note holder. We shared important information for those who buy, sell, or invest in notes.

Need help from a real estate agent? How to tell who is qualified? How can you be sure that if the agent is qualified, he or she will represent you and only you? This chapter comes from the heart. Two agents have written it, Bill and George, who each practice what they preach (Single Agency representation) and have been doing so for decades.

Some sellers get finessed into a low down payment deal (10% or less) by agents who tell you not to worry or by buyers who want you to believe they are the only takers for your property. You should worry. Here we showed you why. This is critical information for agents involved in the original structuring of carryback notes or for sellers who are carrying back paper.

We explored different ways, illustrated with forms and examples, of how to reduce the high risks of a low down payment transaction. Also covered was how to reduce the risk of not being paid the balloon payment when it comes due.

We progressed from a 10% down payment offer to an even lower down payment transaction. Here we showed the difference between a "nothing down" deal (with lots of risk) and a "no money down" transaction (with much less risk to the seller). Read this chapter again to be sure you know which alternative you as a seller or agent should use and how to structure the transaction.

Next on our journey through the seller carryback jungle, we showed how you as a seller can change or substitute the security on your note from the property you are selling or have sold, to perhaps an equal or more secure position using a property owned by your buyer. We also explored securing a carryback note with a note owned by the buyer, which is secured by another property.

Then came Broadbent's personal checklist of 15 important points. Learn what he uses when representing a property seller or when buying a note for his own account. There is some new material here, not found on other checklists. **NOTE:** Bill does not buy notes from clients he has represented in real estate transactions.

Having made you aware of note negotiations, transaction structuring, different types of security to use with different amounts of down payment, we discussed the idea of carrying back multiple notes secured by one trust deed or mortgage. For divorces and estate or business partnership buyouts, multiple notes can work wonders!

To conclude, we showed you how to have more security than just a buyer's personal liability. We believe the chapter on the Performance Note alone is worth many times the price of the book. There are some more new ideas here complete with documentation. Don't forget to check with legal and tax counsel before using them.

Added to this new edition are chapters on mobile home notes and on business notes. Each type of note requires that you have some special knowledge in these fields before buying or selling either the product or a related note. Be sure to check these chapters if you think you'll be involved in either a mobile home or business transaction.

Let's review what's been covered. We began at ground zero. Step by step we progressed to an understanding of what you as a seller can do and how you can sell your property faster by understanding both the concepts and mechanics of seller carryback financing. We showed you **how to take back a note or mortgage without being taken** by negotiating for the best position and showed you how to protect yourself when carrying a secured note. If you're buying we also educated you on what you need to know to make seller financing work for a buyer.

To: Real Estate Agents: **A FINAL THOUGHT**

As there are some intricacies to the proper creation of paper secured by real estate, we have repeatedly advised you to seek legal and tax counsel. After you have completed several transactions involving seller carryback paper with professional assistance, you'll learn the important points that apply in your state. As you learn to lay the basic groundwork, future transactions will become easier (for the rest of your life) and will require less review time by professionals. You will build your confidence along with your bank account. You'll have an edge over many of your competitors who are unwilling to learn how to properly use seller carryback financing. When the next money crunch occurs (the authors have lived through many), you'll still be doing business while other agents are dropping out. The principles in this book apply in ALL states, are not a fad and will be used year in and year out as long as we enjoy private ownership of property.

When you have completed an interesting transaction using the techniques in this book, we invite you to send us a summary. We may use it in a future edition of the book and will acknowledge your contribution.

WE WELCOME OTHER SUGGESTIONS.

SUPPLEMENTARY INFORMATION ABOUT THIS SUBJECT

Many computer amortization programs are available. "T Value" which has an excellent reputation is now available in both a PC or Macintosh version. "Financial Genius" by Softflair, Inc. does a good job. For servicing small note portfolios (private investor's) Notesmith (IBM compatible) is excellent. Notesmith may be used on a Macintosh with Soft PC.

Real Estate Digest
Seller Financing
Published by *first tuesday*, Editor: Fred Crane
P.O. Box 20068
Riverside, CA 92516
Phone # 714-781-7300

Very good with _much detail_ on California Law

The Homeowners Guide to Foreclosures
by James I. Wiedemer
Dearborn Financial Publishing, Inc.
520 North Dearborn St.
Chicago, Illinois 60610-4354

In Appendix are Summaries of State Foreclosure Laws

Smart Trust Deed Investment In California
by George Coates
Barr-Randol Publishing Company
Box 4486
Covina, CA 91723

California oriented but many feel that 90% of it applies almost anywhere

Invest in Debt
by Jim Napier
P.O. Box 858
Chipley, FL 32428

A CLASSIC. It belongs in every investor's library

THE PAPER COURSE
Peter Fortunato
e-mail: Papercrse@aol.com
P.O. Box 8804
Federal Capital Corporation
Madeira Beach, FL 33738

*A _very advanced_ seminar that **IS NOT** ABOUT INVESTING OR BROKERING PAPER. Peter teaches how to use paper creatively in the acquisition and disposition of real estate. You really need to understand this book before taking Peter's course.*

The brochures (examples 20, 21 and 22) reproduced on pages 186 through 195 can be purchased in quantity from: PrintMasters, 1375 Greg St. #102, Sparks, NV 89431. (702) 359-5601, Fax (702) 359-5602. Please contact this source directly rather than the authors.

ADDENDUM

The following information and document reproductions complement the subjects presented in this book.

ARTICLE 15 OF THE CALIFORNIA CONSTITUTION
USURY

§ 1. INTEREST RATES

SECTION 1. The rate of interest upon the loan or forbearance of any money, goods, or things in action, or on accounts after demand, shall be 7 percent per annum but it shall be competent for the parties to any loan or forbearance of any money, goods or things in action to contract in writing for a rate of interest.

(1) For any loan or forbearance of any money, goods, or things in action, if the money, goods, or things in action are for use primarily for personal, family, or household purposes, at a rate not exceeding 10 percent per annum; provided, however, that any loan or forbearance of any money, goods or things in action the proceeds of which are used primarily for personal, family or household purposes; or

(2) For any loan or forbearance of any money, goods, or things in action for any use other than specified in paragraph (1), at a rate not exceeding the higher of (a) 10 percent per annum or (b) 5 percent per annum plus the rate prevailing on the 25th day of the month preceding the earlier of (i) the date of execution of the contract to make the loan or forbearance, or (ii) the date of making the loan or forbearance established by the Federal Reserve Bank of San Francisco on advances to member banks under Sections 13 and 13a of the Federal Reserve Act as now in effect or hereafter from time to time amended (or if there is no such single determinable rate of advances, the closest counterpart of such rate as shall be designated by the Superintendent of Banks of the State of California unless some other person or agency is delegated such authority by the Legislature).

No person, association, co-partnership or corporation shall by charging any fee, bonus, commission, discount or other compensation receive from a borrower more than the interest authorized by this section upon any loan or forbearance of any money, goods or things in action.

However, none of the above restrictions shall apply to any obligations of, loans made by, or forbearance's of, any building and loan association as defined in and which is operated under that certain act known as the "Building and Loan Association Act," approved May 5, 1931, as amended, or to any corporation incorporated in the manner prescribed in and operating under that certain act entitled, "An act defining industrial loan companies, providing for their incorporation, powers and supervision," approved May 18, 1917, as amended, or any corporation incorporated in the manner prescribed in and operating under that certain act entitled, "An act defining credit unions, providing for their incorporation, powers, management and supervision," approved March 31, 1927, as amended or any duly licensed pawnbroker or personal property broker, or any loans made or arranged by any person licensed as a real estate broker by the State of California and secured in whole or in part by liens on real property, or any bank as defined in and operating under that certain act known as the "Bank Act," approved March 1, 1909, as amended, or any bank created and operating under and pursuant to any laws of this State or of the United States of America or any nonprofit cooperative association organized under Chapter 1 (commencing with

Section 54001) of Division 20 of the Food and Agricultural Code in loaning or advancing money in connection with any activity mentioned in said title or any corporation, association, syndicate, joint stock company, or partnership engaged exclusively in the business of marketing agricultural, horticultural, viticultural, dairy, live stock, poultry and bee products on a cooperative nonprofit basis in loaning or advancing money to the members thereof or in connection with any such business or any corporation securing money or credit from any federal intermediate credit bank, organized and existing pursuant to the provisions of an act of Congress entitled "Agricultural Credits Act of 1923," as amended in loaning or advancing credit so secured, or any other class of persons authorized by statute, or to any successor in interest to any loan or forbearance exempted under this article, nor shall any such charge of any said exempted classes of persons be considered in any action or for any purpose as increasing or affecting or as connected with the rate of interest herein before fixed. The Legislature may from time to time prescribe the maximum rate per annum of, or provide for the supervision, or the filing of a schedule of, or in any manner fix, regulate or limit, the fees, bonuses, commissions, discounts or other compensation which all or any of the said exempted classes of persons may charge or receive from a borrower in connection with any loan or forbearance of any money, goods or things in action.

The rate of interest upon a judgment rendered in any court of this state shall be set by the Legislature at no more than 10 percent per annum. Such rate may be variable and based upon interest rates charged by federal agencies or economic indicators, or both.

In the absence of the setting of such rate by the Legislature, the rate of interest on any judgment rendered in any court of the state shall be 7 percent per annum.*

The provisions of this section shall supersede all provisions of this Constitution and laws enacted thereunder in conflict therewith.

Amended November 6, 1979

* Effective July 1, 1983 the California legislature increased the rate of interest on judgements to 10%. Code of Civil Procedure § 685.010.

WHAT EVERY SELLER
(and Agent)
SHOULD UNDERSTAND ABOUT MARKETING
REAL ESTATE

IF YOUR PROPERTY HAS NOT SOLD...
consider the relationship below
between price and terms

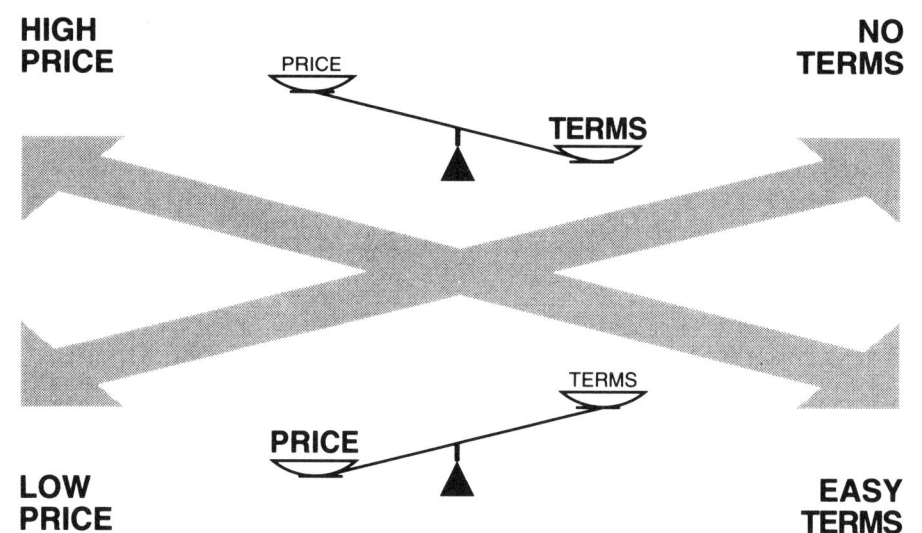

The price of any product is whatever another person will pay for it. Ultimately the marketplace determines the value or price of any product. Cost does not determine value, nor should it influence the current price.

Terms vary with the marketplace. Terms include down payment, number and amounts of payments, interest rate, and length of the loan. Terms are also relative to current market conditions in the area in which the property is located.

This brochure was written to explain the basic concept of creative real estate marketing. Reproduction of this material without the written consent of the author is prohibited.

WHO'S WHO IN CREATIVE REAL ESTATE, INC.
P. O. Box 23275, Ventura, CA 93002
(800) 729-5147
"Dedicated to raising public awareness of the Real Estate Professional"

Suppose an adjustment in price or terms does not work. How else can you expand the market for your property?.....

TO BROADEN THE MARKET FOR YOUR PROPERTY, ask yourself: Can I accept something other than cash for my equity?

Equity is **the market value of the property, less the total loans on the property.** The **Seller's equity** is ultimately determined not by the Seller or his Agent, but rather by a Buyer or **Taker** in the marketplace under current market conditions. A Taker is a Buyer who acquires property using assets (equity) other than cash.

A Buyer will buy your property using money. **Many more people (Takers)** will acquire your property using assets other than cash. Examples include but are not limited to land, mortgages, a rental house, office building, motel, airplane, motor or mobile home, etc. This brochure explains the most common methods of broadening the market for your property. **The more flexible you are, the more Takers you will find.**

THERE ARE ALWAYS MORE TAKERS IN THE MARKETPLACE WITH NOTES AND/ OR EQUITY THAN CASH BUYERS!!! As you read down the chart below, each step downward increases the number of people who can and will take your property.

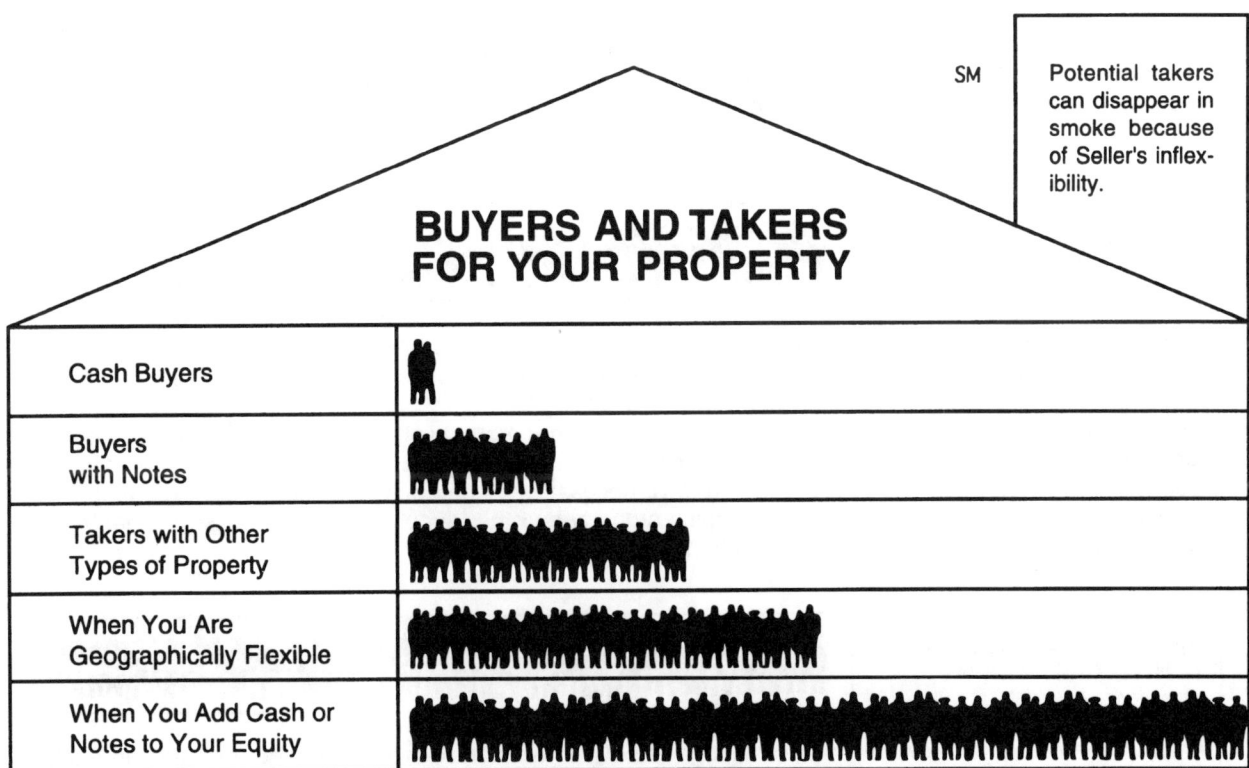

NUMBER OF TAKERS

WHAT EVERY SELLER AND AGENT SHOULD UNDERSTAND

Cash Buyers	

Many Sellers ask for cash. Everyone understands cash, and few understand other possible alternatives. Occasionally, there is a Buyer who will pay cash for the equity. More often a transaction requires some cash from the Buyer, plus a loan from a bank or savings and loan to "cash out" the Seller's equity. In recent years, there has been a trend toward stronger credit requirements by institutional lenders. Fewer Buyers qualify for loans. Finding an all cash Buyer for your property has become more difficult.

Buyers With Notes	

People in this category pay some cash down and the Seller carries back a note for a portion of the purchase price. This Seller carryback note is frequently secured by the property being sold. Sometimes takers will have a note that they carried back on the sale of the other property. They may be willing to assign this note to you instead of all or part of a cash down payment. Takers often have significant equity in property they own and want to keep. They may be willing to write a note secured by a trust deed or mortgage on their property in your favor. This note could become a partial or full down payment on the property you wish to sell. **For every cash Buyer for your property, there are probably 5 to 15 takers who would take your property if they could use trust deed or mortgage notes instead of a cash down payment.**

Takers With Other Types of Property	

Since there are more takers in the marketplace with equity than there are Buyers with money, as you move away from a cash Buyer requirement, you can expect more offers on your property. **For every cash Buyer for your equity there are probably 15 to 30 or more people in the marketplace who would acquire your equity using some property they own in exchange for your equity.** Obviously, you do not have to accept just any equity offered. Can you consider equity in other property? Do you see how this broadens the market for your property? Why not expand the market for your property by considering the equity in other property?

When You Are Geographically Flexible	

Assume you own a three unit apartment building. You are willing to accept property, provided the property is in your local community. You have broadened the market for your three units by your willingness to accept property in your community. Your area preference will be somewhat of a limiting factor. If you would consider property anywhere in your county, there would be more takers. If you would consider property anywhere in the state, there would be even more takers, and for property anywhere in the country many, many more takers. If you are offered income property some distance from where you reside, then it is necessary to locate suitable property management. There are real estate Agents who specialize in managing property for other people and do not engage in the typical brokerage functions of buying, selling and exchanging real estate.

When You Add Cash or Notes to Your Equity	

Certain properties attract few takers even though the owner will consider an exchange for equity in another property, anywhere. Sometimes the addition of more desirable assets or equities by the Owner/Seller makes a transaction feasible. The addition of trust deeds, cash, or mortgages with your equity makes the overall situation more attractive to a taker.

WHAT EVERY SELLER AND AGENT SHOULD UNDERSTAND

SUMMARY

The concepts mentioned here are designed to give you a brief insight into a few creative marketing techniques and principles. These concepts can help broaden the market for your property and solve your present ownership problems. Sometimes you must take more than one step to get from where you are now to where you want to be.

There are many more concepts, techniques, and formulas which are beyond the scope of this brochure. These concepts evolved over the past few decades into a unique specialty, creative real estate. The creative real estate concepts referred to here are truly innovative, with built-in safeguards for both Buyer and Seller. The practitioners of this newer method have traveled to seminars, devoted hundreds of hours of study at a cost of thousands of dollars to learn more ways to help clients, both Buyers and Sellers, meet their property needs. **If you are having difficulty finding a cash Buyer for your property, why not consider discussing your situation with someone who understands creative methods of marketing real estate.....?**

WHAT TO LOOK FOR WHEN SELECTING AN AGENT

A winning personality and a firm handshake are not useful criteria to determine the marketing expertise of an Agent. It may be in your best interest to avoid a relationship when the Agent fails to carefully explore what you actually need. The Agent you seek should be one whose concern generates pertinent questions about you and your objectives. That Agent will provide you a number of alternatives to use in developing a successful marketing strategy. An effective marketing strategy goes beyond placing ads in the newspaper, insertion in a Multiple Listing Service, or holding an Open House.

Selecting a real estate Agent who will represent only your interest is vital when structuring a real estate transaction. Numerous details, technical hurdles and special provisions are encountered in every transaction. To best protect you, the Agent you select must be more concerned with how the transaction affects you, rather than how soon s/he can get paid.

The precision and care of the concerned, professional Agent may cause your transaction to start a little more slowly. But, is it not better for you to have your Agent make a thorough investigation of all aspects of the documents and potential transactions before acting?

You can spot the professional Agent by the thoroughness of her or his approach. Often your needs may be substantially different from what you think you want. An Agent who uses the counseling approach, one of listening to you, and gathering information from you, is on the right track. The counseling approach will stimulate your thinking and possibly develop more desirable alternatives that might otherwise be overlooked.

Select a professional Agent to represent you who is:

1. Thorough in his or her search for detailed information concerning your needs.
2. Interested in why you need to change ownership at this time.
3. Concerned about what you want to accomplish.
4. Knowledgeable about the price and terms that can be obtained in today's market.
5. Willing to realistically interpret current market conditions even when that reveals something you may not want to hear.
6. In constant pursuit of education, continually upgrading his or her knowledge by attending appropriate seminars. (Don't be afraid to ask your Agent about his/her educational program).
7. **Trained in alternative marketing strategies, understands and is capable of explaining and utilizing the concepts outlined in this brochure to help you accomplish your objectives.**

When you find these characteristics in an Agent, your chances for a comfortable, successful and profitable transaction are excellent.

Who Does Your
Real Estate Agent Represent?

Introduction by
P. Roy Vallarino
Attorney at Law • Specialist in Real Estate Law and Taxation • San Rafael, California

A common practice among people interested in purchasing real estate is to engage the services of a real estate broker/agent to do the initial searching. A well prepared agent is personally familiar with many properties, has access to the Multiple Listing Service and can save you time and effort by finding and showing you the properties that best suit your needs.

Compensation for the agent is usually provided from the sales price out of the seller's proceeds of sale. This always raises the question of "who is the agent working for?" Who is really paying the agent's commission and to whom does the agent owe fiduciary duties?

You should understand that the term "buyer's agent" may be a misnomer. In fact, and in law, unless a buyer employs an agent the buyer's agent usually does not represent the buyer.

Even though you, the buyer, instructed an agent to locate property for you, that agent is usually considered by the law to be a subagent of the seller and responsible for protecting and promoting the seller's interests.

You, the buyer, believe the agent negotiating a property transaction is representing you, when in reality that agent is legally and in fact working for the seller. Part of that representation of the seller is to insure that the agent negotiates, on behalf of the seller, the highest purchase price and the best terms for the seller, not the best deal for you, the buyer.

Real estate agents, by their day-to-day activities, parallel the professional activities of lawyers. However, in most cases they do not understand, nor do they adopt the professional obligation of undertaking the sole, exclusive and proper representation of only one of the parties to a real estate transaction.

It would be unheard of to have one attorney representing both the Plaintiff and the Defendant in a lawsuit. Daily, real estate agents attempt to represent both parties to a real estate transaction. Most real estate transactions have as many adversary elements in their negotiation as we find in typical legal litigation.

A "Single Agency" format where the real estate agent represents only one party to a real estate transaction is THE ONLY SOLUTION to fulfillment of the fiduciary obligations of a real estate agent, thereby assuring proper representation of the client, whether buyer, seller, or lessee.

An increasing number of enlightened real estate agents believe that you (as a buyer) may desire and need proper representation in real estate transactions and would rather employ a real estate agent solely to represent you, not the seller. You become *the Client,* thereby authorizing the agent to fully represent you in negotiating with other real estate agents or sellers. This Single Agency concept applies not only to the purchase of all types of real estate, but also to business opportunities and to representation of tenants in search of suitable, commercial, industrial, and office space to lease.

I recommend the following articles by Bill Broadbent which will give you a further explanation of one of the "sole representation" concepts being practiced today by enlightened and truly professional real estate agents. The "Buyer's Broker" concept is explained and reasons are detailed why you should consider this representation alternative when you are planning to purchase real estate, a business, or leasing property, long term.

P. Roy Vallarino

FINDING THE RIGHT PROPERTY FOR YOU
William R. Broadbent

To understand the benefits of employing a buyer's broker (to the buyer), let us examine what takes place the way a typical real estate transaction is normally carried on in the marketplace today.

Bob Buyer walks into the office of Joe Real Estate and expresses interest in purchasing a particular type of property. After a brief "qualifying conversation," Joe is satisfied that Bob is financially capable of purchasing what he says he wants, and his "wants" are not unrealistic, in terms of the marketplace. What happens next?

1. Joe checks his office listings to see if there is anything remotely close to Bob's "want," and probably shows him anything even halfway in the ballpark. If Joe gets lucky and Bob happens to like it, then Joe gets a larger fee. We will assume that Joe has nothing in his listing inventory that Bob likes. What happens next?

2. Joe opens his Multiple Listing Book and reviews it to see if other local brokers have anything listed that he could sell to Bob and share a commission with the other real estate firm. We will assume that Bob is not interested in anything in the Multiple Listing book. What happens next?

Joe racks his brain, and suddenly remembers a FSBO (for sale by owner) that might fit. Joe inspects the property (it is a natural for Bob) and tells the owner, Susie Seller, that he has a potential buyer, and asks if she would give him a listing on her property. At this point Susie unloads on poor old Joe. Not only will she not give him a listing, but she hates brokers and would not pay a broker $5, much less 5 or 6 percent, or whatever it is they charge.

Joe retreats a broken man. Will Bob ever get to see Susie's property, through Joe Real Estate? (Remember, it was a natural). Not on your life! Joe may not be the smartest man in town, but he certainly is not dumb. Why should he introduce a willing buyer to a willing seller without any protection for his commission?

Joe briefly recalls another property that could fit Bob's situation, but it is not on the market at all, and the owner, Mabel Maybe, is well known in real estate circles for being represented by an attorney who seems to be notorious for killing real estate deals. After the tongue lashing he got from Susie Seller, he figures another battle is not worth the effort, and vows to show Bob only properties that are already listed.

Bob may not realize it, but due to the manner in which real estate is normally carried on, he is being excluded from a segment of the market. Unless he happens to stumble across Susie Seller, or Mabel Maybe, he will probably not end up with either of their properties.

As a buyer of real estate who is willing to work through a broker, Bob will end up paying the commission on whatever he eventually buys, since the brokerage fee is built into the price of the property he will be purchasing. With this thought in mind, Bob might well consider engaging the services of a creatively trained real estate practitioner who would represent him as a buyer's broker with the broker negotiating net with the seller, and receiving his commission from Bob.

Perhaps Bob would still decide to use Joe Real Estate. With a buyer's broker contract protecting his commission, Joe could then go into the marketplace on Bob's behalf and negotiate with the Susie Sellers, Mabel Maybes, or anyone else with the property most suitable for Bob. The buyer's agency relationship opens up the ENTIRE MARKETPLACE for Bob (no exclusions), and Joe has the best opportunity to come up with the best property that produces the most benefits for Bob, because he does not need to restrict himself only to listed properties.

There are a number of benefits and reasons why Bob should consider employing a buyer's broker, but **the biggest benefit of buyer's agency is that it opens up the entire marketplace for the buyer**, whereas, he (Bob Buyer) is currently excluded from certain properties, as we have seen in the situations mentioned in this article.

A growing number of professional real estate practitioners are utilizing this concept for the benefit of their clients. If you are a buyer, and the idea appeals to you, discuss it with your broker.

© 1989 William R. Broadbent

MISMATCH?

QUESTIONS AND ANSWERS ON
EMPLOYING A "BUYER'S BROKER"

Q. Who really pays the brokerage fee in a real estate transaction?

A. While the fee or commission may be deducted from the seller's proceeds, it is really "built-in" the price and therefore is paid by the buyer. Most sellers think in terms of "net" to themselves and add on commission to their listing price or sales price.

Q. Who really receives the representation?

A. The seller, provided of course, that the broker is living up to his Employment Agreement (listing) as the seller's agent.

Q. Can't I (as a buyer) get representation by dealing with a broker other than the listing broker?

A. Yes, provided that two things are done:
1. You employ in writing an agent from another firm to represent you, and,
2. The agent you employ rejects in writing any listing agent's offer of subagency.

Q. For which client is a broker going to devote his time, effort, ability and overhead?

A. In representing sellers, the broker spends most of his time on exclusively listed properties and little or no time on open listings or uncontrolled situations. The broker who has been employed (under contract) by a buyer to locate a specific or non specific property will concentrate his time to fulfill this obligation. A good broker will spend little time and effort with uncontrolled buyers who are shopping with every other broker and "for sale by owner" in town. In this latter case he will only try to sell his own exclusive listings.

Q. Under a "Buyer's Broker" contract, can my agent collect two fees?

A. No! Usually, the employment contract precludes the broker from accepting a fee from anyone other than his client. The transaction is on a "net" basis to the seller with the "Buyer's Broker" negotiating the best possible price. The buyer then evaluates the benefits to be obtained in view of the combined "net" price and his broker's fee. If the seller pays a fee to the listing broker he does so out of the "net" price.

Q. What if the broker I employ as "Buyer's Broker" turns out to be unproductive?

A. The contract can provide for cancellation on reasonable notice with protection for the broker on any properties previously submitted to the buyer.

Q. Will the "Buyer's Broker" arrangement save me any time?

A. Yes. Since the buyer's objectives and capabilities are explained to only one broker, this saves time. It also keeps the buyer's affairs more confidential. Because of the closer broker/client relationship, the broker can eliminate many weak possibilities and wasted hours and the buyer need inspect only properties with the "right benefits."

Q. What can I (as a buyer) expect from my "Buyer's Broker?"

A. 1. More conscientious representation.
2. A more thorough job;
   a. A seller's broker is interested in a ready, willing, and able buyer - no questions asked.
   b. A "Buyer's Broker" has a great responsibility. Because his fee is protected, he seeks the best property in the best location, with minimum problems and maximum benefits to accomplish his buyer's objective.
3. A better negotiated transaction. Dealing direct with the owner or listing broker may put you at a competitive disadvantage. A "Buyer's Broker" becomes YOUR negotiator. He can often negotiate a price down to the "real world" and save you more than his fee!
4. Preliminary negotiations. If you wish, the "Buyer's Broker" may submit preliminary offers on your behalf subject to your inspection and final written approval.
5. Anonymity! Selling prices tend to become very firm where the buyer is a well known real estate investor, wealthy individual or large corporation. The "Buyer Broker" can now act as agent for the undisclosed principal.
6. After a successful transaction the "Buyer's Broker" becomes an important contributor to the buyer's continuing real estate program.

Q. Can compensation to the "Buyer's Broker" be based on something other than a percentage of the purchase price?

A. Yes. Frequently "Buyer's Brokers" work on a flat fee! In some cases they can be employed on an hourly basis, but in such cases their fee is usually not contingent upon the outcome of a transaction. Sometimes a combination of contingent and noncontingent fees is used.

Q. Will I get maximum exposure to suitable properties using this "Buyer's Broker" approach?

A. ABSOLUTELY, AND THIS IS THE BIGGEST BENEFIT OF ALL. Normally a good broker will show a buyer only listed properties in order to protect his commission and avoid having "customers" go around him.

Since the "Buyer's Broker" is contractually protected on his fee he can contact owners of any and all properties that will benefit his client, even those not "on the market." A buying broker who doesn't have to cloud up his approach to an owner by asking for a commission usually has a better psychological relationship with the owner. It is amazing how some owners who have not publicly expressed any interest in selling suddenly come to life if they think they can "save a commission." Some brokers who have exclusive listings on excellent, desirable properties frequently try to avoid dealing with other brokers because they want to keep the entire commission for themselves. The buyer knows what he is willing to pay for the property, including his broker's fee and the benefits to be derived from the acquisition. If the benefits are there, why should the buyer concern himself with what the seller does with his money?

Q. How do I select the right broker to represent me in the capacity of a "Buyer's Broker?"
A. Ask people in related fields (Attorneys, C.P.A.s, Bankers, Title Insurance people) who are the most knowledgeable and experienced real estate agents in the community. After a few inquiries, several names will be repeated over and over. Concentrate further inquiries on these individuals and learn their specialties, methods of operation and expertise. Select the one who seems to be best qualified for your purposes, and make an appointment to discuss your situation. If the two of you decide not to work together make an appointment with the remaining one and counsel with him or her. Usually, one or the other will be just who you need to help you. When you feel you have found the right Broker to represent you, then stop searching, place your trust and confidence in that person just as you do with your doctor, attorney and C.P.A., and work with him or her to accomplish your objective.

The primary source of agents capable of representing buyers is the **Buyer's Broker Registry,** a special section of the national, professional directory, WHO'S WHO IN CREATIVE REAL ESTATE, P.O. Box 23275, Ventura, CA 93002. Listees have been employed and paid by buyers.

REALITY

Buyers DO NOT get a free ride under the traditional brokerage system. A commission is built into the price of the property being purchased. The Buyer actually pays the commission while the Seller gets the representation. Since you, the buyer, are paying the commission anyway, **WHY NOT GET THE REPRESENTATION?**

AGENCY DISCLOSURE DOCUMENT
Which do you prefer to be - A CUSTOMER OR A CLIENT?

The distinction between client and customer has been blurred by misuse in everyday real estate practice. Agents typically refer to their buyer as "client." In law, however, the client is the principal who employs the broker to be his agent.

DEFINITIONS:
Customer: (1) A person who purchases goods or services (Webster's Dictionary).
         (2) One without proper representation in real estate under the Law of Agency (WHO'S WHO IN CREATIVE REAL ESTATE's definition).

Client: (1) A person under the protection of another (Webster's Dictionary).
     (2) A person who engages the professional advice or services of another (Webster's).

In a typical real estate transaction, all agents involved split a commission paid by the seller (client) and are either agents of the seller or agents of the seller's broker (subagents). A buyer usually has "customer status" in real estate transactions and is entitled to honesty by the agent but does not receive the same representation that he would receive if he were a client. The agent CAN be an advocate for a client but not for a customer.

By law the listing agent represents the seller (client). A buyer (customer) should avoid discussing any confidential information with a seller's agent or subagent, unless he would be willing to disclose that information directly to the seller. At the beginning of their first meeting, a buyer, for his own protection, should determine from the agent whether they might work together on a customer or a client basis.

THE PRIMARY PURPOSE OF THE FOLLOWING DESCRIPTION OF AGENCY IS TO INFORM YOU OF <u>YOUR</u> <u>REPRESENTATION</u> <u>ALTERNATIVES</u>.

IN THE EVENT WE DECIDE TO WORK TOGETHER to attain your objective, we must determine which method of representation should be employed toward that end. Four alternatives are currently available.

1. SELLER AGENCY ALTERNATIVE:
Seller agency is the customary method of representation in use throughout the nation today. A listing agent represents the seller. A selling agent works with the buyer but is paid by and represents the seller. Because agency lines are not clearly drawn, a tangle of conflicts emerges which has been and is even now being wrestled with by organized real estate associations, the courts, and the federal government.

Under the law of agency, no agent may work against the best interests of his principal. Since the listing contract is signed by the seller, the listing agent legally is the agent of the seller.

Normally, this listing contract appoints any selling agent as a subagent, i.e., an agent of the seller's agent. A fiduciary relationship (involving a confidence or trust relationship), established between seller and subagents, does not permit any of the subagents to work against the seller's best interests. In real estate, this fiduciary responsibility means that neither the agent nor subagents can legally negotiate for the interests of the buyer in areas of conflicts of interest such as: price, terms, carry-back financing, special conditions, dates of possession, and personal property to be included.

Under seller agency conditions, buyers are usually shown only listed properties.

Unless the buyer employs his own agent to protect and represent him, the buyer is without adequate representation. In the event the buyer wants representation when making an offer to purchase a listed property, he should employ his own agent to review the transaction and represent him. The buyer should pay his agent's fee. This fee may be on a percentage basis, flat fee basis, or an hourly basis. Payment of an hourly fee is not contingent upon whether the transaction closes.

THE BUYER MAY ELECT TO PROCEED WITHOUT REPRESENTATION (customer status). If the buyer chooses customer status, he must realize that the seller's agent or subagents owe the buyer honesty and full disclosure of any detrimental aspects of the property, but cannot negotiate on his behalf. The seller's agent or subagents legally cannot disclose to the buyer any information confidentially disclosed to them by their principal, the seller. Confidential information includes, but is not limited to, the seller's possible willingness to accept a different price, terms, financing, conditions, and personal property included in the transaction.

2. DUAL AGENCY ALTERNATIVE:
Some listing agents try to represent the buyer as well as the seller. Such dual representation is legal provided both buyer and seller give their **informed** **consent** **after** **full** **disclosure**. Practically speaking, it is extremely difficult to protect and promote the interests of both buyer and seller, whose objectives may be in conflict with each other. Very few situations justify the risks inherent is a dual agency.

Owner Will Carry © 1998 by Bill Broadbent, SEC, CCIM, & George Rosenberg

3. SINGLE AGENCY ALTERNATIVE:

"Single Agency" means that an employed agent represents only one principal in any transaction, whether a sale, purchase, lease, exchange of real properties, or a business opportunity.

Under the single agency method, the principal employs the agent to represent him and him only. The principal pays a mutually agreeable fee to the agent either noncontingent for time spent or contingent upon completion of a transaction. The "single agency broker" does not normally collect his fee from another principal or agent unless directed to do so by the single agency broker's principal in their employment agreement.

The biggest benefit to a buyer in employing his own agent and agreeing to pay that agent's fee is that the agent's search for the right property for the buyer is no longer limited to "listed" properties. As his fee is protected, a buyer's agent can negotiate on properties that are "for sale by owner" or seek out properties that are not on the market, or are in foreclosure or probate.

As he represents only one party, the "single agency broker" is in a prime position to negotiate the best possible price, terms, and conditions for his client. He owes only honesty and full disclosure of detrimental facts to the other principal. This alternative may result in a much better transaction for the principal of the single agency broker even when the single agency broker's fee is considered.

If the principal is a seller, the agent must notify his client that he, the single agency broker, will probably not sell the property himself. Rather, he will market it in such a manner that other licensees working with buyers will most likely procure a sale of the property.

The single agency method of representation is not commonly practiced as yet by real estate agents nationally. A buyer may be located by another agent, who may not practice "single agency" and who may expect to receive his share of the commission paid by the seller. In this event, the single agency broker and his principal will consider the other agent as being the buyer's agent who represents the buyer. The buyer's agent may collect his fee from the seller or the seller's agent with the seller's permission.

4. CONSULTING ALTERNATIVE:

The unrepresented individual is at the mercy of an adversary who may be inept, clever, or greedy. A buyer may employ an agent as a consultant on an hourly fee basis to represent him in the event he has located a property he wishes to buy. An unrepresented seller who has received an offer to purchase from an agent representing a buyer may employ another agent as a consultant to review the transaction and represent the seller on an hourly basis. The fee of each agent is payable by his principal whether or not the transaction is consummated.

Real estate consultants are often employed to provide counseling and guidance in various real estate situations when no transfer of title is anticipated.

A "single agency broker" representing his client can usually suggest to an unrepresented customer the names of several local consulting agents from whom the unrepresented customer may wish to select someone to represent him.

PLEASE FILL IN THE INFORMATION BELOW FOR OUR RECORDS:

Name: _____

Address: _____ Phone: _____

I have received and read a copy of the brochure(s):* (Please initial below)

_____ * WHO REPRESENTS **YOU**... WHEN YOU ARE BUYING OR SELLING REAL ESTATE? © 1985
_____ * YOUR REPRESENTATION ALTERNATIVES © 1982, © 1986, © 1990
_____ * WHO DOES YOUR REAL ESTATE AGENT REPRESENT? © 1974, © 1979, © 1981, © 1990
and discussed my representation alternatives with

_____ of _____
(name of agent)   (name of real estate firm)
PLEASE INITIAL ONE CHOICE BELOW:
_____ I believe I am knowledgeable enough to represent myself. In the event we decide to work together, I prefer CUSTOMER STATUS and acknowledge that the above agent is not representing me.
_____ I desire CLIENT STATUS representation. In the event we decide to work together, I will enter into a separate written agency agreement with you.

_____ Date _____
(signature)
_____ Date _____
(signature)
*These brochures are copyrighted. Unauthorized reproduction is prohibited.
TO ORDER: WHO'S WHO IN CREATIVE REAL ESTATE, P.O. BOX 23275, VENTURA, CA 93002
(800) 729-5147

Owner Will Carry © 1998 by Bill Broadbent, SEC, CCIM, & George Rosenberg

SELLER'S PROPERTY DISCLOSURE STATEMENT
(Including the main structure and any outbuildings)

This document provides disclosures with respect to the property known to the Seller as of the date of this statement. It is not a warranty of any kind and is not a substitute for property inspections by experts which the Buyer may wish to obtain. Buyer understands and acknowledges that the broker(s) in this transaction cannot warrant the condition of the property or guarantee that all defects have been disclosed by the Seller.

PROPERTY ADDRESS _____

SELLER'S NAME _____

1. TITLE AND ACCESS
a. Is the property currently leased? .... ☐ Yes ☐ No
b. Has anyone right of refusal to buy, option, or lease the property? .... ☐ Yes ☐ No
c. Do you know of any existing, pending or potential legal actions concerning the property or Owners Association? .... ☐ Yes ☐ No
d. Has a Notice of Default been recorded against the property? .... ☐ Yes ☐ No
e. Any bonds, assessments, or judgements which are liens upon the property? .... ☐ Yes ☐ No
f. Do you own real property adjacent to, across the street from, or in the same sub-division as subject property? .... ☐ Yes ☐ No
g. Any boundary disputes, or third party claims affecting the property (rights of other people to interfere with the use of the property in any way)? .... ☐ Yes ☐ No

2. ENVIRONMENTAL
Are you aware of the following with respect to the property?
a. Any noises from airplanes, trains, trucks, freeways, etc.? .... ☐ Yes ☐ No
b. Any odors caused by toxic waste, gas, industry, agriculture, animals, pets, etc.? .... ☐ Yes ☐ No
c. Formaldehyde gas emitting materials, especially urea-formaldehyde foam insulation? .... ☐ Yes ☐ No
d. Asbestos insulation or fireproofing? .... ☐ Yes ☐ No
e. Elevated radon levels on the property? .... ☐ Yes ☐ No
f. Elevated radon levels in the neighborhood? .... ☐ Yes ☐ No
g. Use of lead-base paint on any surfaces? .... ☐ Yes ☐ No
h. Contamination of well or other water supply? .... ☐ Yes ☐ No
i. Any past or present flooding or drainage problems? .... ☐ Yes ☐ No
j. Any past or present flooding or drainage problems on adjacent properties? .... ☐ Yes ☐ No
k. Any standing water after rainfalls? .... ☐ Yes ☐ No
l. Any sump pumps in basement or crawlspace? .... ☐ Yes ☐ No
m. Any active springs? .... ☐ Yes ☐ No
n. Is property located wholly or partially within Flood Hazard Zone, as determined by the National Flood Insurance Program? .... ☐ Yes ☐ No
o. Is the house built on landfill (compacted or otherwise)? .... ☐ Yes ☐ No
p. Is there landfill on any portion of the property? .... ☐ Yes ☐ No
q. Any soil settling, slippage, sliding, or similar problems? .... ☐ Yes ☐ No
r. Any sinkholes or voids on or near the property? .... ☐ Yes ☐ No
s. Any depressions, mounds, or soft spots? .... ☐ Yes ☐ No
t. Any pending real estate development in your area (such as common interest developments, planned development units, subdivisions, or property for commercial, industrial, sport, educational, or religious use)? .... ☐ Yes ☐ No
u. Any federal or state areas once used for military training purposes, within one mile of the property? .... ☐ Yes ☐ No
v. Traces of concrete, metal, or asphalt indicating prior commercial or industrial use? .... ☐ Yes ☐ No
w. Proximity of property to former, current or proposed mines or gravel pits? .... ☐ Yes ☐ No
x. Proximity of property to former or current waste disposal sites? .... ☐ Yes ☐ No
y. Ravines or earth embankment that may indicate former dumping? .... ☐ Yes ☐ No
z. Pipelines carrying oil, gas, or chemicals underneath or adjacent to the property? .... ☐ Yes ☐ No
aa. Existence of pipeline rights-of-way or easements over or adjacent to the property? .... ☐ Yes ☐ No
bb. Discoloring of soil or vegetation? .... ☐ Yes ☐ No
cc. Oil sheen in wet areas? .... ☐ Yes ☐ No

3. STRUCTURAL
a. Approximate age of the house: _____
b. Do you know of any condition in the original or existing design or workmanship of the structures upon the property that would be considered substandard? .... ☐ Yes ☐ No
c. Do you know of any structural additions or alterations, or the installation, alteration, repair, or replacement of significant components of the structures upon the property, completed during the term of your ownership or that of a prior owner without an appropriate permit or other authority for construction from a public agency having jurisdiction? .... ☐ Yes ☐ No
d. Do you know of any violations of government regulations, ordinances, or zoning laws regarding this property? .... ☐ Yes ☐ No
e. Do you know of any excessive settling, slippage, sliding, or other soil problems, past or present? .... ☐ Yes ☐ No
f. Any problems with retaining walls cracking or bulging? .... ☐ Yes ☐ No
g. Swimming pool out of level? .... ☐ Yes ☐ No
h. Do you know of any past or present problems with driveways, walkways, sidewalks, patios (such as large cracks, potholes, raised sections)? .... ☐ Yes ☐ No
i. Any significant cracks in any of the following: .... ☐ Yes ☐ No
   ☐ foundations, ☐ exterior walls, ☐ interior walls, ☐ ceilings, ☐ fireplaces, ☐ chimneys, ☐ decks, ☐ slab floors, ☐ garage floors?
j. Any slanted floors? .... ☐ Yes ☐ No
k. Any distorted door frames (uneven spaces between doors and frames)? .... ☐ Yes ☐ No
l. Any sticking windows? .... ☐ Yes ☐ No
m. Any sagging exposed ceiling beams? .... ☐ Yes ☐ No
n. Any structural woodmembers (including mudsills) below soil level? .... ☐ Yes ☐ No
o. Crawl space, if any, below soil level? .... ☐ Yes ☐ No
p. Any structures (including play structures, tree house, etc.) that could be hazardous? .... ☐ Yes ☐ No

FORM 110.11 (10-91) COPYRIGHT © 1991, BY PROFESSIONAL PUBLISHING CORP. 122 PAUL DR. SAN RAFAEL, CA 94903 (415) 472-1964 **PROFESSIONAL PUBLISHING**

Owner Will Carry © 1998 by Bill Broadbent, SEC, CCIM, & George Rosenberg

Property Address _____

4. ROOF, GUTTERS, DOWNSPOUTS

a. Type of roof: ☐ Tar and Gravel, ☐ Asphalt Shingle, ☐ Wood Shingle, ☐ Tile, ☐ Other _____. Age of roof: _____

b. Has roof been resurfaced? _____ If so, what year? _____

c. Is there a guarantee on the roof? _____ For how long? _____ By whom? _____

d. Has roof ever leaked since you owned the property? _____
   If so, what was done to correct the leak? _____ ☐ Explanation attached.

e. Are gutters and downspouts free of holes and excessive rust? _____

f. Do downspouts empty into drainage system or onto splash blocks? _____

g. Is water directed away from structure? _____

5. PLUMBING SYSTEM

a. Source of water supply: ☐ Public, ☐ Private Well. If well water, when was water sample last checked for safety? _____
   Result of test: _____ ☐ Explanation attached.

b. Well water pump: _____ Date installed: _____ Condition: _____ Sufficient water during late summer? _____

c. Are water supply pipes copper or galvanized? _____

d. Are you aware of below normal water pressure in your water supply lines (normal is 50 to 70 lbs.)? _____

e. Are you aware of excessive rust stains in tubs, lavatories and sinks? _____

f. Are you aware of water standing around any of the lawn sprinkler heads? _____

g. Are there any plumbing leaks around and under sinks, toilets, showers, bathtubs, and lavatories? _____ If so, where? ☐ Explanation attached.

h. Pool: Age: _____ Pool Heater: ☐ Gas, ☐ Electric, ☐ Solar. Pool Sweep? _____ Date of last inspection: _____
   By whom? _____ Regular maintenance? _____

i. Hot Tub/Spa: _____ Date of last inspection: _____ By whom? _____

j. ☐ City Sewer, ☐ Septic Tank: ☐ Fiberglass, ☐ Concrete, ☐ Redwood. Capacity: _____ Is septic tank in working order? _____

k. Any repeated need for sewer and drain cleaning or repair, resulting from root overgrowth in plumbing or septic system? _____

6. ELECTRICAL SYSTEM

a. 220 Volt? .... ☐ Yes ☐ No

b. Is the electrical wiring Copper? .... ☐ Yes ☐ No

c. Are there any damaged or malfunctioning receptacles? .... ☐ Yes ☐ No

d. Are you aware of any damaged or malfunctioning switches? .... ☐ Yes ☐ No

e. Are there any extension cords stapled to baseboards or underneath carpets or rugs? .... ☐ Yes ☐ No

f. Does outside TV antenna have a ground connection? .... ☐ Yes ☐ No

g. Are you aware of any defects, malfunctioning, or illegal installation of electrical equipment in or outside the house? .... ☐ Yes ☐ No

7. HEATING, AIR CONDITIONING, OTHER EQUIPMENT

a. Is the house insulated? .... ☐ Yes ☐ No

b. Type of Heating System: _____

c. Is furnace room or furnace closet adequately vented? .... ☐ Yes ☐ No

d. Are fuel-consuming heating devices adequately vented to the outside, directly or through a chimney? .... ☐ Yes ☐ No

e. Heating Equipment in working order? .... ☐ Yes ☐ No

f. Solar heating in working order? .... ☐ Yes ☐ No

g. Air Conditioning in working order? .... ☐ Yes ☐ No

h. Does Fireplace have a damper? .... ☐ Yes ☐ No

i. Provision for outside venting of clothes dryer? .... ☐ Yes ☐ No

j. Water Heater in working order? .... ☐ Yes ☐ No

k. Is heater equipped with temperature pressure relief valve, which is a required safety device? .... ☐ Yes ☐ No

l. Electric garage door opener in working order .... ☐ Yes ☐ No

m. Burglar alarm in working order? .... ☐ Yes ☐ No

n. Smoke Detectors in working order .... ☐ Yes ☐ No

o. Lawn Sprinklers or drip irrigation in working order? .... ☐ Yes ☐ No

p. Water Softener in working order? .... ☐ Yes ☐ No

q. Sump pump: in working order? .... ☐ Yes ☐ No

r. Are you aware of any of the above equipment that is in need of repair or replacement or is illegally installed? .... ☐ Yes ☐ No

8. BUILT-IN APPLIANCES

a. Are you aware of any built-in appliances that are in need of repair or replacement? .... ☐ Yes ☐ No

9. CONDOMINIUMS — COMMON INTEREST DEVELOPMENTS

a. Please check the availability of copies of the following documents: ☐ CC&Rs, ☐ Condominium Declaration, ☐ Association Bylaws,
   ☐ Articles of Incorporation, ☐ Subdivision Report, ☐ Current Financial Statement, ☐ Regulations currently in force.

b. Does the Condominium Declaration contain any resale restrictions? _____

c. Does the Homeowners Association have the first right of refusal? _____

d. Please check occupancy restrictions imposed by the association, including but not limited to: ☐ Children, ☐ Pets, ☐ Storage of Recreational
   Vehicles or Boats on driveways or in common areas, ☐ Advertising or For Sale signs, ☐ Architectural or decorative alterations subject to
   association approval, ☐ Others: _____

e. In case of a conversion, have you an engineer's report on the condition of the building and its equipment? _____

f. Monthly/annual association dues:$ _____ What is included in the association dues? _____
   _____

g. Has your association notified you of any future dues increases or special assessments? _____
   If so, give details: _____ ☐ Explanation attached.

h. Are all dues, assessments, and taxes current? _____

i. I shall provide a statement from the Condominium Homeowners Association documenting the amount of any delinquent assessments, including
   penalties, attorney's fees, and any other charges provided for in the management documents to be delivered to Buyer. _____

j. Security: ☐ Inter-com, ☐ Closed circuit TV, ☐ Guards, ☐ Electric gate, ☐ Other: _____

k. Parking: Does each unit have its own designated parking spaces? _____

l. Sound proofing adequate? _____ Are there noisy trash chutes? _____

m. Property Management Co. _____

Seller(s) Initials [_____] [_____]

Owner Will Carry © 1998 by Bill Broadbent, SEC, CCIM, & George Rosenberg

EXHIBIT 38, Page 3 of 3

Property Address _____

10. OWNERSHIP

a. Are you a builder or developer? .... ☐ Yes ☐ No

b. Are you a licensed real estate agent? .... ☐ Yes ☐ No

c. Have all persons on the title signed the listing agreement? .... ☐ Yes ☐ No

d. Please list all persons on the title who are not U.S. citizens: _____
_____

11. PERSONAL PROPERTY INCLUDED IN THE PURCHASE PRICE

a. The following items of personal property are included in the purchase price: _____
_____

b. Are there any liens against any of these items? _____ If so, please explain: _____

12. HOME PROTECTION PROGRAM

a. Do you want to provide a Home Protection Program at your expense? .... ☐ Yes ☐ No

13. REPORTS

a. Have you received or do you have knowledge of any of the following inspection reports or repair estimates made during or prior to your ownership?

REPORT	YES	NO	BY WHOM?	WHEN?	REPORT AVAILABLE?
Soils/Drainage					
Geologic					
Structural					
Roof					
Pest Control					
Well					
Septic					
Pool/Spa					
Heating					
Air Conditioning					
House Inspection					
Energy Audit					
Radon Test					
City/County Inspection					
Notice of Violation					

14. OTHER DISCLOSURES

a. In addition to the disclosure statements made herein, the following facts are known or suspected by me/us which may materially affect the value or desirability of the subject property, now or in the future: _____ ☐ Explanation attached.

The foregoing answers and explanations are true and complete to the best of my/our knowledge and I/we have retained a copy hereof. I/we herewith authorize _____ , the agent in this transaction, to disclose the information set forth above to other real estate brokers, real estate agents, and prospective buyers of the property.

Seller agrees to hold harmless all brokers and agents in the transaction and to defend and indemnify them from any claim, demand, action or proceedings resulting from any omission or alleged omission by Seller in this Disclosure Statement.

Dated: _____ Seller: _____ Seller: _____

The undersigned Buyer understands that this document is a disclosure of Seller's knowledge of the condition of the property as of the date signed by the Seller. It is not a warranty of any kind and is not a substitute for property inspections by experts which the Buyer may wish to obtain. Buyer understands and acknowledges that the brokers in this transaction cannot warrant the condition of the property or guanantee that all defects have been disclosed by the Seller.

I/we acknowledge receipt of this SELLER'S PROPERTY DISCLOSURE STATEMENT, including additional explanations, if any, attached hereto.

Dated: _____ Buyer: _____ Buyer: _____

I am satisfied with the above SELLER'S PROPERTY DISCLOSURE STATEMENT.

Dated: _____ Buyer: _____ Buyer: _____

I am NOT satisfied with the above SELLER'S PROPERTY DISCLOSURE STATEMENT and herewith rescind my offer to purchase above property.

Dated: _____ Buyer: _____ Buyer: _____

I reserve the right to have the property inspected by the following professional(s) _____
_____

and to submit a copy of the inspection report(s) to Seller's agent on or before _____

Dated: _____ Buyer: _____ Buyer: _____

FORM 110.13 (10-91) COPYRIGHT © 1991, BY PROFESSIONAL PUBLISHING CORP. 122 PAUL DR. SAN RAFAEL, CA 94903 (415) 472-1964  **PROFESSIONAL PUBLISHING**

Owner Will Carry © 1998 by Bill Broadbent, SEC, CCIM, & George Rosenberg

WHERE TO USE A REAL ESTATE BROKER AS A CONSULTANT

A fallacy which many consumers, property owners and potential investors believe is that real estate brokers work only on commissions based on the buying or selling of property. Often, people involved in the purchase or sale of real estate need only minor assistance with a transaction rather than full service brokerage. Also, property owners or investors need information about real estate where no buying or selling activity occurs. They need information from a knowledgeable real estate agent, but the traditional commission system of compensation seems (and probably is) inappropriate.

AGENT NEED NOT = COMMISSION

The consulting alternative is applicable many, many situations. Capable real estate agents who charge for their time and knowledge are not concerned whether clients buy, sell, or exchange. Real estate consultants represent only their client's interest. They review specific situations and are paid by the client. Payment is usually an hourly fee, similar to the manner in which attorneys and accountants are paid.

Unlike a brokerage fee that is contingent upon a transfer of title, a consultant's fee is not contingent upon a closing. Consultants are paid for their expertise and time. Real estate agents holding national designations such as S.E.C., Society of Exchange Counselors; CCIM, Certified Commercial Investment Member of the Commercial Investment Real Estate Institute; CRE, American Society of Real Estate Counselors; should be among the better qualified agents to assist the public in a consulting capacity concerning real estate investments.

Some due diligence is required on the part of the consumer who is looking for a real estate consultant. Here are some suggestions. In an effort to try to distance themselves from the mediocre image of the average real estate agent, some agents have added "consultant" to their business cards and or advertisements. In many cases they have no special training, experience or credentials and have not been employed as a consultant or been paid consulting fees. Free advice may be abundant but is usually worth what you're paying for it.

When searching for a real estate consultant don't be afraid to ask qualifying questions, such as.
What is your area of expertise and experience?
What special education and training have you completed that would help qualify you as a consultant?
Can you provide references from real estate oriented professionals such as.
(Attorneys, Accountants, Brokers, Escrow & Title people who are familiar with the quality of your work?)
Can you document cases you've handled as a consultant that illustrate how your services have benefited clients?
Do you consult on property situations outside your local area.
Who do you normally represent in a real estate transaction. One party or both?
A good consultant should be an advocate solely for your interest,

A few examples where people have effectively employed a real estate agent/consultant for transaction assistance include but are not limited to:

Negotiating real estate acquisitions and dispositions. These include, but are not limited to buying, selling, exchanging, financing, splitting ownership interests. They may involve the structuring of seller carryback financing so that the paper is safe and saleable at a good price if in the future the seller needs to sell their note(s). The consultant may know private or institutional sources for funding non-traditional loans. **Whenever negotiations are anticipated, the client will get the most for their money by meeting with the consultant prior to preliminary discussions with the other party. Even though preliminary discussions may not be legally binding, experience has shown time and again that advantages are usually lost due to the inexperience of the client.**

An unrepresented individual in a real estate transaction may be at the mercy of an adversary who is more knowledgeable, inept, clever, or greedy. A buyer may employ an agent/consultant on an hourly fee basis to represent him in the event he has already located a property he wishes to buy. An unrepresented seller who has received an offer to purchase from a buyer, or an agent representing a buyer, may employ a qualified agent in a consulting capacity to review the transaction and represent the seller on an hourly fee basis.

As the principles involved in real estate decisions transcend county and state boundaries, the location of the property is seldom important to the consultant.

A consulting agent, educated in creative real estate techniques, may be able to provide valuable transaction structuring in situations which will benefit the client. The consulting agent does not give legal or tax advice, but will alert the client to situations which should involve the client's attorney or accountant. Experienced consulting agents usually know who the better real estate oriented attorneys and CPAs are for clients who have not established relationships with appropriate counsel.

Some agent/consultants do not charge for a preliminary interview. This gives each party an opportunity to determine if they wish to work together. Real estate is more complicated than most people perceive. You should consider the consulting alternative. It can prevent costly mistakes, solve problems, and provide objective input that will assist in the decision making process.

"The best investment you can make is professional advice, provided you have found a true professional."

Florida millionaire

INDEX

INDEX

INDEX

INDEX

NOTES

NOTES

NOTES

NOTES

NOTES

NOTES